ROVER P6

2000, 2200, 3500

THE COMPLETE STORY

OTHER TITLES IN THE CROWOOD AUTOCLASSICS SERIES

ROVER P6

2000, 2200, 3500
THE COMPLETE STORY

James Taylor

THE CROWOOD PRESS

First published in 2020 by
The Crowood Press Ltd
Ramsbury, Marlborough
Wiltshire SN8 2HR

enquiries@crowood.com

www.crowood.com

British Library Cataloguing-in-Publication Data
A catalogue record for this book is available from the British Library.

ISBN 978 1 78500 721 7

Typeset by Jean Cussons Typesetting, Diss, Norfolk

Printed and bound in India by Parksons Graphics

CONTENTS

INTRODUCTION AND ACKNOWLEDGEMENTS

The Rover P6 was unquestionably one of the best saloon cars to come out of Britain in the 1960s. It combined a wealth of technical innovation with a distinctive appearance that incorporated exactly the right degree of Italianate sharp-suited appearance for its time. It was, and remains, a great car to drive, and all these qualities were combined with the space and practicality of a four-seat family saloon. All right, legroom in the rear was a little tight, but it was fine while the children were still young…

For anyone new to the car, it is worth briefly running through its innovative aspects. It used base-unit construction, a type seen elsewhere only on the revolutionary Citroën DS. It had all-round independent suspension, with a De Dion rear end, and disc brakes all round with the rear pair mounted inboard. Its four seats provided the style and comfort previously known only to owners of saloons in the 3-litre class. It delivered 100mph (160km/h) performance with fuel economy that was excellent for the time – and it held a promise of the future, as Rover made their intention to produce a gas turbine-powered version very clear from early on. Sadly, that intention never became reality, but instead owners were treated to the superb performance of a model powered by a lightweight V8 engine.

My interest in the P6 was triggered in 1981, when I bought the Panelcraft convertible prototype. As I had already been interested in Rovers more generally for five years or so by then, I soon began to appreciate just what an excellent car the P6 really was. I went on to have my share of P6s over the years. In date order, they have been the 1965 convertible, a 1968 2000SC Automatic, a 1970 2000SC Automatic (spares only), a 1972 2000SC, a 1975 2200SC and a 1975 3500S.

For most of the 1980s, the P6 was still a cheap old car, but by the early 1990s the late John Blunsden at Motor Racing Publications reckoned there was sufficient enthusiast inter-est to merit a book on the subject. So he asked me to write *Rover P6, 1963–1977*, which was published in 1993. Nearly twenty years later, there was still no other book on the subject, but enthusiasts had discovered a good deal of new information and some colleagues encouraged me to prepare a new edition. With help from three of them, Nick Dunning, Al Worsfold and Chris York, a revised edition appeared in 2012, this time published by Brooklands Books.

There was still more information coming out of the woodwork, however, and it was clear that the time was right for a new book. So here it is, and I will say right now that it incorporates a lot of new research, both by me and by Chris Wilson and Andries Griede. I will also say that rewriting some of the original was more than a little difficult – pointless, even, where there was nothing new to say – and so if any sentences or even whole paragraphs seem familiar to readers of the original 1993 book, the reason is that I could see no reason to change them.

It is customary to add a list of acknowledgements at this point. As I know this book is tight for space, I will simply scoop up all the P6 enthusiasts who have provided valuable information or pictures into a single big thank you. They know who they are. But there have also been many former Rover people who have helped, and I think it is important to record who they have been. Sadly, many of them are now no longer with us.

So, for the record, these are the Rover people to whom I have spoken directly about the P6 story over a period of some forty years:

David Bache	Chief styling engineer
Gordon Bashford	Design engineer
Gerry Boucher	V8 engines team
Chris Bramley	Gas turbine engineer

Eric Branson	Research Department
John Carter	Engine development
Lou Chaffey	Rally team mechanic
Dan Clayton	Competitions Department
Roger Crathorne	Land Rover engineer
Maureen Hill	PA to David Bache
Spen King	Advanced design and gas turbine work
Bruce McWilliams	Head of RCNA
Jimmy McWilliams	Public relations at RCNA
William Martin-Hurst	Managing director
Tony Poole	Styling Department
Gordon Reed	P6 project engineer
Frank Shaw	Head of Transmissions Department
Jim Shaw	Brakes specialist
Brian Terry	Engine Test Department
Lyn Thomas	Suspension and NVH engineer
Richard Twist	Engine development
Dave Wall	V8 engines team

I have also corresponded with:

Tony Cleminson	Triplex
Richard Fishwick	NVH engineer
'Nobby' Fry	FLM Panelcraft
Ted Gawronski	P6 project engineer
Mike Green	Son of RCNA engineer Dick Green
Roger Harding	New Zealand Motor Corporation

A. Lowe	AE Brico, fuel injection development
David McMullan	Crayford
A. B. Smith	Managing director
Jack Swaine	Head of the Engines Department

Finally, through the efforts of others, I have been able to tap into the memories of:

Gerry Beddoes	AE Brico, fuel injection development
Anne Hall	'Works' competition driver
Colin Elmer	P6 inspection superintendent
Roger Clark	'Works' competition driver
Rob Lyall	Rover steering specialist
Peter Willmer	Rover transmissions engineer

Obviously, steering a way through sometimes conflicting memories has been my responsibility, and I hope the result is an accurate reflection of what really happened. But I would never think of describing what is in this book as definitive, and I hope that any reader who can add to the story or correct what I have said will feel free to let me know by contacting the publishers.

One final thing: if you get half as much fun out of reading this book as I have done in writing it, then my publisher should have charged you at least twice as much when you bought it…

James Taylor
Oxfordshire, September 2019

TIMELINE

September 1956   First meeting to discuss the specification of the future Rover P6 model

October 1963   P6 introduced as the Rover 2000

March 1966   2000TC model introduced (initially for export)

October 1966   2000 Automatic introduced

April 1968   Three Thousand Five introduced

October 1969   North American 3500S introduced

October 1970   New Look range introduced

October 1971   3500S (manual) model introduced

October 1973   2200SC, 2200SC Automatic and 2200TC replaced equivalent 2000 models for most markets

June 1976   First Rover SD1 variants (3500) introduced to replace P6 range

February 1977   End of Rover P6 production

CHAPTER ONE

DESIGN AND DEVELOPMENT, 1956–1963

Although the start of work on what would become the Rover P6 can be traced quite accurately to a meeting held on 21 September 1956, Rover's first ideas about such a car were actually discussed at least three years earlier. A central factor was the success of the Land Rover, introduced in 1948 as a product primarily for export that was intended to tide the company over until the difficult trading conditions of the post-1945 period came to an end. In practice, the new vehicle had been such a success that it had become Rover's primary product by 1951.

With it had come increasing profits, and these had encouraged the Rover board to consider bringing out a second range of cars alongside the P4 models that had been introduced in 1949. They envisaged a smaller and cheaper car to be built in larger volumes, one equivalent in size to cars like the contemporary Vauxhall Velox.

However, as those discussions progressed and the first scale models of the new car were produced in the styling studio, it became clear that the plan had a flaw. Once again, the Land Rover was the cause: booming demand and the need for extra assembly facilities meant that Rover could not satisfy that demand and create the assembly plant needed for a brand-new high-volume car as well. So the plan for a second car range was radically rethought during 1955. What was already known as the P5 model changed from a medium-sized, high-volume car to a larger, low-volume luxury model – and in that guise it entered production as the Rover 3-litre in 1958.

However, the idea of a smaller Rover that would be built in higher volumes did not go away. By 1957, with Land Rover sales still booming and providing much of the necessary finance, the Rover board were prepared to look again at the possibility of such a car. Not the least of their concerns was the medium-term need to prepare a replacement for the P4 model, which was already beginning to look old-fashioned next to some of its rivals from other makers. If Rover could

In the post-war period, Rovers had been deliberately conservative and were aimed at the well-to-do professional classes. This is a 1964 110, the last of the well-loved P4 range. AUTHOR

Above the P4 in the Rover range was the P5 3-litre, a more modern luxury saloon that nevertheless maintained the Rover traditions of conservatism and discretion. This 1959 model is typical of the breed. WIKIMEDIA COMMONS

combine the two ideas and replace the P4 with a smaller, high-volume model, that would make perfect sense.

Along with all this came the idea that the new Rover should incorporate the very latest technology. Although Rover's mid-1950s cars made the company appear staid and traditional, behind the scenes it was highly innovative. It was Rover who had led experiments with gas turbine propulsion for road cars, developing its first experimental car in 1950 and using it to claim a world speed record in 1952. Since then, further development had led to a quite remarkable prototype of a small gas turbine coupé in 1956, which combined a rear-mounted gas turbine engine with an advanced structure and drive to all four wheels.

Other development work, initially in connection with the aborted volume-car project, had focused on chassis-less construction with a steel skeleton structure and unstressed skin panels — an idea put forward by manufacturing director Olaf Poppe. So it was not surprising that some of these new ideas should be submitted when discussions began in earnest about the new high-volume Rover in 1957.

Most importantly, although the thought was not recorded in any contemporary documents, Rover knew that it faced a major challenge with its new car. What were high volumes to Rover were low volumes to the established makers of high-volume saloons like Vauxhall and Ford, and so the new car would have to offer something very different in order to establish a place for itself in the market. Advanced technology seemed like the ideal answer: it would give the Rover what is today called a unique selling point (USP).

IN THE BEGINNING

In the mid-1950s, the two outstanding figures at Rover were

the brothers Spencer and Maurice Wilks, who had guided the company's fortunes since the early 1930s. Spencer Wilks, the older brother, had been managing director since 1933, while Maurice Wilks had run the Engineering Department since 1931. However, times were changing. On the one hand, the success of the Land Rover and Rover's consequent

Maurice Wilks was Rover's technical director in the 1950s, and became its managing director. He oversaw the early thinking on the P6 project. ROVER CO. LTD

Robert Boyle was Maurice Wilks' deputy, and
was appointed Rover's chief engineer when
Wilks became joint managing director in 1956.
He initiated the P6 project. ROVER CO. LTD

Spen King was a nephew of the Wilks brothers
and was involved with gas turbine experiments in
the 1950s, later becoming head of Rover's future
products think-tank. He had a substantial input to
P6 – initially because there were thoughts of making
a gas turbine-powered version available. ROVER CO. LTD

Gordon Bashford had designed the 'package' for every
post-war Rover and became Spen King's deputy in the
department that became New Vehicle Projects. He was
responsible for the overall layout of the P6. ROVER CO. LTD

expansion demanded changes in the way the company was
managed; and on the other hand, it was time to give some
of Rover's very able younger engineers the opportunity to
influence the company's future.

So in a series of top management reshuffles during 1956,
Maurice Wilks was appointed joint managing director
with his brother. Although he would continue to keep a
fatherly eye on Engineering, he appointed as Rover's new
chief engineer his deputy, Robert Boyle. Below Boyle he
also appointed two new senior engineering managers. These
were Dick Oxley, whose task was to oversee Rover car
engineering, and Tom Barton, whose job focused on Land
Rovers.

Meanwhile, there remained a number of separately
managed departments within Rover Engineering – notably
Engines, under Jack Swaine; Transmissions, under Frank

Peter Wilks was another nephew of the Wilks brothers and a cousin of Spen King. He held a senior position in the Engineering Department, and later took over as its director. ROVER CO. LTD

Shaw; Research, under Brian Silvester; Gas Turbines, under Spen King; Styling, under David Bache; and Design Research, under Gordon Bashford. These positions remained unchanged when Spencer Wilks became chairman in 1957 and finance man George Farmer was appointed as joint managing director alongside Maurice Wilks.

Thus it was Robert Boyle who called that meeting on 21 September 1956, which was intended to initiate thinking about a new Rover car, to be known as the P6. Present were Peter Wilks (Boyle's deputy and a nephew of the two senior Wilks brothers), Gordon Bashford, David Bache, Jack Swaine, and Olaf Poppe, who was still running Rover Manufacturing. Spen King did not attend the meeting, but received a copy of the minutes and became fully involved in all subsequent planning meetings.

Boyle told his colleagues that Rover needed to start work on a new car, and that 'in broad outline this had to be a vehicle substantially cheaper as regards both tooling cost and

selling price than the P5' – the 3-litre saloon that would not reach the showrooms for another two years. The meeting agreed a target weight of 24cwt (2,866lb or 1,219kg) with alloy panels and 25cwt (2,800lb or 1,270kg) with steel panels, and that the new car's cost before purchase tax should be no more than £800. This would make it a direct rival for the Austin A105 (£799 in October 1956), Wolsley 6/90 (£806) and Standard Vanguard Sportsman (£820). These were all relatively expensive and prestigious saloon cars, although none was quite in the Rover price bracket, which at the time ranged from £865 for the cheapest 60 saloon up to £1,130 for the most expensive 105R De Luxe.

With the record of the September meeting came an outline specification that contained some quite radical proposals. There was to be base-unit construction, a De Dion rear suspension, and an engine of between 2 and 2.5 litres – ideally a 4-cylinder but 'silence and smoothness are primary considerations'. All these ideas survived into the production model. Those that did not included front-wheel drive with a two-speed automatic gearbox, rack-and-pinion steering, 13in wheels, the possibility of plastic body panels and 'doors possibly partly in the roof for access'.

That initial meeting was not precise about the size of the proposed new car, but for the next meeting – on 1 October – Boyle had prepared a document that described it as 'possibly similar in general proportions to the Ford Consul'. He specified a 105in (2,667mm) wheelbase, actually 5in (127mm) longer than that of a Mk 1 Consul but still one size down from the 111in (2,819mm) of the P4's wheelbase and the 110.5in (2,807mm) of the planned P5's wheelbase.

Through this meeting and a number of others in November, December and the early part of January 1957, Boyle and his colleagues discussed the initial proposals on the table and more. At the third meeting, on 19 November, Boyle asked for future meetings to be referred to as PX meetings rather than as P6 meetings. Perhaps this was to restrict speculation within the company about what might be happening, because to anyone who worked at Rover, the P6 name immediately suggested a new product destined to follow the P5.

During this period, Boyle asked for a number of studies to be made. Engine designer Jack Swaine, for example, was to investigate three engine configurations – a V6 and in-line engines of both 4 and 6 cylinders. Specifically, Boyle wanted him to re-examine the experimental 2-litre V6 that had been drawn up for P5 in the days when it was envisaged as a smaller car than P4, and he wanted Swaine to think about developing a lightweight aluminium alloy version of it. He

WHY CALL IT P6?

In late 1945, Maurice Wilks began work on the design of a new post-war Rover, which he called Model P. This was a completely new type of name for Rover – the pre-war cars had simply been called 10hp, 12hp, and so on – and the most likely theory is that the P stood for post-war. (Wilks seems to have liked these single-letter codes. He used M for a proposed post-war miniature car, T for the gas turbine models and J for a mule prototype based on the Jeep that eventually developed into the Land Rover.)

Model P did not materialize, but the one that followed it logically became model P2, even though it was actually a very limited update of the last pre-war Rovers. Next came P3 in 1948, marrying a new engine and chassis to what was essentially still pre-war styling with separate wings and running boards.

The P3 was a short-lived model, and the proper post-war model arrived in 1949 as the P4. Engine and chassis were both further developments of those pioneered in the P3, but the new full-width, three-box body styling was completely new to Rover – and upset many traditionalists.

The P5 was initially intended to be a smaller, higher-volume car positioned below the P4, but actually became a more upmarket, lower-volume model released in 1958. It was still being developed when Rover started work on their new high-volume model, which logically took the next code name of P6.

The P-series of code names continued until the end of Rover's days as an independent company. P7 was a further development of P6, which is described in Chapter 4; P8 was intended to replace P5 but was cancelled by British Leyland because it would have been a direct rival for the Jaguar XJ6. Then there was the P9, a sports car developed from the P6BS (*see* Chapter 8), which was cancelled because it was another direct threat to Jaguar; and finally the P10, which started life as the replacement for the P6 and became SD1 under British Leyland.

also wanted him to look at the 4-cylinder Mercedes-Benz 190 engine (an ohc type of 1897cc with 75bhp) as 'a good example of about the best that can be done'. Other subjects of study were to be the 6-cylinder Mercedes-Benz 220S engine (ohc, 2195cc, 100bhp) and the 6-cylinder Mays-head Ford Zephyr engine (ohv, 2553cc, 127bhp).

1957: A SLOW START

The start of serious thinking about Rover's new model had coincided with the early days of a major international crisis. In July 1956, President Nasser of Egypt nationalized the Suez Canal, and Israel, Britain and France responded by sending invasion forces to 'liberate' this critical international waterway. Nasser then sank blockade ships in it to prevent trading vessels passing through, and although the United Nations then intervened to restore peace in the region, oil supplies were seriously disrupted.

In Britain, petrol prices rose sharply and rationing was introduced in mid-December, the ordinary car user being limited to enough for 200 miles (320km) a month. Sales of new cars slowed dramatically; Ford and Vauxhall reduced production and introduced a four-day working week, and

Rover sales inevitably suffered. Clearly there was not much point in planning for a new model if the Suez Crisis was going to have long-term effects. On 23 January, Peter Wilks wrote a memo to say that all PX planning would be suspended until further notice. He asked for any ideas to be forwarded to Gordon Bashford, who would bring them to Maurice Wilks' notice when the time was right.

Fortunately, the crisis began to ease, and the ban seems to have been lifted fairly quickly. Within a couple of months, Robert Boyle had drawn up a 'Suggested Specification for P6'. There was no more talk of PX. He now expected the car to have rear-wheel drive, still with a two-speed torque converter transmission. He expected Rover to manufacture the base-unit in house as a 'composite structure using steel, light alloy and other material such as waterproof plywood… as dictated by cost, weight and performance'. Its bolt-on skin panels were to be of light alloy.

Boyle envisaged 4-cylinder and 6-cylinder derivatives of the P6, with engines that shared common bore and stroke dimensions, a chain-driven overhead camshaft and a die-cast light-alloy cylinder block. The 4-cylinder was to have 80bhp, five main bearings and a 1.8-litre swept volume, while the 6-cylinder was to be a 2.7-litre engine with seven main bearings and 120bhp.

This was the outline specification that he put to an engineering policy meeting on 19 April, no doubt seizing the opportunity created by the end of petrol rationing, which followed the reopening of the Suez Canal that month. Chairman Spencer Wilks and the two recently appointed joint managing directors, George Farmer and Maurice Wilks, agreed that he should go ahead with what he had in mind. That meeting also agreed that Boyle should find a new office for Gordon Bashford – whom he had made responsible for the layout of the new car – close to Spen King in the Gas Turbine Department to allow maximum co-operation between them.

This was a new and exciting development, and it marked the formal start of a plan to develop a gas turbine-powered variant of the P6 saloon. Rover had already built a number of successful gas turbine cars, but all had been engineering test-beds. Pressing his department's interests, King now wanted to build a new gas turbine car that would be a viable production possibility. The cost of developing a purpose-designed model would be too great, and so King wanted to get a gas turbine engine adopted as a production option for the new P6 saloon. This was why he needed to work closely with Bashford, whose overall design for the base unit was to leave room for the 2S/140 gas turbine engine that King's team were already developing.

The idea that there should be both 4-cylinder and 6-cylinder models now became more firmly embedded in the plan, and on 13 May a document outlining Rover's 'suggested future car programme' envisaged a 4-cylinder P6/A model and a 6-cylinder P6/B model. The first P6/A prototype was to be on the road by March 1959 and cars were expected to be on sale from October 1960. The P6/B programme was undated, and was presumably expected to follow at a later date.

This was all well and good, but there was still no agreed specification for P6, and paperwork from the first half of 1957 reflects this confusion. The 6-cylinder engine, for example, is called a 3L7 in some papers – but that was actually the P5 3-litre IOE engine and not the planned new ohc type at all. By June, the idea of a two-speed torque converter gearbox had been dropped, but some papers refer to a conventional four-speed manual box as standard while others suggest that a new three-speed type then being developed might be fitted. Expected options were the P5's overdrive and Borg Warner automatic gearboxes. Frank Shaw's transmission engineers probably breathed a sigh of relief when they were finally asked to focus on a new four-speed all-synchromesh gearbox for the P6.

Gordon Bashford, frustrated by this lack of clear direction from his management, spoke to Robert Boyle and Peter Wilks on 12 June in an attempt to pin down a specification for the P6, but all he got was another set of different ideas! So P6 remained undefined until the autumn, when Bashford, Wilks and Boyle met in Boyle's office on 30 September and established 'certain terms of reference for P6'. They agreed a number of actions, and Peter Wilks drew up a dated engineering programme on 11 October, which was adopted with minor changes and issued to relevant people at Rover on 29 October.

At last, things were getting under way. Rover management now agreed to aim for an October 1961 Earls Court show launch for the new car. The company advertised for a project engineer and recruited Ted (Tadeusz) Gawronski from Ford specifically to lead development of the new car; his experience with cars produced in much higher volumes than Rover was used to was no doubt expected to be invaluable. Gordon Reed became his deputy as Assistant Project Engineer, and a pair of more junior Technical Assistants completed the development team.

Robert Boyle had already concluded that Rover could not manufacture the base units in house after all, and so he and Gordon Bashford visited Pressed Steel in November to arrange for that company to supply base units and panels in quantity by July 1961. By the end of the year, Gordon Bashford had completed the preliminary mock-up and layout work, although there were still some stray ideas around. Among these were an air suspension system, which Brian Silvester's Research Department engineers investigated as an eventual alternative to the steel springs planned for the first production cars.

The Base Unit

Base-unit construction, in which the mechanical components and unstressed skin panels are bolted to a stressed steel skeleton, had first been proposed at Rover in 1951 by Olaf Poppe – four years before Citroën had announced it on their revolutionary DS model. It was ideally suited to the long model life for which a small company like Rover had to plan, because styling facelifts to the unstressed skin panels would be cheap and simple to make.

This method of construction also appealed to Gordon Bashford, because it both saved the weight of a separate chassis and offered the torsional rigidity that he considered so important in car design. Follow-ing Poppe's suggestion, he built a first experimental base unit in 1952 using the dimensions of the then-current P4 saloon so that direct compari-sons could be made. By mid-1954 he had built one up into a mobile test rig, using P4 60 running gear and an experimental strut suspension.

Base-unit construction had been part of the specification for the origi-nal 'small' P5, but a monocoque was chosen when that car became larger and heavier. Nevertheless, Bashford remained convinced of the sound-ness of the base-unit principle, and he championed it for P6.

For Pressed Steel, the Rover base unit was a new challenge. Not only was it the first base-unit structure they had been asked to build, but Rover also demanded very tight manufacturing tolerances because they wanted to minimize the amount of hand-fitting necessary on the assembly lines. To achieve the nec-essary 'first time' panel fit, Pressed Steel planned to put every base unit through a large automated drilling jig that ensured all the bolt holes for the outer skin panels would be in exactly

This is the very first full-size base unit, which would be built up as P6/1. The unusual front suspension design can be clearly seen. The tyres are tubeless crossply types on 13in steel disc wheels. ROVER CO. LTD

This schematic drawing shows the unstressed skin panels that bolted to the P6 base unit.

the same place every time. Pressed Steel engineers kept in close touch with Rover designers as details of the base unit evolved during the P6's development.

From this policy of easy panel fitting came the idea of easy panel replacement, and Rover decided to provide ready-painted P6 skin panels from the factory that could be bolted straight on to reduce the cost of accident repair work. This system continued in use until the late 1960s and perhaps longer, but brought with it additional complications for stock-ing the panels as the number of colour options increased.

1958: P6 TAKES SHAPE

The issue of a preliminary specification for the P6 on New Year's Day 1958 was almost symbolic of a new beginning.

Some fifteen months after that first discussion about the P6 in Robert Boyle's office, the car was formally expected to be a high-performance lightweight four-seater of advanced design on a 103in (2,616mm) wheelbase. It was to sacrifice none of the traditional Rover engineering quality or ride comfort, but it would be lighter and cheaper to run than the P4 that it would replace.

Work on the P6 during 1958 was aimed at just two tar-gets. By July, all information needed to build a base unit and suspension units for static tests was to be available. By December, the main styling features were to be established and enough information available to permit manufacture of a set of body panels for the first running prototype. That put much of the onus onto David Bache's Styling Department because the base unit could not be finalized until certain elements of the styling had been determined.

In fact, Bache had put down his first thoughts on P6 styling in a memo dated 12 December 1957. These show how much emphasis he placed on simplicity: 'In view of the very nature of the P6 specification,' he wrote, 'it lends itself ideally to be a simple classical form, devoid of all superfluous ornament.' In the longer term, such a style would be 'most helpful for a future revision (facelift) policy'. Bache envisaged

David Bache ran the Styling Department. He had been responsible for the P5, for various P4 facelifts, and would lead the styling for the P6. ROVER CO. LTD

'a clean elegant form with all character lines expressed by the medium of sculpture in the basic panels, with no external rubbing strips. The general form flows forward creating vivid movement with a new and unused character.'

With simplicity went good aerodynamics, which Bache reasoned would improve both performance and stability. Good high-speed handling would be important in the coming age of the motorway, and Bache's designs for the P6 therefore all aimed to get the centre of air pressure far enough rearwards to ensure straight-line running at high speeds. Aerodynamics also influenced the design, and from the start the bonnet and windscreen planes were designed to provide optimum pressure at the base of the windscreen, where the air intake for the heating and ventilating system would be located.

Sketches and photographs from Bache's styling studios show that there was a good deal of American influence on the early P6 proposals – unsurprising at a time when American car design was in the ascendant. Several had pronounced tail fins, and some of the bold tail-light designs proposed were wholly unlike anything seen in the European motor industry. The dimensions, though, were firmly European, and there was European influence in the shapes of the roof line and the nose, both of which clearly took their inspiration from Citroën's 1955 DS saloon.

By the middle of January 1958, Bache's team were making quarter-scale models of various styling proposals; by the end of March these were ready for formal viewing and selection of a theme; and by the middle of July, the favoured theme had been turned into the first full-size P6 clay

Bache's ideas for the shape of the P6 were translated into a series of scale models. The dart-like shape of early proposals is clear on the one nearer the camera. AUTHOR'S COLLECTION

Those scale models showed a different proposal on each side. This is side A of model no. 2; some of the differences on the side B proposal (otherwise 2B) can be seen. ROVER CO. LTD

THE CITROËN INFLUENCE

The Citroën DS represented the cutting edge of automotive design at the time Rover began thinking seriously about the new model that would become the P6, and so it should be no surprise that it had a considerable influence on the new car from Solihull. Introduced at the Paris Salon in October 1955, the DS pioneered base-unit construction, and featured all-round disc brakes with a full-power hydraulic system, together with a revolutionary interlinked suspension that was operated from the same high-pressure hydraulic circuit as the brakes. High-pressure hydraulics were also used for the steering and clutch.

The Citroën had a 4-cylinder, 2-litre engine, which was an elderly design that was the car's only major disappointment, but it did drive the front wheels rather than the rear wheels, and this was still seen as quite avant-garde even though Citroën had espoused front-wheel drive as long ago as 1934. One result of this layout was that the passenger cabin was quite remarkably spacious for the size of the car.

The Citroën DS had some important influences on the design of the P6.
KLUGSCHNACKER/
WIKIMEDIA COMMONS

Rover certainly considered using front-wheel drive for their new car, although they abandoned the idea quite early on. They enthusiastically followed Citroën's lead by using base-unit construction (which they had been looking at independently for some years), and they also chose to use an all-disc braking system. The high-pressure hydraulic system was a step too far, although Rover certainly did experiment with full-power brakes, testing them on a pair of P4 105R saloons during 1957. The Citroën's famed 'magic carpet ride' almost certainly persuaded Rover to pay careful attention to the suspension of their new car, choosing a De Dion rear axle to give most of the benefits of an all-round independent layout.

Then there was of course the influence of the Citroën's shape on David Bache's styling for the P6. His original design had a low, sloping nose that recalled the Citroën (although the Rover always had a conventional boot instead of a sloping rear like the French car). The shape of the Rover's roof and glass area was also undeniably influenced by the DS, and a comparison of the bright trim around the top corners of the windscreen on the two cars is further confirmation of the Citroën influence.

It is again no surprise that Rover should have bought a Citroën to study, although of course they had a fleet of competitor cars of all types. Their Citroën was not in fact a DS but the cheaper and less complex ID19 model, which lacked some of the high-pressure hydraulic systems. The car was registered to Rover as XUE 431 on 5 February 1958; for the record, it had commission number 9-560085 and engine 20701225, and was sold on through Stratton Motors on 11 August 1960.

styling model. As a next stage, this was handed over to the jig shop, where a team led by Cyril Nicholls had hand-built a prototype base unit by the end of October. This was then put through a series of static tests, mainly to determine its torsional rigidity.

Here is P6/I during early testing. No wind tunnel was available, so the aerodynamic performance was measured by means of tufts of wool attached to the car. ROVER CO. LTD

The early base unit design was pillarless, with a deep panel at the rear that added strength and formed a box-like boot. This is base unit no. 4 undergoing torsional testing at Pressed Steel. It would never be built into a complete car. PRESSED STEEL CO.

1959: THE FIRST PROTOTYPES

Skin panels, gearbox and engine all became available in the closing months of 1958, and the first running prototype of the P6 was on the road by the end of February 1959. To the Engineering Department it was known as P6/I, but in terms of the overall P6 programme it was known as a Phase I prototype. The plan was to build four Phase I cars to the 1958 specification, to incorporate the lessons learned from these into the Phase II prototypes, and then for the Phase III prototypes to have the final modifications before production began. At least, that was what the Rover engineers hoped. In practice, there would also be a Phase IIIA, a Phase IV and a Phase IVA before the P6 entered production, and along the way there would be plans for a radical future redevelopment that became known as Phase X!

The construction of the first P6 prototype should have signalled the end of Gordon Bashford's involvement with the project. His job, after all, was to develop new concepts and no more. However, Maurice Wilks wanted to ensure that the radically new engineering that would go into the P6 should lose nothing in the transition from drawing board to production line, so he asked Bashford to remain in close touch with the project right up to the pre-production stage. As a result, the P6 would always be very much Gordon Bashford's baby.

The four Phase I prototype cars were built in the first nine months of 1959 and were numbered P6/I to P6/4. They all had a sloping nose with frog-eye headlamps, a pillarless passenger cabin with frameless door windows, a 100in (2,540mm) wheelbase and a 'box' boot with

By the time of the fifth prototype in late 1959, Rover had greater confidence in the strength of the base unit and the depth of the rear panel was reduced. This appears to have been the only car built with twin headlamps on the original sloping nose. ROVER CO. LTD

full-depth tail panel for rigidity. All of them had the new 2-litre 4-cylinder ohc engine and all-synchromesh gearbox that would be carried through to production, but they had disc front brakes and inboard rear drums because a satisfactory all-disc system was not yet available. Suspension and steering were generally similar to the eventual production designs, although the Phase I cars had crossply tyres on 13in wheels instead of radials on 14in wheels. It was probably one of these cars that achieved 109mph (175km/h) at the new MIRA test track near Nuneaton.

Inevitably, there were problems. 'When we put the first car on the road, it was a shocker... terrible!' Gordon Bashford told the author. 'It vibrated, it was noisy, and tyres were a problem. You've got to remember it was a lot of new ideas incorporated into one vehicle.' Pavé testing revealed structural problems, too: the weight of the full fuel tank, located under the boot floor, caused the joint between the A-post and the cantrail to flex and crack because the pillarless construction failed to absorb the stress loading. The frameless side windows also gave trouble.

Then there were objections to the Phase I car's appearance, especially to its futuristic sloping nose design. 'Maurice Wilks thought the public wouldn't like it,' Spen King told the author. As a result, David Bache was asked to draw up a 'proper' front end, and as early as July 1959 he was working on the squared-off, twin-headlamp nose that would lend the production P6 such distinction. Even that was a bit radical

for some tastes, as all earlier Rovers had incorporated a recognizable old-style radiator grille.

Not all of these problems had been rectified by the time of the first Phase II prototype, which was probably built in 1959. The sloping nose remained, although it now incorporated the four frog-eye headlamps that had been tried on a full-size mock-up in April. The passenger cabin was still pillarless and the door glasses were still frameless, and the fuel tank was still under the boot floor. However, the clumsy rear end shape of the Phase I cars had been refined, the roof had been redesigned with a more pronounced rearward curve, and the interior trim had been extended to leave none of the bare metal in the passenger compartment that had characterized the first four cars.

Interior Design

David Bache's Styling Department began work on a full-size model of the P6's passenger compartment early in 1958. The driver's compartment (seat, facia and controls) was initially developed on a separate model, and the finished details were then transferred to the full passenger compartment buck.

Bache's aim was to allow the driver maximum comfort and convenience to give him or her the best chance of retaining full control of the car at all times. He was a pioneer in applying the science of ergonomics to car design,

This interior proposal is a full-size model, and shows the early design of lightweight seats and the twin-nacelle proposal for the instruments; in this case, the dials have been taken from a P5. The 'shin bins' and central grouping of the switchgear are already in the plan. ROVER CO. LTD

ponents to minimize injury in an impact. Below the parcel shelf he sited angled drop-down 'shin bins', which were padded and would collapse under impact to reduce leg injuries. At the same time, he designed most of the P6 dashboard to be made from injection-moulded plastic, a relatively new medium in the motor industry. These large mouldings reduced the amount of hand assembly typical on car production lines, so lowering costs. He designed injection-moulded plastic retainers for the wood finishers on the doors, reducing the amount of hand fitting traditional to Rovers. And, of course, all the plastic components contributed to weight saving.

Rover owners expected leather upholstery, but Bache's team developed a new lightweight seat design that was half the weight of a traditional P4 or P5 seat. They began by sculpting the seat in clay to ensure its form was physiologically correct, and then designed the mechanical details within the agreed contours. A new patented frame was created to absorb impact loads in a collision and so minimize injuries, and it incorporated infinite rake adjustment for the first time in a Rover. The first lightweight seat prototype was ready in March 1959, and seats of this design went into many of the early P6 prototypes. They can still be seen in the surviving gas turbine prototype, T4. Unfortunately, they were not carried through to production. No details are known, but it seems that the visually more luxurious production design was called for some time around 1962.

and this was reflected in some of his design solutions. For example, he made the steering column adjustable to suit drivers of different sizes; he set the speedometer as far from the driver's eyes as possible because most people have difficulty in changing focus from road to instruments quickly; he sited cold-air vents carefully to prevent drowsiness; he used modern 'idiot lights' instead of gauges because they were impossible to ignore; and he used different designs for different dashboard switches to make them easier to distinguish in the dark.

The P6 interior was also designed to simplify production of both left-hand-drive and right-hand-drive cars. The handbrake, gear lever, radio and switches were all mounted centrally. Bache reversed the traditional positions of glove box and parcel shelf to give a full-width parcel shelf onto which the instrument pod could be mounted on either side. The original design had all the instruments contained in two large circular pods ahead of the driver, and both mock-ups and prototypes had P5 dials. However, the production layout with its ribbon speedometer was settled in December 1960, and the first car to have it was probably P6/12, ten months later.

Bache's design also took account of the trend towards safety features, with rounded or soft edges to interior com-

1960: MORE DELAYS

For the second time in its short history, political problems now had an impact on the P6 programme. The British government were pursuing a policy of creating employment in depressed areas of the country by encouraging manufacturers to build new factories there and refusing planning permission for new factories in existing prosperous areas. The Midlands was a prosperous area, and Rover were denied permission to build the new factory at Solihull that they had always seen as essential to the P6 project.

Rover moved rapidly to resolve the problem. The company acquired a 120-acre (48ha) site on the former airport at Pengam, near Cardiff – a choice probably influenced by their new production director, William Martin-Hurst, who was also chairman of the Welsh Development Board. By October 1960, they had gained planning permission for a satellite plant there and for an extension to some existing buildings on the north of the Solihull site.

Building the new factories from scratch meant that the P6's launch would be delayed by two years from its original target of October 1961. While Rover management were probably less than happy, the engineers were more positive. As Gordon Bashford remembered, 'We were under some pressure because of some development problems on P6 relating to structure and vibration, so in my opinion a delay was a godsend.' One consequence was that any plans for further Phase II prototypes were cancelled, and Rover moved straight to Phase III for the next cars.

Spen King also believed that this delay allowed Rover to take a second look at the P6 project. King had now become much more directly involved with P6 after a management reshuffle in 1960, which had put him in charge of what was now called New Vehicle Projects. This was in fact Gordon Bashford's old design research team, now supervised directly by King instead of reporting both to Robert Boyle as chief engineer and to Roland Seale as head of the drawing office.

'We now had time for a rethink,' he told the author. 'I was keen on looking at front-wheel drive, so I asked Gordon to draw up some layouts for me.' This second look probably began in December 1960 and became known as Phase X. Like the main programme, it allowed for both 4-cylinder and 6-cylinder derivatives of the car, but it did not go beyond the drawing board. The main reason was that the delay caused by the new factory

allowed Rover to develop out the problems that had shown up on the prototypes and to make the P6 much more refined in its existing rear-wheel-drive form.

Much of this refinement work was carried out on the next pair of prototypes. Planning for the Phase III cars had begun in the early autumn of 1959, before the Phase II car was on

After Maurice Wilks had vetoed the sloping nose design as too radical, David Bache redesigned the front end. This is the full-size mock-up, pictured on the roof of the Styling Department in May 1960. There are quarter-bumpers at the front, and there is still a kick-up at the waistline on the rear window, although the pillarless design has been abandoned. ROVER CO. LTD

The visual redesign required a redesign of the base unit, too, and here a scale model is being prepared. AUTHOR'S COLLECTION

COMPARING NOTES

In 1960 Rover became aware that Standard-Triumph were developing a new 2-litre saloon for release at about the same time as their own. After what was probably some high-level negotiation, the two companies got together to compare notes, probably to determine the risks involved in putting two essentially similar models onto the market at the same time.

Rover discovered that the new Triumph 2000 was going to have a 6-cylinder engine and that it would be far more conventional than their P6. What neither company realized was that they were both working on cars that would start a new market trend – the so-called 'executive saloon' market that would become important during the 1960s.

Special Talago badges were made up to disguise the prototypes when they went out on road test. It appears that each car had only two, one on the rear and one on the left-hand front wing. This one was kept as a memento by deputy project engineer Gordon Reed (who later took over as project engineer). AUTHOR

the road, and they were to have some major differences. Their fuel tanks were to be repositioned over the rear axle to overcome the stress problems at the front of the base unit, and they were to have a conventional full centre body pillar with framed door tops and the new squared-off front end. At some stage during the design process, their wheelbase was lengthened from the original 100in (2,540mm) to a nominal 103.5in (2,629mm), probably to restore passenger cabin space taken up by the relocated fuel tank. With this redesign, Phase III became Phase IIIA, and in practice no Phase III cars were ever built. Both P6/6 and P6/7 were put on the road in July 1960 as 103.5in wheelbase Phase IIIA cars.

Ted Gawronski checks the tyres by the roadside during the 1960 Continental test. The half-height rear panel and a proposed design of rear over-riders are both very clear here. TED GAWRONSKI

Prototype number P6/7 was taken on a Continental proving trip by Peter Wilks (left) and Ted Gawronski (right) during 1960. Note how the design of the rear door windows has been changed to incorporate a quarter-light. This picture was probably taken in Spain.
TED GAWRONSKI

The next stage in the P6 test programme was high-mile-age endurance testing, and much of this would be done on public roads. Keen to keep their new car secret for as long as possible (in order to protect sales of the existing models), Rover chose an elaborate disguise. It was not enough to register the cars away from Solihull, as had been done with the earlier prototypes, because the cars still carried the Rover name on the licence discs in their windscreens. This time, they set up an entirely fictitious car company that would register the cars, and developed badges to go with it. The company was called Talago, a name thought up by project engineer Ted Gawronski and based on his initials of TLG.

Over the summer of 1960, P6/7 went on a long continental road test with Peter Wilks and Ted Gawronski. Closer to home, it achieved a best speed of 107.8mph (173.5km/h) for the flying quarter-mile and a mean of 104.8mph (168.7km/h) during maximum speed runs on the M1 motorway, where the police used to allow testing early in the morning before traffic had built up. These were good figures: although an earlier prototype had reached 109mph (175km/h), P6/7 was heavier, thanks to those extra 3.5in (89mm) in its wheelbase, and it had a less aerodynamic front-end design. Besides, 100mph (162km/h) was still a magic figure that was unattainable by most family saloons in the early 1960s.

Meanwhile, the older prototypes remained in use for some types of development work. Under Phase III of the P6 programme, for example, P6/3, P6/4 and P6/5 were to be fitted with Delaney-Gallay heater-demister units to see if these were a viable alternative to the Smith's type. But Phase IIIA did not last for long. Phase IV began on 18 November 1960.

The Engine and Gearbox

Jack Swaine's brief for the new Rover engine called for a 4-cylinder type of between 1700cc and 2000cc. The performance target for P6 was 100mph (162km/h), and this had to be allied to good fuel economy. Swaine calculated that the new engine needed about 90bhp in view of the overall weight target for the P6. Minimum weight was a given, along with a low overall height so that David Bache could have his sloping nose design.

That low overall height was not going to be easy to achieve with the modern ohc design that Swaine wanted to use. He had to argue his case for this with Maurice Wilks, who was initially strongly opposed to the idea, probably thinking of the long timing chain that would be needed when he insisted that such an engine would be noisy. Swaine got his way in the end, designing a two-stage chain drive with double roller chains in each one and a tensioner to take up wear. He also pointed out that wide-throated valves in an ohc design would give good breathing, with low reciprocating weight and light valve spring loadings.

Engine and gearbox viewed from the left-hand side; this one was taken from an early (suffix B) production car. The forward exit of the exhaust outlet probably restricted power a little.

NICK DUNNING

The height issue also limited the length of the pistons' stroke. An oversquare design would have limited low- and mid-speed performance, so Swaine chose an equal bore and stroke of 85.7mm, which gave an overall displacement of 1978cc. Steeply inclined inlet ports and vertical inlet valves would have given the best gas flow, but this would also have given overall height problems. So Swaine chose to cast the inlet manifold into the cylinder head in the form of an open gallery, with its top face closed by a bolted plate.

Cost ruled out an all-alloy engine, although an alloy cylinder head was affordable and followed existing Rover practice. An aluminium sump was affordable, too, and Swaine made it as deep as he could, meeting the block along the crankcase centreline. Bolting the sump through to the base of the gearbox maintained rigidity of the engine-and-transmission assembly, while a steel sandwich plate sealed off the rear of the block and sump from the clutch housing.

Working with his assistant, Norman Bryden, Swaine reduced the weight of the iron block by designing it with two large 'windows' in the sides, where strength was less critical. These were then covered with 16-gauge blanking plates. The timing cover was also cast in one with the block, access being through holes filled by blanking plugs with rubber seals. Swaine had no hesitation in choosing a five-bearing crankshaft (three-bearing types were more common in 1958) to ensure smooth running. When torsional vibration problems showed up at 5,200rpm on test during 1960, Norman Bryden sought advice from Stewart Tressilian at Bristol Siddeley Engines in Coventry. However, in the end Rover did not adopt his suggestion of a four-bearing crankshaft with counter-weights in place of a centre main bearing; instead, they used a Holset rubber damper on the nose of the five-bearing crankshaft.

Combustion chamber design was influenced by the need for compactness, with the whole squish area within the bore. The ohc design with in-line valves ruled out a conventional hemispherical chamber in the cylinder head, and Swaine told the author that 'bathtub' designs proved unsatisfactory. So Rover used a Heron-head design, with the combustion chamber in the piston crown and a flat cylinder head face. Early fears of high piston operating temperatures proved unfounded, but a cutaway piston top was designed after tests on a single-cylinder development rig showed that the valves would hit the pistons at TDC if the engine was over-revved to the point of valve bounce.

With a single SU carburettor and a 9:1 compression ratio, the new 2-litre engine developed 90bhp gross at 5,000rpm –

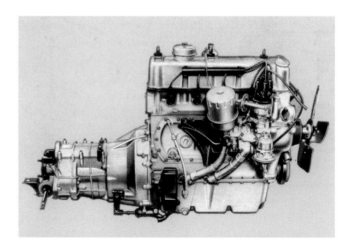

From the other side, the high-mounted oil filter is a notable feature. It simplified servicing – and had been tried before on the early Rover P4 engines.

almost as much as the 6-cylinder Rover 90 engine produced from 2.6 litres. The engine was a viable concern by the end of 1958, although considerable detail refinement followed before production – such as using a nylon adjusting arm to cut out secondary vibrations from the rubber-mounted dynamo.

This engine drove the rear wheels of the P6 through a new four-speed all-synchromesh gearbox drawn up by Frank Shaw in the Transmission Department, who reported to Roland Seale, the head of the Rover drawing office. Despite the good fuel economy that was a P6 design target, the additional weight and cost of a bolt-on overdrive (as used in existing P4 and P5 Rovers) probably prevented one from being specified for the new car. Nevertheless, experiments with an overdrive did follow during the early 1960s (*see* Chapter 8).

1961: PHASE IV

It was on 24 October 1960 that Maurice Wilks formally proposed to the Rover board that the P6 should be put into production. His fellow directors agreed and set a new launch target date of October 1963 – just two years after that originally planned. And in December 1960, the New Vehicle Projects team turned their thoughts to the next stage of the P6 programme, which was the 6-cylinder derivative that had been planned since the beginning. In practice, it became the P7, and its story is told in Chapter 4 of this book.

Nearly there! P6/9, built in 1961, still had front quarter-bumpers but was very recognizably the car that would enter production less than two years later. ROVER CO. LTD

There was, however, still plenty of development work still to be done on the 4-cylinder P6. Five more base units were sanctioned under Phase IV, but only four of them were built up as P6 prototypes. These were numbered P6/8, P6/9, P6/11 and P6/12, the missing number 10 becoming Spen King's gas turbine-engined prototype and being renumbered as T4/10 (there is more about this car in Chapter 8). All of them were built up during 1961, and all of them had a new rear end with a bootlid that opened down to bumper height: it was by now clear that the P6 base unit was strong enough without the additional transverse panel at the rear. To counter the extra weight introduced when the wheelbase had been extended under Phase IIIA, the Phase IV cars had lower first, second and third gear ratios that improved acceleration. That 104mph (167km/h) top speed achieved in 1960 was going to be enough.

It was during this stage of the programme that the P6 made the important switch from crossply tyres to radials. Spen King recalled radial tyres being suggested to Rover by Dunlop, with whom the company had long-standing links:

> *Rex Marvin [Rover's chief development engineer] and I looked at radials for the P6, but they increased road noise enormously – and the P6 was already a noisy car. So we examined a Peugeot, which was the best there was then for low road-noise on radials. That had compliance built into its suspension, and so I designed some compliance into the P6's suspension and we standardized on radials. The handling was much better after that.*

One of the last changes before production was that the ventilation outlets on the rear pillars were deleted. Here is one, on the car that survives as P6/16. AUTHOR

In fact, Dunlop had been touting for business without having the product: only Pirelli made the 165 × 14 radial size that Rover needed for the P6. Nevertheless, Dunlop agreed to produce the right size specially for Rover, and Rover agreed to dual-source its tyres so that the first production P6s came with either Dunlop SP tubeless or Pirelli Cinturato tubed tyres as original equipment.

It was Dunlop, too, who came up with the definitive P6 braking system. As early as the outline specification of 1 October 1956, Robert Boyle had wanted power-assisted disc brakes in the car's specification, and before Phase I had begun in 1959, Rover had approached both Girling and Dunlop about an all-disc system to suit the 13in wheels then planned for the P6. An all-disc system made by Lockheed was certainly under consideration during Phase I, although it is doubtful that it was ever installed on a car. However, by October 1961, Dunlop had come up with a power-assisted all-disc system that would suit the P6 as then conceived. With this in the programme, Phase IVA began.

Another important design change in this period was prompted by William Martin-Hurst, who at that stage was production director. It seems to have been in the early summer of 1961 that he told Maurice Wilks that he thought the boot was too small, and the record of an executive directors' meeting dated 20 June 1961 refers to a 50 per cent increase in boot capacity. A deeper boot was probably then tried out on one of the Phase IV prototypes. The base-unit press tooling had already been ordered from Pressed Steel, but Wilks bit the bullet and had it altered to make the boot deeper. At the same time, the spare wheel well was moved from the right-hand side to the left.

Suspension Design

The suspension design of the P6 was one of its most advanced and interesting features, and lay behind its excellent ride and handling qualities. Gordon Bashford had proposed as early as January 1958 that suspension stresses should be borne by the front and rear bulkheads, which were the most rigid pressings in the base-unit structure. A rubber-in-torsion

The inboard rear disc brakes reduced unsprung weight and so contributed to the excellent ride quality – although they were not easy to work on.

suspension medium was subsequently briefly discussed but rejected because the accompanying mechanical leveller was likely to be rather heavy.

The front suspension was designed to meet Spen King's need for a wide engine bay to accommodate his gas turbine engine. Bashford drew it up with an upper link pivoted from the bulkhead, a horizontal coil spring parallel to it, and a very short lower locating link. He kept the steering linkage clear of the engine bay by running it along the bulkhead, and an anti-roll bar was clamped to the top links, again minimizing intrusion into the engine bay. As fitted to the first P6 prototypes, the system had a forged bottom wishbone, but this was changed for a cast type in 1959 or 1960.

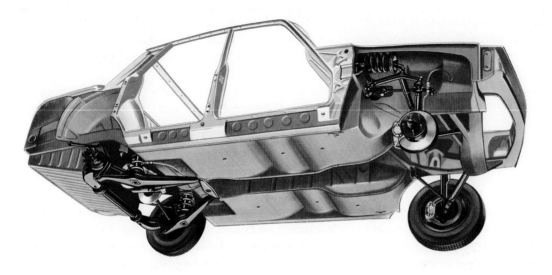

The suspension design was quite remarkable for a saloon car, with a De Dion rear end and a custom-designed arrangement at the front that left a wide engine bay.

An early proposal for an independent rear end with swing axles (as used by Mercedes) lost out to Bashford's plan for a De Dion tube with a sliding joint, fixed-length driveshafts and a Watts linkage to locate the axle. Although this increased unsprung weight compared to conventional independent rear suspension, its ability to keep the rear wheels parallel to each other and vertical to the road at all times gave great handling advantages.

No production Rover had ever had a De Dion suspension, but Bashford, King and Peter Wilks were all keen motor sport enthusiasts and were convinced of its merits as a result. King and Wilks had used a De Dion axle in their home-built Rover Special single-seater racing car some years earlier, and King had incorporated one into his 1956 Rover T3 gas turbine prototype. Bashford, meanwhile, had also used De Dion axles in the Djinn and the Mezzolitre, two single-seaters he had designed for club racing in the early 1950s.

Peter Wilks told *Autocar* magazine in a 1969 interview that Maurice Wilks had initially been:

> dead against… the De Dion back end, which he thought was a quite unjustified expense. We took the view, though, that for the sake of an extra £35 – which is about what it costs – it was well worth it just to be able to write De Dion into the specification of the car, even if it hadn't turned out to be any better. We did in fact succeed in creating an image of engineering innovation which had an impact which the car might otherwise not have had.

From the start, Bashford mounted the rear brakes inboard next to the differential housing, where they did not affect unsprung weight. Early prototypes had rear drums with their front discs (a disc-drum set-up did not reach production on other Rovers until autumn 1959), but an all-disc system became available during 1961 and was carried through to production.

1962: A PROPER NAME

The four Phase IVA prototypes were numbered P6/13 to P6/16 and were put on the road during the first five months of 1962. They had the all-disc braking system, radial tyres, the Smith's ribbon speedometer, the deeper boot, and the final production-style panelling. Probably two had left-hand

More mock-ups were needed, and this one, built up at Pressed Steel, served as the model from which the dimensions of the production panels were taken. Behind it, under the cover, can be seen a Jaguar E-type bodyshell, which was of course another Pressed Steel product. PRESSED STEEL CO.

drive, as exports were expected to be an important element in P6 sales. Tests showed that everything was now satisfactory, and the full technical specification was settled in May 1962.

New Vehicle Projects now bowed out of the picture. Although Spen King and Gordon Bashford continued to look at future developments of the P6, the basic 4-cylinder model was now handed over to the department headed by Dick Oxley, chief engineer (cars), whose task was to refine the car and make it ready for production. 'He didn't much like P6 when it was handed over to him,' Spen King told the author, with a smile.

So far, the P6 had no name other than its project code, and it was William Martin-Hurst again who in 1962 proposed to call it a Rover 2000. As he explained to the author some twenty years later, Rover's sales division wanted to call the new car a Rover 2-litre, but Martin-Hurst pointed out that the logical name for the anticipated 6-cylinder variant would then be Rover 3-litre, a name already used for the big P5 saloon. So he suggested calling the 6-cylinder car a Rover 3000 and the 4-cylinder car a Rover 2000. These names, the first of their type in Rover history, were in use by August 1962 when a full-size mock-up was photographed wearing Rover 2000 badges.

THE P6 PROTOTYPES

Phase I prototypes

Number	Registration number	Registration date	Engine number	Remarks
P6/1	WUL 432	24 Feb 1959	2L/OHC/3	Airflow work, possibly towing tests
P6/2	WXY 963	1 May 1959	2L/OHC/5	Probably pavé test car
P6/3	XLF 666	1 Jun 1959	2L/OHC/6	Probably pavé test car
P6/4	See note	1959	See note	Base unit only; see note

Phase II prototype

Number	Registration number	Registration date	Engine number	Remarks
P6/5	XYK 5	c.Nov 1959	P6/9/7	Probably pavé test car

Phase IIIA prototypes

Number	Registration number	Registration date	Engine number	Remarks
P6/6	193 AYK	12 Jul 1960	P6/9/10	Unknown uses
P6/7	146 AYN	22 Jul 1960	P6/9/11	Continental road test, 1960; maximum speed tests on M1

Phase IV prototypes

Number	Registration number	Registration date	Engine number	Remarks
P6/8	8 BLR	1 Feb 1961	P6/9/13	Probably included wind tunnel tests; engine to experimental Land Rover 695 EAC, probably in November 1962
P6/9	9 BLR	1 Apr 1961	P6/9/12	Unknown uses
T4/10	6427 WD	1 Nov 1961	2S/140/II no 1	T4 gas turbine car. Still exists
P6/11	11 CXK	1 Sep 1961	Not known	Noise testing, door seal development, tyre testing
P6/12	12 CYX	c.1 Nov 1961	P6/9/16	Bootlid spare wheel mount trials; probably towing trials

Phase IVA prototypes

Number	Registration number	Registration date	Engine number	Remarks
P6/13	13 DLH	1 Jan 1962	P6/9/19	Unknown uses
P6/14	14 DLT	1 May 1962	P6/9/21	Probably left-hand drive; boot capacity trials
P6/15	15 DYF	c.Aug 1962	Not known	Unknown uses, probably including testing in Norway
P6/16	16 DYF	10 Aug 1962	P6/9/24	Left-hand drive; continental test and NVH work

Notes

P6/4 This may have been the base unit used for torsional tests by Pressed Steel in August 1959. It may also have been used for experimental CKD packaging and was probably the one pictured in this condition on 30 April 1960. It was probably never built up into a running prototype.

P6/16 This car was sold to a Rover employee in 1964 and was converted to RHD. It was rebuilt with a new base unit and V8 engine with manual gearbox in approximately 1970. It still survives and has been made to look as much like a P6 prototype as possible.

Colours All the P6 prototypes were painted in a dark grey colour that was chosen because it was unlikely to attract attention when they went out on the road. It suited the shape of the P6 very well and was exactly the sort of colour that that would appeal to traditional, conservatively minded Rover owners. So, ironically perhaps, it was chosen as a production colour and was then named City Grey.

Engine numbers The significance of the number 9 in the engine numbers used in P6/5 and later prototypes is not known for certain, but it is likely to have indicated a 9:1 compression ratio.

Talago models Company records for P6/6, P6/7, P6/9, P6/14 and P6/16 show that these cars were registered as Talagos. Photographs show Talago badges on P6/5, P6/7, P6/9, P6/12 and P6/13. These badges were certainly used on the first two off-tools cars (see Chapter 2) as well.

CHAPTER TWO

THE 'SHARK'S-TOOTH' 2000, 1963–1966

Pressed Steel's Cowley works began to deliver base units and panel sets to Solihull towards the end of 1962, and from these Rover assembled twenty-five pilot-production cars between January and the end of April 1963. These were described within the factory as off-tools prototypes. Two cars were completed in January; known to the Engineering Department as P6-A1 and P6-A2, these also had the production-style identities of 400-00001A and 400-00002A. P6-A3 to P6-A5 followed in February, and then in March came B-batch cars that incorporated minor production improvements. The first two were P6-B6 and P6-B7, and there may have been more with these numbers, but the

The very first production car came off the lines in January 1963, and was photographed on a snowy day that month. The full production specification was not yet in place, and 400-00001A (known internally as P6-A1) had a grille badge that was different from the production type, wheel trims with vaned ribs instead of grooves, and other differences. It was originally Willow Green, but was later repainted City Grey. ROVER CO. LTD

batch identifier had gone by the time of the twelfth car off the line, which was numbered P6-12 on the Engineering Department fleet. This was, of course, not the same car as prototype P6/12 built in 1961, which was still in use for development work. One car (400-00018A) was 'completed' as a CKD (completely knocked down) type.

WEARING DISGUISES

All the early off-tools and production cars were retained at Solihull. Most became engineering test vehicles, and several went out on public roads before the car was announced. Rover continued to take quite elaborate precautions to protect their identity, and all those road-registered during 1963 gained London rather than Warwickshire registrations. The first five became 101 FGO and 102–105 FJJ. A further batch of London numbers, 106 FLK to 154 FLK, was used for many of the early 2000s, although the numbers were not allocated consecutively and some were used up on early volume-production models – 143 FLK, for example, went onto car number 400-00122A. Prior to the public launch in autumn 1963, the 2000s that went out on the roads were stripped of badges and other identifying features, and some wore Talago badges as well. P6B-7 (400-00007A, 107 FLK) was sent out to France to allow Rover's importers, Franco-Britannique in Paris, to get an idea of the forthcoming new model, and for that trip it wore Triumph hubcaps, less their distinguishing centre badges.

Despite Rover's precautions, however, the security around the Rover 2000 did not remain entirely unbreached. In May 1963, the Norwegian *Teknikens Värld* magazine carried a picture of an unbadged 15 DYF (prototype P6/15), which they suspected was a Rover. Then in its September

The second of the 'FLK' cars was 400-00007A, which was built in March 1963 and became 107 FLK. This was a B-batch car (known internally as P6-B7), and still had several differences from the eventual production cars. It went out to Franco-Britannic Autos in Paris, Rover's French distributors, wearing no badges and with other disguise features. This and several other pictures of the car were taken in secret and no doubt against company instructions! AUTHOR'S COLLECTION

This rear view of 107 FLK shows the very early angled exhaust tailpipe, the offset reversing lamp, and a Talago badge on the bootlid, as used on the prototypes. There is a second Talago badge on the front wing – although, again as on the prototypes, there was not one on the opposite side. AUTHOR'S COLLECTION

Those wheel trims were part of the disguise, and were never intended for production. They are in fact de-badged Triumph hubcaps with slotted outer trim rings – as would become available on Triumph's own rival 2000! This car was painted in Turquoise, a colour not carried through to production. AUTHOR'S COLLECTION

Very noticeable in this underbonnet view are the detachable plates on the inner wings, which were presumably thought necessary for working on the suspension. They were deleted for production, when the inner wings were painted black rather than in the body colour, as here. AUTHOR'S COLLECTION

This is 107 FLK again, in this case showing the De Dion rear end. The very early style of exhaust system is also clear in this view. AUTHOR'S COLLECTION

1963 issue, *Motor Sport* carried a reader's photograph of 111 FLK and coyly asked its readers if they could identify this car, which wore a 'Falago' (sic) badge on its bootlid and which its driver had described to the inquiring photographer as 'a foreign prototype'. The launch of the new car was by then only a month or so away and no doubt the *Motor Sport* staff knew exactly what it was, but they were probably anxious to retain cordial relations with the Rover Company as well as to publish a photograph that might help to sell a few more copies of the magazine!

COLOUR AND BADGE CHOICES

Minor details were still changing on these pilot-production and early production cars. Among them were the hubcaps, which on P6-A1 had radial 'fins' that were replaced by indentations on production models; the shape of the exhaust pipe was simplified; and the reversing light moved from the right to the centre below the bumper. Several cars had front

and rear quarter-lights with the catch half-way up the glass instead of at the bottom (this position was also tried on at least one prototype of the P5 3-litre Coupé in 1962); and between March and May 1963 a number of paint colours were tried out that were not carried over to the final launch selection.

Twenty of the early cars (the last one was 400-00052A) were painted in colours that were not used on production cars. This was a normal process that allowed the proposed colours to be assessed on full-size cars before a final choice was made. None of these cars passed through dealers' showrooms, and none was made available to the public. There were six non-production colours, which were Arabian Blue (used on three cars), Cobalt Blue (two cars), Gull Grey (two cars), Mallard Green (one car), Steel Grey (six cars) and Turquoise (six cars).

The final choice of paint colours for production ranged from the conservative (City Grey and White) to the eye-catching (Wedgwood Blue and Willow Green). There is a story that Willow Green was proposed by Maurice Wilks' wife, and was matched to her favourite candles. More verifiable is that the very first off-tools car (P6A-1, 400-00001A, 101 FGO) was painted in Willow Green. It was recorded as

The very first production car, and perhaps
a few others, had this style of grille badge.
It was not adopted for production.

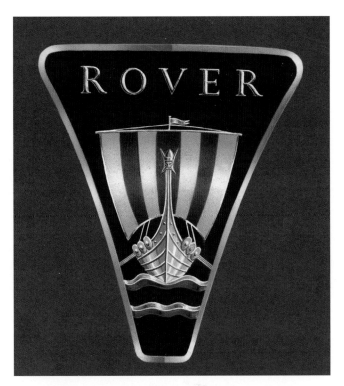

This rendering of a proposal for the P6 grille
badge was done by Tony Poole in the Styling
Department in December 1962. A small
number of badges was made to this design, but
again it was not adopted for production.

This is one of the trial batch of badges with
the red and white sails. CHRIS WILSON

such by the Despatch Department and was photographed
on 22 January 1963; although the photographs were in black
and white, they clearly show a light colour. Such a colour
would have drawn attention to the car on public roads, of
course, and at some point 101 FGO was repainted City Grey
– or perhaps its skin panels were simply changed for grey
ones. When it passed later into the ownership of Rover's
brakes specialist Jim Shaw, he had no idea of its original colour and was sure it had been City Grey from new!

It also took some time for the design of the grille badge to
be settled. No one ever doubted that it would be a version
of Rover's well-established Viking ship emblem, but at least
two different styles were drawn up and made (probably in
small trial batches of around half a dozen each) before the
final design was chosen. One of these early designs had an
all-red sail on the Viking ship and a very different style of
lettering for the Rover name. This one was used on the first
off-tools car, 101 FGO. Tony Poole in the Styling Department drew up the second one – and he may well have done

the first one as well. This was very similar to the production type but had sails with alternate red and white stripes, and all lettering was silver. One badge from the trial batch of this design was later fitted to the Rover TCZ prototype (*see* Chapter 8).

INTRODUCING THE 2000

The 2000 was introduced to the company's dealers at an event held at Rover's Solihull factory in early October 1963, and this was closely followed by the formal press launch on 8 October 1963, also at the factory. Attendees were given a presentation about the car and a tour of the assembly lines, and some also took the opportunity of a brief test drive. Sadly, Maurice Wilks had died a month earlier, and it was his successor, William Martin-Hurst, who gave the speech of welcome. Recognizing that information about the new Rover had already leaked out, he acknowledged the restraint of his press guests 'for keeping so securely under your hats much information which I know has been available to you for some time'.

A handful of journalists from the leading British motor-

ing magazines had in fact already road tested 2000s during September in order to meet early deadlines, but working to an agreed embargo date for publication. The cars they were lent were a small number of City Grey examples, probably beginning with 400-00076A. These had come off the assembly lines in August – ahead of others with lower commission numbers that would eventually go out to dealers for sale to the public – and most probably had FLK registrations; certainly, 144, 148 and 149 FLK were among them. While on loan to the journalists, the cars' badges were removed, although in some cases it seems probable that only the triangular grille badge and the Rover letters on the boot lid were actually taken off.

The next stage in the launch was the Earls Court Motor Show in London, which opened on 16 October. Rover displayed four examples of the new model on their stand, the centrepiece being one specially finished in gold (car number 400-0100A) and one car being a white demonstration cutaway that displayed the 2000's key features. The other two were a white car with optional Webasto sunroof and an HMV radio, and a Copperleaf Red example with an extra-cost Pye radio. For good measure, there was a Wedgwood Blue car with a radio on the Pressed Steel stand as well.

The Rover stand at the 1963 London Motor Show (then held at Earls Court) featured one of the gold cars (behind the curved wall on the right), a cutaway base unit, plus a white car that can be seen in the middle of the stand. AUTHOR'S COLLECTION

The new Rover 2000 was introduced to Rover dealers at an event held in the factory at Solihull. These are senior Rover figures at the table, with managing director William Martin-Hurst (in glasses) clearly visible. The car on the stage is one of the two that were specially painted in gold for the launch events. AUTHOR'S COLLECTION

This is the cutaway exhibit on the Rover stand at Earls Court. William Martin-Hurst is showing it to HRH Princess Margaret and her husband, Antony Armstrong-Jones, the Earl of Snowdon. ROVER CO. LTD

THE SHOW CARS

Rover prepared a special demonstration cutaway of the 2000 for the launch of the 2000, along with two cars that were specially painted in gold.

The white cutaway 2000 first appeared on the Rover stand at Earls Court in 1963 and then on the Rover stand at the 1964 New York Motor Show. According to the November 1965 issue of the company magazine, *Rover & Alvis News*, it appeared that autumn at an international roads and traffic exhibition held in Munich, West Germany, on a stand dedicated to car safety. The magazine reported that the authorities who organized the exhibition actually bought the cutaway afterwards, but its subsequent use and fate are unknown.

The two gold-painted cars had commission numbers 100 and 101. They did duty at the dealer and press launches in Solihull, on the Rover stand at the Earls Court Motor Show in October, at the Scottish Show in November, and then again at the New York Motor Show in April 1964.

Only one gold car was displayed at each event. As far as it is possible to tell, no. 100 was displayed at the Earls Court Motor Show and was subsequently shipped to New York for the US launch of the car in 1964. Number 101, meanwhile, was at the press launch at Solihull, and then during the Earls Court show was probably held as a back-up car at Rover's Seagrave Road Service Department in London (which was conveniently close to the show venue). It then went on to do the Scottish Show in Glasgow that opened on 7 November 1964, appearing on the stand of James Gibbon & Sons, who were the major local dealers. It may then have accompanied 100 to New York, again as a back-up car.

Both cars were recorded back at Solihull on 12 May 1964. One may subsequently have spent some time at the Pengam works. The eventual fate of no. 101 is not known, but no. 100 was registered as EXC 525C in March 1965 and went to Rover engineer Dan Clayton. It still survives.

The gold car shows off its interior on the Rover stand at Earls Court. The angled exhaust tailpipe was still in use at this stage. AUTHOR'S COLLECTION

One of the gold cars also appeared at the Scottish Motor Show, where the Rover stand was set up by James Gibbon Motors of Glasgow. It is seen here in the company of a darker coloured example and a P5 3-litre Saloon. AUTHOR'S COLLECTION

One of the gold cars, 400-00100A, still survives and has been restored to original condition. NICK DUNNING

LAUNCH MEMORABILIA

Journalists who attended the October 1963 press launch of the Rover 2000 were given a number of small promotional items. These included a small silver keyring with a model of the 2000 on a chain, a branded biro with a sliding section that opened to reveal the 2000 name, and a 1/43 scale model of the car finished in gold (like the real one that William Martin-Hurst had presented) and mounted on a wooden box with a marble lid. The box contained cigarettes, branded with the Rover 2000 name. The model was made by Corgi Toys, and a number of unmounted examples were given to the engineers who had worked on the car, but the gold version did not become available when the Corgi model reached the shops. A set of branded cufflinks may also have been among the launch gifts.

The gold model is seen here on the marble lid of the presentation box. These cigarettes, displayed at the British Motor Museum, are the only known survivors of those given away in 1963. HARVEY ANNABLE

Several of the FLK-registered cars were used for publicity purposes. This is 148 FLK in an advertisement from February 1964.

By the time of the Earls Court show, production was running at 250 cars per week, and Rover's aim was to build it up as rapidly as possible to the full plant capacity of 550 cars per week. Only then could export variants be accommodated on the lines. There were, of course, teething problems in production, but in his statement to Rover's annual general meeting on 17 November 1964, chairman George Farmer was able to say that: 'production is rising steadily towards our planned maximum production rate. In the meantime, such has been the reception given to this exciting new model that we are not able to give our customers as quick delivery as we would have wished.'

The Solihull despatch records show that the first 2000s had been sent out to dealers at the beginning of October. The first six cars were in City Grey or White, and left Solihull on 4 October bound for Henlys in London, Atkinson & Co in Huddersfield, Crabtree and Nicol in Sheffield, Moores of Brighton, Longton Garage of Longton and Andrews Garage in Derby. Numerically the earliest dealer car was 400-00053A, a white car that went to Rosenfields of Manchester on 17 October. Nevertheless, the Rover 2000 did not become generally available in Rover dealers' showrooms until the following January, and initial demand had been so overwhelming that there were waiting lists for the car by the spring of 1964. There were stories of brand-new examples changing hands for more than the list price. From then on, at least in Britain, demand for the 2000 and its later derivatives would exceed supply right up until the replacement models were announced, thirteen years later.

EARLY OPTIONS

The new Rover 2000 was offered in a range of five colours, with a choice of five interior colours, and there were two different colours of headlining to complement the main interior colour. Not all of these colours were a great success: Willow Green did not sell well, and Copperleaf Red displayed a tendency to fade. It was replaced by a reformu-

lated paint, which then caused problems for repairs because it was a slightly different shade from the original.

There was a range of extra-cost options to go with the car, too, and notable among these was a streamlined roof rack that David Bache had designed specially to suit it. There was also a kit to mount the spare wheel on the bootlid, apparently introduced at the insistence of William Martin-Hurst. Not content with getting the boot enlarged during

The early five-colour paint range was re-created here by P6 enthusiasts Nick Dunning and Chris Wilson. Clockwise, these are Wedgwood Blue, White, City Grey, Willow Green and Copperleaf Red.
CHRIS WILSON

Toggle switches were standard on the dashboard of these cars, but this one was a rarity. As the label shows, it was for the optional auxiliary driving lamp or lamps. NICK DUNNING

This early production car from 1964 is in Copperleaf Red and carries some extras. All 2000s had rear mudflaps but the front ones were an extra-cost option – as were the two round Notek lamps under the front bumper. The roof-mounted radio aerial was a standard fit for the UK but the door mirror is an aftermarket accessory. NICK DUNNING

173 JWD was an early 1964 car that was registered by Rover and was used by one of the company's engineers. It was pictured here with one of the stylish roof racks that David Bache designed as an accessory for the 2000. AUTHOR'S COLLECTION

A Webasto sunroof became an approved aftermarket option. This one is seen on JXC 200C (400-11252B), a Willow Green car that served as VIP transport at the factory with the registration number ROV 1. NICK DUNNING

the prototype stage in 1961, he proposed this method of increasing the P6's luggage capacity still further. It seems to have been developed quite quickly during the early part of 1963, and by May that year a prototype installation was in place on development car P6/12.

A radio was an extra-cost accessory, and cars without one had a blanking plate to fill the standard opening. Early plates were black metal with a metal Viking ship badge, but plastic ones with a gold badge replaced them in summer 1964. A heated rear window cost extra, as did Irvin front and rear seatbelts (which tended to get into a dreadful tangle), and a round Notek auxiliary driving lamp could be mounted under the front bumper. An approved aftermarket fitment was a Tudor Webasto fabric sunroof.

2000s FOR EXPORT

Rover had always planned to limit sales to the home market for the first six months after the 2000's launch, which allowed early teething troubles to be caught and dealt with close to home and quickly. Left-hand-drive 2000s started coming off the assembly lines in February 1964, and right-hand-drive export types the following month. The 2000 was formally launched into Europe at the Geneva show in March 1964 and into the USA (see Chapter 9) in the late summer of that year.

Steering position apart, there were no major differences between these early export 2000s and the home market cars – although cars bound for North America did acquire a

The county borough of Solihull began issuing XC registrations in January 1964, and these quickly became associated with the Rover Company. AXC 511B is an early 2000 (400-02998A) that was registered in April 1964 but was destined for export. ROVER CO. LTD

Left-hand-drive cars began to appear in the spring of 1964. This one was registered as AXC 89B at the factory in May, and was 403-00086A. ROVER CO. LTD

series of special features as time went by. From late 1964 or early 1965, Rover also introduced a low-compression (7.5:1) engine that could cope with poor-quality petrol but, with less than 90bhp, would certainly not have shown the handling qualities of the 2000 to their best advantage. Export sales were not spectacular in these early years, and there can be little doubt that the 2000's adequate but not sparkling performance – even with the 9:1 compression engine – counted against it when it was compared with cheaper cars produced locally.

It seems to have been around the middle of 1966 before the first Rover 2000s were shipped abroad as CKD (completely knocked down) kits of parts for assembly overseas. Records are unfortunately sketchy, but there is more about this aspect of the P6 story in Chapter 13.

PRESS REACTIONS

The first press reports on the Rover 2000 appeared in the week leading up to the opening of the 1963 Earls Court Motor Show. They were all enthusiastically positive. 'After two weeks' and 1,650 miles' experience in this new Rover, we rate it as one of the outstanding cars of the decade,' was *Autocar*'s opinion in its issue dated 11 October. 'A short spell of driving the car showed it to be possessed of quite exceptional handling qualities,' said *Motoring News* of 10 October. 'The only problem which seems likely to trouble Solihull will be that of an overloaded order book.'

'From the point of view of ride we would put it in the top three amongst European cars irrespective of price,' said *Motor* in its 9 October issue. It went on to add that the Rover had 'striking' high-speed stability, that the engine's flexibility and fuel consumption were 'impressive', and that the brakes were 'amongst the best we have tried'. *Motor Sport*'s schedule meant that it was the November issue, available during October, that carried that magazine's report, but the testers pronounced themselves 'almost unreservedly

Rover were very proud of the 2000's crash performance, and included a picture of this one in an advertisement for the car in the USA. 9999 WD was an early car that was allocated to Lt Col Peter Pender-Cudlip, who ran Land Rover military sales, and he walked away from what looks to have been a very serious collision. Very clear here is the early 'shark's-tooth' front valance – albeit somewhat bent.
ROVER CO. LTD

THE RIVAL 2000

The Triumph 2000 had been designed and developed at the same time as the Rover and was released about a week after it. Not only was it considerably cheaper than the Rover, but it also had a twin-carburettor 6-cylinder engine and overdrive gearbox, which to some buyers gave it the edge, at least on specification. Yet the two cars were so closely competitive that the British motoring press often ran comparison tests, going on in later years to compare the more powerful derivatives of both models.

Generally, the Rover came out marginally ahead in these comparisons, but the Triumph actually sold better. Triumph also broadened their car's appeal when they made an automatic gearbox option available by summer 1964, which was two years before Rover did so. However, in comparison tests the Rover was generally found to handle better. It had a significantly higher top speed of 104mph (167km/h) as against the Triumph's 98mph (158km/h), was quicker in the upper speed ranges (though slightly slower away from rest), offered greater comfort and, of course, had been designed with passenger safety in mind. As *Car* magazine put it in a September 1965 comparison of the two cars, 'one thing you can't put a premium on is safety – and as far as design for safety is concerned the Rover doesn't have any competitors at any price or in any size range. Not on this side of the Channel, anyway.'

enthusiastic' about the 2000, commenting that, 'It is astonishingly fine value and we shall be very surprised if Rover do not have to increase their production from the planned 550 a week.'

All agreed that comfort was of a very high order, fit and finish up to Rover's usual excellent standards, and performance extremely good for a 2-litre family saloon. Disappointingly, perhaps, Rover's efforts to incorporate safety features into the 2000 went largely unremarked: *Autocar* did mention the padded backs to the front seats, but that was all.

There were criticisms in those early press reports, too. *Motor* worried about tyre noise, heavy steering at low speeds and the noisy and notchy gearboxes in the two cars it tested. *Motor Sport* also noted that the gearboxes in its two test cars were poor, but reported that Rover were already modifying

production cars because so many of the early gearboxes had been faulty. *Autocar* found fault with the angle of the brake and clutch pedals, with road noise and with the steering-column stalk controls; and *Autosport* of 11 October also noticed 'a little road noise' on poor surfaces. Yet all these were minor niggles, and none detracted from the overall verdict of the motoring press that, in the 2000, the Rover Company had produced a very significant car indeed.

EVOLUTION, 1963–66

The Rover system during the P6 era was to identify major production changes that affected servicing of the cars by means of a letter suffix to their serial number. In these first three years, major changes coincided with the start of each new model year, so that the early cars were all suffix A types, the 1965 models introduced in September 1964 had suffix B, and the 1966 models introduced in September 1965 had suffix C. That neat arrangement was disrupted after March 1966, however, and the model year changes rarely coincided with major production changes again. It was also in March 1966 that the front valance panel was changed, and the early type with vertical air intakes disappeared. This visual distinction of the early cars has led to the popular description of them as 'shark's-tooth' types.

There were very many minor changes to the Rover 2000 in its first three years of production, and yet a 1966-season model was hard to tell from a 1964-season car at a glance. The full details of all the changes would make tedious reading (and they can be found in Rover service newsletters and

The 'shark's-tooth' front valance was replaced by this new and smoother design in early 1966. GXC 914C (400-17888C) was a very early example, registered in September 1965 and earmarked for publicity photographs. ROVER CO. LTD

Very early production cars had a spare wheel cover with a handle like this one. This is on 145 FLK (400-00080A), which became a Publicity Department car. AUTHOR

in parts catalogues), but it is worth summarizing the more important changes here. By this stage, P6 development was being led by Gordon Reed, who had been Ted Gawronski's deputy on the original team. When Gawronski left Rover around the time of the 2000's launch, Reed was his natural successor. Reed would remain in charge of P6 development matters until the end of the car's production, and he remembered that he was still being consulted on P6 matters by the time he retired in 1982!

As some early road tests had reported, there was a problem with the first gearboxes. Many years later, Roger Crathorne recalled the problem with the faulty gearboxes. A Rover apprentice at the time and soon to become involved in the project that would later produce the Range Rover, he remembered that Rover embarked on a crash programme that involved changing the gearbox on every new car before it left the factory. This was a major operation, and several engineers were taken off non-urgent work and allocated full-time to it. The job lasted for several weeks, until a revised gearbox specification began to come through on production models, and Crathorne was sure he could have changed a gearbox in his sleep by the end of it. Every replacement gearbox was marked with a splash of orange paint to identify it, and this mark has been found on some early cars more than half a century later.

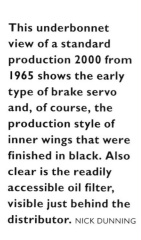

This underbonnet view of a standard production 2000 from 1965 shows the early type of brake servo and, of course, the production style of inner wings that were finished in black. Also clear is the readily accessible oil filter, visible just behind the distributor. NICK DUNNING

The suffix A cars had a separate steering idler and damper... NICK DUNNING

... which were replaced by this combined Armstrong idler and damper unit on the suffix B models introduced in September 1964. NICK DUNNING

Exhaust noise was among the 2000's biggest problems in the model's early years. Spen King remembered that an acceptable level of refinement had been attained on the prototypes, but had then been lost when the exhaust system was redesigned for production. As a result, there were several minor changes over the first three years, both to the system itself and to its mountings. These changes did reduce noise transmitted to the interior, but the 2000's characteristic exhaust resonance remained unchanged.

During suffix A production in 1963–1964, the visible changes included the deletion of the handle from the spare wheel cover, and, after about 2,000 cars had been built, longer tell-tales on the sidelamp lenses. The main beam headlamps were uprated from the original 37.5 watts to 50 watts, and the starter motor changed from an M45 to an M418 type that gave greater starting torque. The gearbox internals were also strengthened in some areas, and the original fabricated engine mountings were changed to a cast steel type (although not before car number 400-00970A). From May 1964, the front brake shield and dust covers were also redesigned.

With chassis suffix B in September 1964, the most visible change was that the original aluminium-backed wood veneer door and dashboard trims were replaced by printed Formica types. The spare-wheel mounting bracket in the boot changed, too. Under the bonnet, a combined damper and steering idler (made by Armstrong) replaced the earlier Teleflo damper and separate idler, and there were several internal changes to the engine, plus a change to Champion

N9Y spark plugs and a revised distributor advance. The rear suspension also had its share of revisions, gaining new bushes and longer rear springs with revised bump rubbers.

Small things continued to change during the 1965 season. From November 1964, there was a new rear-view mirror that incorporated a courtesy light and a strut to steady it against the windscreen. The front seats were given longer cushions in February 1965, and their runners were reinforced. At the same time came a new instrument cluster, with a 120mph (193km/h) speedometer in place of the original 110mph (177km/h) type, brighter lighting and the brake and ignition warning lights transposed from their original positions. A locking fuel filler cap became standard in June 1965. Mechanical changes during the year affected the driveshafts and the clutch; the valve springs and the timing chain tensioner were both modified; and the radiator pressure cap was uprated to 7psi from the original 5psi type.

The 1966-season cars, which were introduced with chassis Suffix C in September 1965, brought relatively few changes. The most obvious one was to the paint options. Copperleaf Red was withdrawn after giving trouble in service, and in its place came two new colours, Arden Green and Zircon Blue. A green and a blue had clearly been considered desirable because two others had been tried out before the final choice was made: Henley Green was tried on car number 400-02171A and Aztec Blue on 400-02172A, but these cars remained one-offs.

On the inside, there were changes to the controls as well, as the heater grips were increased in size and the petrol reserve and choke control grips took on a hooked shape in place of the earlier circular one. There was a more effective self-cancelling mechanism for the direction indicator stalk, too. If the rubber mounting added to the dynamo bracket was not very obvious, the new 7in Lockheed brake servo that replaced the original 5.5in Dunlop type was very much more so. With it came a change to the brake pad material.

Minor changes continued over the next few months, with a revised steering column shaft to reduce rattle (in November), and then a modified distributor advance curve and gearbox lubrication improvements in January 1966. The suffix C cars then gave way to suffix D types in March 1966, and these are described in the next chapter.

SELLING THE 2000

The Rover 2000 largely seems to have sold itself, although at the start of its life Rover certainly put a lot of effort into

Sets the lead in fine cars for a generation to come

The Rover 2000 – first touring car home and 2-litre touring class winner in the 1965 Monte Carlo Rally – is praised by enthusiastic drivers and the motoring press alike. This is what MOTOR said:
'Comfort is the keynote of this car. From the point of view of ride we would put it in the top three amongst European cars irrespective of price.'
'One has the impression that it was planned by engineers who are enthusiastic drivers and by stylists who put function before decoration, and the result is something of

an object lesson to other manufacturers.'
'The ability to reach 50 m.p.h. in just over 10 seconds and to cover the standing quarter mile in 19.4 seconds puts the Rover on a par with most saloons of up to a litre greater capacity.'
'It is doubtful whether there is any car in which four people can undertake a long journey more comfortably.'
£1,298.2.1 (including P.T.) ex-works.
Ask your nearest Rover dealer for a trial run in the brilliant, world-beating Rover 2000.

ROVER 2000
ONE OF THE WORLD'S BEST ENGINEERED CARS

The Rover Company Ltd., Solihull, Warwickshire. London Office: Devonshire House, Piccadilly. Rover 3-Litre Motoring—Rover Quality Throughout. Makers of the world-famous Land-Rover.

Rover were still using pictures of the FLK-registered cars in mid-1965, when this advertisement appeared in the *Motor* magazine.

establishing a strong image for it. The launch slogan – 'Rover 2000 takes motoring years ahead' – stressed the advanced engineering that had gone into the car, and press advertisements over the next three years supported this theme.

Advertising put special emphasis on safety, too. 'Probably one of the safest cars ever produced' was how the 1964-season sales catalogue put it, devoting two of its fourteen pages to the car's safety features. Interestingly, safety was only rarely mentioned in the early development documents so far discovered (see Chapter 1)!

Traditional Rover customers were probably more interested to learn that the 2000 had won its class in the IBCAM coachwork quality awards at the 1965 Earls Court show. As the sales catalogues put it, the important point was that 'fittings and appointments generally are to the accepted Rover standard'.

PAINT AND TRIM OPTIONS

October 1963–August 1965

There were five paint colours and five interior trim colours. All seat facings were in leather. Headlinings were either Light Grey or Biscuit 'to match', but it is not clear which headlining was standard with each trim colour. The Light Grey option disappeared at the end of Suffix A production in 1964. Carpets matched the main trim colour.

The combinations available were as follows:

City Grey	with trim in	Biscuit, Grey, Red or Tan
Copperleaf Red		Biscuit, Black or Grey
Wedgwood Blue		Biscuit, Black or Grey
White		Black, Red or Tan
Willow Green		Biscuit or Black

September 1965–May 1966

Two new paint colours were added to the range: Arden Green and Zircon Blue. Copperleaf Red was no longer available. The same five interior trim colours were available, always with a Biscuit headlining. Carpets matched the main trim colour.
The combinations were:

Arden Green	with trim in	Biscuit, Grey or Tan
City Grey		Biscuit, Grey, Red or Tan
Wedgwood Blue		Biscuit, Black or Grey
White		Black, Red or Tan
Willow Green		Biscuit or Black
Zircon Blue		Biscuit, Black, Grey or Tan

PRICES AND RIVALS, 1963–66

The totals shown here were basic showroom prices for 2000 models in the UK without extras. Also shown are the basic ex-factory cost and the purchase tax payable.

October 1963

Total	Ex-factory	Purchase Tax
£1,264 9s 7d	£1,046	£218 9s 7d

January 1965

Total	Ex-factory	Purchase Tax
£1,298 2s 1d	£1,073	£225 2s 1d

July 1966

Total	Ex-factory	Purchase Tax
£1,357 9s 10d	£1,073	£254 9s 10d

Note: In July 1966, the 2000 was still the only P6 model on sale in the UK even though the 2000TC had been released for overseas markets.

Rivals

At launch, the Rover 2000 was competing for sales with cars like the Jaguar 2.4-litre Mk 2 at £1,347 17s 1d, the Fiat 2300 at £1,329 14s 7d and the Citroën ID19 at £1,307 19s 7d. Lower down the price range, strong competition came from the Volvo 122S at £1,098 18s 9d, the Triumph 2000 at £1,094 2s 1d and the Peugeot 404 at £1,019 13s 9d. Of these, however, the keenest competition came from the Triumph, which was much cheaper than the Rover: the £170 difference represented 13.5 per cent and was a lot of money in 1963.

The works rally team – which was purely a publicity exercise and is discussed in Chapter 5 – had no major successes before the beginning of 1965 and so its exploits did not feature in the 2000 sales campaign. Even after Roger Clark's magnificent showing in the 1965 Monte Carlo Rally in a works team car, Rover publicity made sparing use of what would undoubtedly have inspired some purple prose and fanfares from other manufacturers.

Sales, meanwhile, were booming. Waiting lists had built up by spring 1964, and that autumn's 'Colour Magazine of the Rover 2000 and 3-litre Saloon and Coupé' (actually a sales brochure) warned that 'delivery dates are still likely to be extended for some time to come although actual periods may well vary in different parts of the country.' Rover's distributors and dealers in the British Isles simply could not get their hands on enough cars to satisfy demand, and so the fact that some export markets were slow became a blessing in disguise; Rover would not have been able to make more vehicles to sell overseas.

Rover 2000 production increased markedly between 1963 and 1966 to meet this demand. From 7,235 cars in the 1964 season, which was affected by strikes and by teething troubles on assembly, production rose sharply to 20,579 for 1965. It then rose again to 25,122 for 1966, although of course this latter figure had been boosted by the arrival of the TC and Automatic models (see Chapter 3) during the year.

ROVER 2000, 1963–66

Engine
Type: Cast iron block and light alloy head
Cylinders: 4
Capacity: 1978cc (85.7mm bore x 85.7mm stroke)
Five-bearing crankshaft
Single overhead camshaft
Compression ratio: 9:1
Carburettor: Single SU type HS6
Max. power: 99bhp SAE (90bhp installed) at 5,000rpm
Max. torque: 121lb ft SAE at 3,600rpm (113.5lb ft at 2,750rpm, installed)
Export only:
Compression ratio: 7.5:1
Max. power: 87.5bhp SAE (80bhp installed) at 5,000rpm
Max. torque: 113lb ft SAE at 3,350rpm (106lb ft at 2,500rpm, installed)

Transmission
Gearbox: Four-speed all-synchromesh manual
Ratios
  1st: 3.62:1
  2nd: 2.13:1
  3rd: 1.39:1
  4th: 1.00:1
  Reverse: 3.43:1
Axle ratio: 3.54:1

Suspension and Steering
Front: Independent suspension with transverse bottom links and leading upper links acting on coil springs mounted horizontally to the bulkhead; anti-roll bar; hydraulic telescopic dampers
Rear: Lower links and coil springs; De Dion tube incorporating sliding joint, with transverse location by fixed-length driveshafts and fore-and-aft location by Watts linkage; hydraulic telescopic dampers
Steering: Adamant Marles worm-and-roller type
Tyres: 165 SR 14 radial
Wheels: Five-stud steel disc wheels with 14in diameter
Rim width: 5in

Brakes
Type: Dunlop discs and callipers on all four wheels, mounted inboard at the rear; handbrake acting on rear discs; servo assistance standard
Size: 10.75in front, 10.25in rear

Dimensions
Wheelbase: 103.375in (2,626 mm)
Overall length: 178.5 in (4,534mm)
Overall width: 66in (1,676mm)
Overall height: 54.75in (1,390mm)
Track, front : 53.375in (1,356mm)
Track, rear: 52.5in (1,333mm)
Running weight: 2,760lb (1,252kg)

Performance
Max. speed: 104mph (167km/h)
0–60mph: 15.1sec

CHAPTER THREE

TC, SC AND AUTOMATIC, 1966–1970

When a new car model is introduced, its designers and development engineers are usually bursting with great ideas for improving it that came along too late to be incorporated in the production schedule. Or sometimes, further developments of the original design are deliberately held over to create improved variants for introduction at a later date. That was very much the case with the Rover P6 and, as the car entered production in 1963, the Rover engineers were already working on the next stages in its development.

These included a 6-cylinder model – called P7 and discussed in the next chapter – and upgrades to the 2000 as well. These upgrades were intended to provide more performance, more luxury features, and an automatic gearbox option. The 6-cylinder car never did reach production, and nor did the luxury or S model, but both the more powerful 2000 and the automatic variant were introduced in 1966. That was a full three years after the P6 had been launched in its original form as the 2000, but it is important to remember that Rover were still a small company by motor industry standards, whose financial and engineering resources had already been stretched by the first-stage P6 project. Accordingly, further development of the range had to proceed slowly.

THE OWNERSHIP OF ROVER

In the meantime, some major changes affected the Rover Company. When the 2000 was introduced in 1963, Rover had been a small but prosperous independent car maker, but changes elsewhere in the motor industry led to a chain reaction of events that brought Rover and many other established marques into the British Leyland combine from 1968.

It had all started in 1965, when the British Motor Corporation (BMC) bought Pressed Steel, the leading supplier of bodyshells that counted Rover among its customers. Rover management, and in particular the company's chairman, George Farmer, became concerned that this might lead to increased costs or other difficulties in getting Rover bodies produced by Pressed Steel. So, early in 1967, Rover agreed to a merger with the Leyland bus and truck group, which already owned rival maker Standard-Triumph and had its own body production facilities.

Meanwhile, Harold Wilson's Labour government had set up an Industrial Reorganization Committee with the brief of creating a more efficient British industrial base through mergers and reorganization. Run by Tony Benn, the IRC became concerned that Britain had no motor industry group capable of countering the major groups in Europe, particularly Volkswagen. Benn also knew that British Motor Holdings (formed in 1966 when Jaguar joined the BMC group) was getting dangerously close to collapse. So, to safeguard both jobs and the industry as a whole, he brokered a merger between the financially strong Leyland group and the ailing BMH. The result formally became the British Leyland Motor Corporation on 17 January 1968.

These mergers left Rover as part of the same group as its key domestic rivals, so clearly something would have to give somewhere. In practice, BLMC management left Rover to their own devices until there were calls on funding. It then had to adjudicate on requests from formerly rival companies, and one result was that two proposed new Rovers (the P8 saloon and the P9 sports car) were cancelled; the P8 had been very close to production but was considered too great a threat to Jaguar's saloons.

These changes did not directly affect the P6 range in the later 1960s, but they did mean that Rover were no longer entirely in control of their own destiny. As funding became harder to obtain, so there would be an impact on the direction that the P6 range would take in the early 1970s.

A HIGHER SPECIFICATION: THE 2000S

The story of the 2000S and 2000TC projects is a very complicated one. In the beginning, Rover intended to develop two separate variants of the 2000 for introduction some time after the car's 1963 launch. One was a luxury model called the 2000S, and the other was a higher-performance model with a twin-carburettor version of the 2-litre engine.

Work began on the 2000S project first, and the earliest clear trace of it is a full-size mock-up completed by David Bache's styling studio in August 1962. This featured wire wheels, a bright trim strip along the body styling crease, rear quarter-panels in a contrasting colour and '2000S' badges. A further-developed mock-up was photographed the following month, but there is no evidence of further progress on the 2000S until more than a year later, in 1964.

In the meantime, development of the twin-carburettor engine had begun during 1963, and the original hope seems to have been to introduce it in a 'performance' derivative of the 2000 at the 1964 Motor Show, just a year after the single-carburettor car had been launched. By November 1963, the aim was to announce the new 2000TC with a five-speed gearbox, which was presumably the ZF type that was also being considered for the P7 6-cylinder car (see Chapter 4).

By December 1963, 'technical difficulties' had arisen with the twin-carburettor project. The record of the executive directors' meeting in December

1963 that heard about them does not elaborate on what they were, but the outcome was a delay in the development programme. By March 1964, it was clear that the projected launch date of that autumn's motor show was no longer realistic, so a date of August 1965 was suggested.

There was then a further change of plans over the summer of 1964, when managing director William Martin-Hurst reviewed work on future P6 derivatives. It seems to have

This August 1962 mock-up for a 2000S model combines very early features (such as the lightweight seats) with new ideas. There are wire wheels, a side trim strip, a contrasting finish for the quarter-panels and (though only just visible here) a new shape for the front valance.

The 2000S prototype car was 169 JWD, seen here in July 1965. The design has evolved a little, and the badges are different. This car has eared spinners on its wire wheels, a feature that would not make production.

been his idea to merge the 2000S and twin-carburettor projects, which were clearly competing for resources. By December that year, the plan was that the 2000S would have the twin-carburettor engine and would be introduced at the London Motor Show in autumn 1965, while a twin-carburettor version of the basic car would follow later. That same month, technical director Peter Wilks wrote to Bruce McWilliams, head of Rover's North American operation, to tell him he hoped the 2000S would be ready for the 1966 New York Motor Show that would open on 9 April that year.

By July 1965, a '2000S to mock-up specs' existed – a real car bearing the registration plate 169 JWD. The host car was an early 2000 (400-01056A) that had been fitted with a pro-totype twin-carburettor engine, numbered 2000TC6. It is not clear whether it had the power-assisted steering, which former test engineer Brian Terry remembers as being in the 2000S specification. Visually, 169 JWD closely resembled the earlier styling mock-up, but it had different badging and lacked the contrasting colour on the rear quarter-panels. The wire wheels and slim side trim strips were there, along with an 'S' motif below the 2000 badge on each front wing. It also had a new design of front apron panel, which would go on to become standard on all 4-cylinder P6s from March 1966.

Inside, the mock-up car showcased several new features that would appear later in P6 production. It pioneered the four-dial instrument panel and the upholstered transmission

Just fifteen 2000S cars were eventually built, and most of them probably did not have the cosmetic features intended for the model. Pictures are very rare, and this one of 410-00009A shows no badges at all at the rear. When pictured, it was in use by A. B. Smith, a Rover board member who would later become the company's managing director. A. B. SMITH

tunnel cover with leather handbrake gaiter that arrived on the Federal 3500S in 1969. The front doors had armrests with map pockets below them, a new design of release handle, and turnwheel adjusters for the quarter-lights – all features further developed for the Federal car. Its wood-rim steering wheel and wooden gearshift grip would later join the options list, and the pleated sections of its seats were upholstered in basket-weave Amblair material – which would enter production for the Federal 2000TC in 1967 (see Chapter 9).

Everything seemed to be on target for an early 1966 launch as a pilot batch of 2000S models was built in October and November 1965. Of the fifteen cars built, three had left-hand drive. All of them went to the Engineering Department, except for one that went to A. B. Smith, then Rover's general manager. Probably none had all the planned 2000S features, and several (including A. B. Smith's car, 410-00009A, HXC 729C) looked like standard 2000 models, though without badges. One left-hand-drive car (413-00003A, FXC 209C) was converted to right-hand drive and did have the padded black leather centre console with leather gaiters, and a car with both PAS and wire wheels that was reported scrapped in Surrey in the early 1980s might have been a 2000S.

However, by mid-1965 Rover was also focusing on devel-oping the 2000 to meet new US safety regulations, and its American arm was asking for versions of the twin-carbu-rettor car with special sporty features to help sales. The Engineering Department was just too busy to deal with all these requirements, and something had to give. The top pri-orities were the twin-carburettor car and its special North American version, and so the 2000S was abandoned by the end of the year. The now-redundant pilot-production cars were diverted to other duties: former engineer Rob Lyall remembers that they were used mainly for mileage work. Two of them were used as the basis of experimental two-door models: 410-00010A (FXC 206C) became the Zagato-bodied TCZ, and 410-00012A became the Alvis GTS proto-type; both these cars are described in Chapter 8.

So, from around November 1965, the 2000S disappeared from Solihull's plans and the Rover engineers and designers focused instead on the car that would become the 2000TC.

DEVELOPING THE 2000TC

There was far more to creating the twin-carburettor engine than a simple bolt-on conversion, because the inlet manifold on the single-carburettor ohc engine was cast integrally with the cylinder head. A complete new head had to be designed, and Jack Swaine's team took the opportunity to improve the manifold's water-heating arrangements and to add a more efficient exhaust manifold as well. Reasoning that many customers were going to make full use of the extra performance and use these new engines to their limit, they also decided to fit an engine oil cooler as standard, finding room for it at the base of the radiator.

The earliest pictures of a prototype engine were taken in January 1964, and by March that year a pair of engines were on test in two of the works rally cars (see Chapter 5), which would have their first public outing on the Alpine Rally in July. Not surprisingly, the rally cars' engines were rather more powerful than those eventually used in the production cars, but they were nevertheless essentially the same. Rover's rallying experience of course fed into the development programme for the eventual production engines.

Meanwhile, the biggest problem with the development of the engine – and probably the cause of those 'technical difficulties' in December 1963 – was the twin-carburettor installation itself. The engines team decided from the start to use a pair of SU HD8 carburettors, which were larger than the single-carburettor engine's HS6 type and were familiar to the Rover engineers from the 3-litre P5 and 2.6-litre P4 110 engines. There was no question that these provided the extra power and performance that was wanted, but they also caused excessive engine vibration. Eventually, test engineer Brian Terry drew up a flexible mounting, which largely took care of the problem; even then, poorly balanced carburettors could give the twin-carburettor engine a most unrefined, un-Rover-like idle.

Getting a satisfactory idle was another long-running problem. Jack Swaine normally insisted on the lowest possible tickover speed for Rover engines, but he had to settle for a 650rpm idle as against the 500rpm of the single-carburettor engine. Nevertheless, a properly set-up twin-carburettor engine would still satisfy Swaine's other standard test of being able to accept full throttle from 10mph (16km/h) in top gear without hesitation.

All this delayed the engine development programme way beyond Rover's original estimate. The amalgamation of twin-carburettor and 2000S projects later in 1964 made no real difference to the engine programme, but the need to develop a special twin-carburettor car for North America introduced yet another delay. Although the 2000TC was announced in March 1966, in practice there were no deliver-

This press-release picture of the 2000TC engine clearly shows the twin carburettors and the tubular exhaust manifold.

ies to customers until the autumn of that year. The new high-performance Rover reached British showrooms in October 1966 – two years after the original target date.

The good news was that by this stage the Rover engineers were happy with the design of the engine. To get the absolute maximum from it, they had specified new pistons that raised the compression ratio to 10:1 from the 9:1 of the standard 2000 4-cylinder. They had also allowed it to rev higher than the single-carburettor type. In production form, the 2000TC engine delivered 124bhp (rated to SAE standards), which was 25bhp or some 25 per cent more than the standard type. This was a very worthwhile improvement, even if the SAE figures were taken on a test bench, and when installed in the car the TC engine actually delivered only about 20bhp extra. Torque was usefully increased, too, to the benefit of acceleration.

DEVELOPING THE 2000 AUTOMATIC

Rover's plans for the P6 range were certainly ambitious. Development work began not only on the high-specification

2000S and high-performance twin-carburettor models, but also on an automatic version of the single-carburettor car.

Rover's executive directors were told as early as December 1962 that an automatic model was to be introduced after the initial release of the manual-gearbox 2000. It appears that the automatic model entered the P6 development programme at the request of the sales division, who knew that many Rover customers were older drivers who were not particularly concerned about performance and handling but were more interested in ease of driving and refinement.

In January 1963, the executive directors learned that Rover hoped to introduce the 2000 Automatic at the start of the 1965 season – which meant at the 1964 Motor Show. However, difficulties soon surfaced, and in June 1963 they were told that the 2000 was now considered unsuitable for an automatic gearbox, although experiments were continuing.

Development engineer Brian Terry remembers some of these early problems. Rover had chosen to use the well-respected Borg Warner Type 35 three-speed automatic gearbox, which fitted comfortably but needed more cooling air to flow around it than was available in the P6's rather narrow transmission tunnel. The bituminous soundproofing on the floor of one of the prototypes melted with the heat from the gearbox after one full day's testing at MIRA!

The solution was a wider transmission tunnel, and once that had been designed there was no more overheating and very little extra development work was needed. The engineers tried a lower 4.3:1 axle ratio to improve acceleration, but this would have reduced the maximum speed and

increased the fuel consumption, which were probably good enough reasons for the 2000's standard 3.54:1 axle gearing to be retained for production. There were further delays to the programme during 1964, and in July that year the executive directors were informed that it had been delayed by a high incidence of service problems on P6. In the end, it was introduced some two years later alongside the 2000TC, which had also suffered multiple delays during development.

ON SALE AT LAST: TC AND AUTOMATIC

Rover were very anxious to get the 2000TC out on sale, and particularly so outside Britain, where customers were showing a keen interest in the P6's possibilities as a sports saloon. So it was announced at the Geneva Show in March 1966, with immediate availability for European markets. The special North American version (see Chapter 9) became available early in the summer, but the car was not introduced to Rover's home market until the autumn, making its debut at the Earls Court Motor Show in October. Although it was a risky strategy to introduce a new model outside the UK first, and one most uncharacteristic of Rover, this did allow production to build up gradually over the second quarter of 1966 while the first cars reached their buyers.

Although the concept of the 2000TC was of a Rover 2000 with the twin-carburettor engine and nothing else, there were some special features for continental European markets. The cars had a new style of squat rubber-faced over-

Discreet in the best Rover tradition: the TC badges on bonnet and wings show what this car is, but at a quick glance the car would have been hard to distinguish from a single-carburettor 2000. NXC 565D was 415-00209B, and was put on the road in September 1966.

Some markets called for different standard features. This early Austrian 2000TC has the overriders used on North American cars, a racing-style wing mirror and a dipping rear-view mirror.

rider, and some had a thin stainless steel trim strip that ran along the body side crease. In tandem with 'TC' badges on the wings, bonnet and rear panel, this made them readily distinguishable from the single-carburettor cars – a factor that Rover's European distributors considered important. On the inside, every early 2000TC also had a rev counter, tacked rather crudely onto the dashboard in a housing next to the instrument panel.

Most export examples had the 10:1 compression engine, which demanded 100-octane petrol, although there was also a 9:1 compression version available for countries where high-octane fuel was not available. The low-compression engine was rated at only 117bhp SAE (which shows how much difference that high compression made), but it still gave usefully more performance than the low-compression single-carburettor cars with which it was likely to be compared.

The British motoring press reported on the specification of the 2000TC as soon as it appeared at the Geneva Show, but Rover did not grant them any test drives until the car actually went on sale in Britain. Home market cars did not have the special overriders or the side trim strip of the export models, but they had the 10:1 compression engine as standard. They also had a much tidier rev counter installation, allegedly redesigned after Rover had seen how the Swiss coachbuilder Graber had done one for the drophead 2000 that he displayed at Geneva (see Chapter 8). All 2000TCs for all markets took on the redesigned rev counter installation that autumn.

The earliest 2000TC models had a rev-counter rather crudely tacked onto the end of the instrument panel. These were rare on right-hand-drive cars like this one, and were soon replaced by a neater design. CHRIS WILSON

Rover's intention with the 2000TC had been to exploit the performance potential of the P6 'chassis', and in that aim it certainly succeeded. A home market model would reach 60mph (97km/h) from a standing start in under twelve seconds, which was nearly three seconds faster than the single-carburettor model; and it would go on to 112mph (180km/h) as compared with the basic car's 104mph (167km/h). Despite increases in noise levels and in fuel consumption – up to 25mpg (11.3ltr/100km) from the 30mpg (9.4ltr/100km) attainable with the original 2000 – the 2000TC became a major success. Although it was out-sold in Britain by the

The later design of pod for the rev-counter and clock is seen here on a 2000TC with the optional wood-rim wheel and wooden gearshift grip. Clear in this picture are the early type of static seatbelts. The car also has a balance control for the front and rear radio speakers (beside the front speaker panel) and the optional rubber floor mats. The small plate in the corner of the dash reads 'The Rover Co Ltd, Engineering Test Car'. This car was not on the engineering fleet, but its current owner had saved the plate from his time with Rover! DENIS CHICK

OXC 388D was a 2000TC that David Bache used for styling development. It was a 1966 car with right-hand drive (number 415-01837B) and is seen here with US-style Gold Band tyres on Rostyle wheels, a US-style side trim strip and overriders, and a bright red paint that was clearly intended to demonstrate that this was a sports saloon. Some of these features later appeared on standard production cars outside North America. Not visible here is that this car also had a prototype petrol injection system (see Chapter 8).

single-carburettor 2000, it came a close second even though it was more expensive to buy, insure and run. More than 35,000 examples were sold in the home market between 1966 and 1970, and this success, allied to strong TC sales overseas, made clear to Rover that performance sold P6s and that the plans they had for a bigger-engined models were on the right lines.

The contrast between the 2000TC and the 2000 Automatic that followed it in autumn 1966 could hardly have been greater. Its specification was exactly the same as that of the single-carburettor 2000, with just an automatic selector gate inside and an 'Automatic' badge on the bootlid to distinguish it from its sibling. Where the TC was designed for perform-ance, the Automatic most certainly was not.

It was also a car that tended to polarize opinions, and there were certainly some people at Rover who felt that it should never have gone into production at all. Per-formance and refinement were the main sources of discontent. Its 0–60mph time of nearly eighteen seconds negated most of the dynamic advantages designed into the P6's suspension, steering and brakes, and a driver who pushed the car hard was rewarded with an increase in the levels of exhaust noise that was enough to discour-age a repeat of the exercise. Nevertheless, the 2000 Automatic did provide the ease of driving that its (typically elderly) buyers expected, and was a very pleasant car to drive as long as there was no rush.

The cost of its bought-in automatic gearbox meant that this car was always the most expensive of the three 2000 variants, and it went on to become a very slow seller outside Britain. However, sales of around 3,350 a year in Britain up to 1970 were enough to justify its existence to Rover while the single-carburettor car sold around 9,000 a year in the home mar-ket and the TC very nearly as many.

ROVER
2000
AUTOMATIC

From autumn 1966 there was a 2000 Automatic as well. As this sales brochure shows, it looked exactly like the manual-gearbox car (although there was a distinguishing badge on the tail).

WIRE WHEELS AND ROSTYLES

Rover decided to emphasize the sporting nature of the 2000TC by making a wire wheel option available for it. This had been tried out some years earlier during development of the 2000S, when the wheels on the mock-up car (169 JWD) had eared spinners as well. Though fashionable in the 1960s, these were not carried through to production. Instead, the production centre cap was a ten-sided nut, and a special spanner was provided in the car's tool kit to suit it.

The wire wheels required special splined hubs and were only ever made available as a build option for the 2000TC. Although a mock-up of a wire-wheeled North American

TC was built, the wheels were never offered as an option across the Atlantic.

Nevertheless, North American buyers did want stylish wheels and, as Chapter 9 explains, Rover met that demand by buying in two different locally manufactured styles for the 2000TC. In the meantime, the British maker Rubery Owen had designed a chromed and painted steel wheel that looked like a more expensive alloy type and promoted the right sporting image. David Bache chose to use these 'Rostyle' wheels, in a 15in size, for the Rover 3.5-litre (P5B) models that were introduced in autumn 1967.

Once Rostyle wheels had become available, Rover chose a 14in version to replace the bought-in wheels on North American TCs. The company also made them available as an optional extra for P6 models in other markets from the start of the 1968 model year, and standardized them on the Three Thousand Five for some continental European markets when that model was introduced in spring 1968 (see Chapter 7). However, the take-up rate of Rostyles in Britain was very low indeed, and it seems likely that Rover dealers were not encouraged to promote their availability, perhaps because of limited supplies.

PRESS REACTIONS

The 2000TC

The 2000TC went down extremely well with road testers on the European continent. *Auto Visie* in the Netherlands called it 'one of the best examples of a modern, handsome, manageable… high-class car which can be found today'. In Denmark, meanwhile, the *Berlingske Tidende* said, 'This car is so wonderful that it is…really beyond description.'

The wire wheel option for the 2000TC certainly gave the car a sporting air. This example shows the production design, with octagonal hub spinners.

Back in Britain, however, where road testers were perhaps more familiar with the Rover range, the TC's refinement was called into question. As *Motor* of 1 October 1966 put it after testing the Rover press demonstrator, MXC 403D:

In the TC quietness is the one real victim sacrificed to performance, for the noises produced by the engine – mechanical at low speed, exhaust at higher speed and particularly at wide throttle openings, with various resonant combinations in between – are always in attendance. To the sporting driver they are purposeful enough to be perfectly acceptable, but the motorist who has always thought of a Rover as being totally refined should be prepared for something different.

Bill Boddy also tried MXC 403D for *Motor Sport*, and he reported on it in that magazine's December 1966 issue. He found it 'amply endowed with performance', and did not altogether accept the view that the TC was less refined than the single-carburettor 2000, even though it had 'considerably increased engine noise when accelerating hard'. He found it 'rather a thirsty car, for I never obtained better than 22.3mpg [12.7ltr/100km] on long runs, and this fell in traffic conditions, averaging out at 21.9mpg [12.9ltr/100km]'.

The test car also had a very lumpy idle and misbehaved in London traffic on one occasion, 'stalling unless revved up, emphasising imperfections of throttle linkage, clutch take-up and play in the transmission by the Rover's erratic progress'. But all was soon forgiven: 'Once clear of the con-

ROVER **2000** AIR CONDITIONING

Rare in Britain, thanks to the climate, was an air-conditioning system by Delaney Gallay. This was the sales brochure that promoted it.

gestion, the trouble cleared up, and did not re-occur, and I formed a very high opinion of this outstanding British car'.

The 2000 Automatic

In Britain, relatively few road tests of the 2000 Automatic were published, because magazine editors tended to focus on the more exciting models and especially on the 2000TC,

SOME SPECIAL TCs

As early as autumn 1966, Rover prepared a left-hand-drive 2000TC specially for King Hussain of Jordan, a long-standing Rover customer who bought large quantities of Land Rovers for his armed forces. This car had non-standard twin driving lights (much larger than the optional Notek type and carried above the bumper) and was also fitted with air-conditioning, which had just become available as an option.

In Portugal, meanwhile, the TC was given a special treatment by the Rover importers, who fitted their own instrument panel in the centre of the dash with three auxiliary gauges. They moved the clock to the corner of the passenger's side of the dashboard, where it was sunk into the wood trim in a manner similar to that on the contemporary P5 3-litre Mk III.

In Portugal, the importers offered a unique pod to give a more sporting air to the 2000TC. It was also offered for the Three Thousand Five (and the one pictured is in such a car).

which on the home market was of course released at the same time. It was *Autocar* that published the first test of a 2000 Automatic, in its issue dated 30 September 1966. The magazine rehearsed the usual praises of the P6's handling, comfort, high standard of finish, ventilation, interior and facia design, visibility, lighting and so on, and reported a small niggle about the lack of a rest for the driver's left foot in the new two-pedal car. However, when the testers came to describe the automatic gearbox, the praise turned to almost palpable disappointment.

If the operation of the gearbox was beyond reproach, there was a serious loss of performance as compared with the manual-gearbox 2000. The D2 position, with its intermediate-ratio start, gave such a slow take-off as to be almost useless, and the overall lack of acceleration was especially noticeable in the vital overtaking range between 30mph and 60mph (48–96km/h). The car seemed to be noisy, too – doubtless because the engine was revving harder to over-

come the slip of the torque converter – and there was so much exhaust throb that the testers suspected a leak. Making the best of what they clearly thought was a bad job, they summed the car up by saying that, in spite of its poor acceleration, it could still return high average speeds once it was on the move, and that the excellence of the basic design went some way towards compensating for the 2000 Automatic's lack of urge.

Motor tested the same car (NXC 228D, 405-00005D) in its issue of 14 January 1967 and confined its comments to the gearbox and its effect on the car. Like *Autocar*, it could not fault the operation of the three-speed automatic, but added that this type of gearbox was not best suited to the 2000's engine, which developed its best torque at fairly high crankshaft speeds. It spoke of substantial losses in both performance and economy, and complained that the engine now seemed fussy because it had to work harder when overtaking in the intermediate gear of the automatic box rather than the third gear of the manual box. Even though Rover's press garage seemed to have adjusted the kickdown linkage on the test car to give more rapid acceleration (the *Motor* testers wrote of a very delicate kickdown pressure which took a while to get used to), the verdict was still the same: the car was abominably slow.

BASE-UNIT COMPLICATIONS

From early on, Rover kept a small number of spare base units as a service 'float' and supplied one in cases where an accident-damaged car was to be rebuilt with a new base unit.

The situation became more complicated in 1966 when the 2000 Automatic was introduced, because the transmission tunnel was wider than on the manual models. Rather than keep supplies of both types of base unit, Rover chose to keep service supplies only of the Automatic type, and developed a conversion kit that allowed a manual gearbox to be fitted to it. Cars rebuilt in this way were inevitably rare, but the base unit was marked as a service type on one known example of an early manual car rebuilt with an Automatic base unit.

This practice probably continued right through to the end of production and beyond. It also seems likely that the 'float' of Automatic base-units was sometimes called on when there was a shortfall of manual types on the assembly lines. This appears to have happened in the case of a 1974 3500S (482-00871D), which was a Solihull-built manual-gearbox car destined for Australia, and which appears to have had an Automatic-type base unit from new.

EVOLUTION: 1966–70

The very first examples of the 2000TC were suffix A types and had the original shark's-tooth valance, but there were relatively small numbers of these and all of them went for export – except for a few examples retained at Solihull for development and testing. From March 1966, the 2000TC switched to suffix B and the single-carburettor model went to suffix D.

The two models shared several specification changes, but the most obvious change in their appearance was a new front apron with horizontal openings in place of the earlier shark's-tooth type. This had been previewed during the 2000S design programme, and supposedly improved stability in side winds. At about the same time, the Notek auxiliary driving lamps were replaced on the options list by rectangular Cibie types. Meanwhile, at the rear, the separate reversing lamp disappeared and new rear light clusters now incorporated a reversing lamp segment on each side, while the displaced reflectors moved to the lower corners of the bootlid. Not so obvious was a reflector disc added to the bootlid channel on each side, to ensure that a red reflector remained visible at the rear even when the boot was open.

From a servicing point of view, the most important alteration was that the electrical system now changed to the negative-earth type that was becoming the European standard, and negative earth labels were added as a warning near the battery and the fuse box. Rover also rationalized the fuse arrangements, grouping all of them under a single cover and eliminating in-line types, but otherwise the only change to electrical equipment at this stage was to link-driven windscreen wipers in place of the earlier cable-driven type.

Less visibly, there were engine changes to commonize the single-carburettor and twin-carburettor types as much as possible. The two engines shared a new and shorter cylinder block and a new composite head-gasket; the main bearings were revised and there was a new crankshaft main-bearing

centre cap, while the pistons now had a thicker wall for the gudgeon pin hole. The air cleaner on the single-carburettor cars was modified so that its intake tube picked up warm air from directly behind the radiator, and a number of cars were built with cast aluminium engine mountings, although the cast steel type was soon reinstated.

There were changes to the interior, too, where the fiddly map-reading lamps under the dash rail were deleted and a new rear-view mirror with integral courtesy light and steady-post was added. The levers for the face-level ventilation flaps were made longer and the flaps themselves gained better sealing, while the clock bezel changed from chrome to matt black. To reduce noise transmission into the cabin – especially important with the TC models – butyl rubber bushes were added to the exhaust mountings at the rear of the engine and the rear of gearbox.

The interior retained its superb combination of modernity and tradition. This is a 2000SC from 1967.

Further changes were introduced as the 1966 season progressed. April brought a larger hole for the gear lever in the transmission tunnel, and a softer gear lever gaiter, together with softer rubbers for the remote linkage and the tie bar fitted between the remote linkage and gearbox. At the same time, the sun wheel and the planet pinion bearings in the differential were strengthened to suit the extra torque of the TC engine, and different venting was introduced for the differential to counter oil loss onto the rear brake discs. In June came modifications to the door and boot locks.

Meanwhile, Rover had embarked on a programme that would see Girling braking components replace the Dunlop items in the P6 range. The Dunlop callipers were prone to seizures that could sometimes lead to cracked discs, and by December 1964 Rover was trying out Girling types. The executive directors' meeting that month was told that a decision about these would be made in February 1965. Whatever that decision was, Girling's acquisition of the Dunlop braking interests later that year somewhat forced the issue, and by the start of 1966 Rover was ready with a programme to change over completely to Girling components on the P6.

The 2000TC was the first model to gain Girling braking components; the suffix A models had Dunlop brakes but the suffix B models had Girling callipers and discs. On the single-carburettor cars, the Dunlop servo, fluid reservoir and master cylinder were all replaced by Girling components from May 1966, but the discs would not be changed until the start of the 1967 model year a few months later. As a result, a good number of cars were built over the summer of 1966 with a hybrid Girling-Dunlop braking system.

The 1967 Models

Rover's main concern as the 1967 season opened in autumn 1966 was probably to minimize complication on the P6 assembly lines as much as possible. The identifying suffix changed to E for the single-carburettor cars in August, and the changes it brought were then in place for the start of 2000 Automatic production.

From the servicing point of view, the most important change was to Girling brake discs and callipers, completing the changeover programme that had begun before the summer. According to *Glass's Guide*, the first single-carburettor car to have these was numbered 400-38509E; they were fitted to all Automatic models, but of course the TCs already had them.

SAFETY AWARD

In June 1966, the Rover Company became the winners of the Gold Medal in the first Automobile Association Motoring Awards. It was awarded for the safety features of the Rover 2000.

The AA awards were launched in 1965 to mark the association's Diamond Jubilee, and consisted of a gold medal and up to three silver medals to be awarded annually for outstanding work in the cause of motoring. Of the first awards, made in 1966, the AA chairman said, 'We noted particularly the volume of work done in 1965 to increase safety in car design and construction and our choice of the Gold Medal winner was largely influenced by this.'

In the award citations, the AA committee described the Rover 2000 as 'a car with many built-in safety features to prevent or reduce the likelihood of injury in the event of an accident'. It went on to say that 'the Rover Company, by designing and constructing a car with a high degree of inherent safety, had developed a car much in advance of its time and had set the pattern for future design in this country.'

Safety became an important preoccupation in the mid-1960s, and Rover carried out crash tests for the first time. This 2000 was rammed into a solid barrier during 1966 to see how well the passengers would be protected in an accident; the passenger compartment has remained intact.

With the change of chassis suffix came a wider use of butyl rubber mountings, which were added to the differential and to the remaining exhaust brackets. There were changes to the exhaust systems as well, as two-can types replaced the earlier three-can systems. In the gearbox, the selector detents were modified, and the clutch friction material changed to a heat-treated type made by Borg and Beck. The accelerator pedal was mounted a little lower than before, on a revised cross-shaft; it had stronger return springs, and a more flexible bulkhead grommet reduced the risk of the linkage sticking. Meanwhile, all engines now had stellite-faced exhaust valves, and a new baffle below the cam-cover breather.

A further change in August 1966 affected the window- and door-operating linkages, which were modified to reduce rattles. Changes then continued into September, when the handbrake mechanism was modified and – more visibly – the vehicle identification plate took on a new shape and moved from the left-hand A-post to the top of the left-hand inner wing under the bonnet.

The 1967 season inevitably brought some changes to the paint options, although less welcome was the deletion of the paint touch-up pencils that Rover had previously supplied with new cars. There were some new interior trim colours, but the range had clearly been rationalized: all headlinings were now in Oatmeal, and all carpets were now brown or grey, although red ones were still supplied with Toledo Red seats.

The bonnet release catch also moved from its original position inside the right-hand-side glovebox to a similar position on the other side. The reason was that Americans (quite reasonably) objected to having to reach right across the car to open the bonnet, and Rover decided to make the new position of the catch standard for all markets to reduce complication on the assembly lines. At least, it became standard for most markets and for most cars: the change could not be made to cars fitted with air-conditioning or those destined for West Germany.

From the start of the 1967 model year, several minor changes were made to improve gearbox lubrication: probably hard use of the new TC models had revealed weaknesses. Then in the early months of 1967 itself, some changes needed for the North American Federal models (see Chapter 9) were standardized across the range. First was a crankcase emissions control system, and second was a pre-engaged starter in place of the original inertia type. This was initially fitted only on left-hand-drive 2000 Automatics (from March 1967), but was later made standard across the whole range.

Meanwhile, the names of the various P6 models had clearly been causing some confusion, and Rover resolved this in February 1967 by changing them. From now on, the basic 2000 would be called a 2000SC and the automatic model would be a 2000SC Automatic. The TC, clearly not causing any problems, remained as a 2000TC. However, the badges on the two single-carburettor models remained unchanged.

It also appears to have been during the 1967 season that Rover made available a 'competition' gearbox with a lower third gear and a lower 4.3:1 final drive. Neither was advertised through normal sales literature, and it is probable that these were actually spares left over from the competitions programme (see Chapter 5) after Rover closed it down in 1966. The most likely scenario is that they were discreetly offered to privateers who were campaigning P6s in motor sport events, and that there were no more than a handful of them.

The 1968 and 1969 Models

Not much changed for the 1968 season in autumn 1967. Production of the new Federal models for North America had begun in July, and these had improved door locks (with

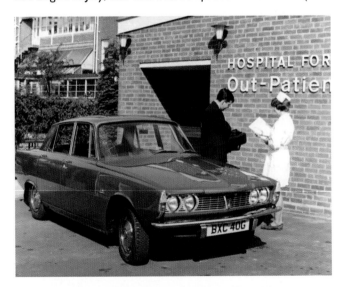

Not much changed externally on the 2000TC between the 1966 and 1969 seasons. This publicity picture links the car to successful professionals – in this case, a doctor. BXC 40G was a September 1968 car, 415-21331D.

pear-shaped faces and spring-loaded keyhole covers) and a bar-type seat slide release, while their sun visors were no longer fitted with vanity mirrors in order to meet collision safety guidelines. Cars for other markets followed suit, so saving Rover complication on the assembly lines, although the bar-type seat adjuster did not become universal until April 1968, when suffix letters changed to F for the SC and Automatic models, and to C for the TC.

As production volumes increased to cope with the new models – TC, Automatic, and soon the Three Thousand Five – and a night shift was started, the production system was stretched to its limits. P6 Inspection Superintendent Colin Elmer remembered many years later that one result was a reduction in the drying time allowed for the base units after they had been painted and before they were built into complete cars. The oven bake used was inadequate, he said, and as a consequence of this moisture could creep in underneath the paint.

In April 1968, the new V8-engined Three Thousand Five model (see Chapter 7) was introduced, and its arrival triggered a number of changes for the 4-cylinder models as well. Most obvious was a new style of hubcap, with twin black rings instead of the single ring of the original type; the twin rings indicated that stronger fixing claws were fitted, an improvement necessary since the arrival of the faster-accelerating TC, where the original trims could rotate under hard acceleration and damage the tyre valve. There were some new paint colours for the V8 car, and these now became available on the 4-cylinder models as well. Meanwhile, the original chromed steel 'ROVER' letters on the bootlid were changed for anodized aluminium ones that retained their appearance better. The 2000TC engines also took on HS8 carburettors in place of their original HD8 types, because these new ones could be more easily tuned to meet the emissions regulations that were clearly going to become more common around the world. Advertised power and torque figures remained unchanged.

There were some new options in April, too, although none of them ever became common. One was a passenger's side grab handle, a rather angular affair that bolted to the dashboard above the glovebox and did not blend in very well with the rest of the interior design. Then there was a metal sliding sunroof designed by the Dutch Coenan company, which was shown on the Sage Green Three Thousand Five on the Rover stand at the 1969 Earls Court Show, although it was also available for the 4-cylinder cars.

The Coenan sliding roof could only be fitted as an after-market accessory by companies with a Coenan franchise, and the only one of those in Britain was the London coach-builder FLM Panelcraft. Fitting the sunroof required a hole to be cut very carefully into the existing roof panel, which probably explains why Coenan were a little choosy about who they allowed to do the job! Over the summer of 1969, Rover made a second sliding roof available as an option, but this one (by Hollandia) was also restricted in its availability.

The main change on the 1969 cars was to flow-through ventilation, which exhausted air from the passenger cabin through flap valves concealed in the rear quarter-pillars. As the opening rear quarter-lights were no longer needed, they were replaced by fixed panes. However, customers seem to have missed the opening quarter-vents, and so the flow-through system was abandoned after just a year in production and the opening windows were reinstated. There were of course also changes to the paint options for the 1969 season, but that was all.

There were some changes to the rear badging for the 1970 season, and this late-registered 2000SC Automatic shows the new style.

The Triplex roof sounded like a great idea, but remained very rare. The cover of the sales brochure shows how it was fitted into a black frame panel – and in this case, the rear pillars were blacked out as well, some time before they were covered in black vinyl on the Series II cars.

The 1970 Models

The 1970 season was not much busier, as Rover were planning major revisions for the following year. The opening rear quarter-lights reappeared and there was a new D-2-1 selector gate for the 2000 Automatic (*see* Chapter 7). The 1970 cars were also distinguished by new badge arrangements. On all models, the Rover name on the bootlid was now in larger anodized aluminium letters and was relocated to the lower left side. The 4-cylinder cars, meanwhile, gained a new '2000' badge, now made of light alloy and set against a black background. There was no variation of this for the TC, which simply had the TC letters above its 2000 badges; Automatic models had an Automatic badge on the bootlid.

Rover also tested the market for a lower-priced entry-level model this year,

This is the view from inside a car with the Triplex roof. On the original picture, it is just possible to see that the windscreen is a heated type – another Triplex 'special' that was tried on the P6 but did not enter production.

The Triplex roof had a cloth lining that could be opened over the front seats, over the rear seats, or removed altogether.

offering a 2000SC with the box-plated Ambla (perforated vinyl) upholstery that had just been introduced on the special North American 3500S. The Ambla upholstery would remain a catalogued option alongside the standard leather for the next three seasons, but was never popular and probably did not encourage very many people to buy this entry-level 2000SC. For most customers at this stage, a Rover would not have been a Rover without leather upholstery.

Perhaps the most interesting new development for 1970 came from Triplex Safety Glass Ltd, with whom Rover had collaborated earlier in the development of heated wind-screens. This was a glass roof option, announced at the 1969 Earls Court Show and clearly a third attempt, after the two sliding sunroofs, to 'let the sunshine in', as a popular song of 1967 put it. Triplex had developed the roof in conjunction with Rover and Roof Installations Ltd of London SW4, which was the only company authorized to install it. It could be fitted to all variants of the P6, new or used, and could be ordered through Rover dealers. Strangely, even though Rover happily displayed a Brigade Red 2000TC with Triplex roof (plus Sundym glass and air-conditioning) on their stand at the Earls Court Show in 1969, they never listed the option in their own sales literature.

Triplex's own October 1969 press release explained that:

The existing roof panel is replaced by a draught and leak-proof glass-fibre perimeter, with a large area of Triplex 'Sundym' toughened glass, tinted green to cut down glare and absorb the sun's rays, therefore reducing the transmitted heat... The Triplex Glass Roof provides 'open-air' motoring without any of the snags – like the slip-stream buffeting your rear seat passengers or having to put the hood up in a sud-den cloud burst. It gives the car, and driving, a new dimension – a feeling of space and light – a unique experience.

The cost is £125 and this includes a zip-in headlin-ing which converts the inside to a normal saloon when you want total privacy or when the South-of-France 'scorchers' make a little shade welcome. The lining, in matching tone to the interior trim, can also be arranged to cover either the front or rear sections of the roof.

Sadly, the Triplex Glass Roof was a not a success, and probably no more than a dozen were fitted to P6s, most

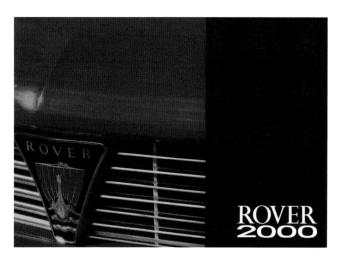

The front end of the P6 was distinctive enough to be all that was needed for recognition on the cover of the sales brochure.

Safety again: in this advertisement, Rover made capital out of their June 1966 safety award from the AA.

of them apparently V8 models, before it was withdrawn from the market in 1971 or 1972. The glass company had probably been counting on Rover sales to get its new product established before making it available for other cars, but in the event it remained unique to the P6. One reason for its failure was probably that it made the interior very hot, even when the headlining was zipped in place. Later, it became apparent that the glue holding the glass roof in place could fail; one car is known to have lost its glass panel at speed.

SELLING THE 4-CYLINDER MODELS, 1966–70

The single-carburettor Rover 2000 was already well established by the start of this period, and from 1966 the main thrust of Rover publicity was on the two new models, the 2000 Automatic and 2000TC. That thrust was switched again after a couple of years, when the new V8-engined models were introduced in April 1968. By then, Rover publicity had done its job and all three 4-cylinder models had become well established among buyers.

Early advertising for the 2000TC in Britain stressed its performance, and one excited advertisement showed it racing a dragster. 'New!' claimed the strapline. 'Rover 2000TC: it boasts Rover quality. And packs Twin-Carb punch.' During 1967, advertisements in English-language magazines sold on the European continent pushed home the quality image with lines like: 'If you know one of the 2000TC's European owners, you've got a shrewd friend.' Yet it was the 1968-season home market advertising campaign that was the most memorable of this period.

With the catchphrase 'a Rover is still a Rover', the cam-

ROVER 2000 AND 2000 AUTOMATIC, 1966–67

ROVER 2000SC AND 2000SC AUTOMATIC, 1967–70

ROVER 2000TC, 1966–70

Engine (2000, 2000SC, 2000 Automatic and 2000SC Automatic)

Type: Cast iron block and light alloy head

Cylinders: 4

Bore and stroke: 85.7mm × 85.7mm

Capacity: 1978cc

Five-bearing crankshaft

Single overhead camshaft

Compression ratio: 9:1

Carburettor: Single SU type HS6 carburettor

Max. power: 99bhp SAE (90bhp installed) at 5,000rpm

Max. torque: 121lb ft SAE at 3,600rpm (113.5lb ft at 2,750rpm, installed)

Export only:

Compression ratio: 7.5:1

Max. power: 87.5bhp SAE (80bhp installed) at 5,000rpm

Max. torque: 113lb ft SAE at 3,350rpm (106lb ft at 2,500rpm, installed)

Engine (2000TC)

Type: Cast iron block and light alloy head

Cylinders: 4

Capacity: 1978cc

Bore and stroke: 85.7mm × 85.7mm

Valves: Single overhead camshaft

Main bearings: Five-bearing crankshaft

Carburettor: Two SU carburettors, type HD8 to 1968, type HS8 thereafter

Compression ratio: 10:1

Max. power: 124bhp SAE (114bhp installed) at 5,500rpm

Max. torque: 132lb ft SAE at 4,000rpm (126lb ft at 3,5000rpm, installed)

Export only:

Compression ratio: 9:1

Max. power: 117bhp SAE (107bhp installed) at 5,500rpm

Max. torque: 125lb ft SAE at 3,750rpm (120lb ft at 3,250rpm, installed)

Transmission (2000, 2000SC and 2000TC)

Gearbox: Four-speed all-synchromesh manual

Ratios

    1st: 3.62:1

    2nd: 2.13:1

    3rd: 1.39:1

    4th: 1.00:1

    Reverse: 3.43:1

Axle ratio: 3.54:1

paign promoted the TC's new high performance image while stressing that traditional Rover qualities had not been lost. So one advertisement for the TC showed the view from the driver's seat as he overtook a lorry, only to find another car appear round a bend. 'Every now and then', read the strapline, 'you have to put your foot down. Then you'll thank goodness a Rover is still a Rover.'

For the 2000SC Automatic, the campaign emphasized stress-free driving. Beneath a picture of several traffic lights at red, the strapline was: 'When you're forever seeing red you'll thank goodness a Rover is still a Rover.' The text went on: 'When you're having more stops than goes. And you're simmering under the collar. You'll thank goodness Rover appreciate the value of things like automatic gear changing. (That way you keep your mind on the driving and your hands on the wheel.)' Then for the single-carburettor manual car, the emphasis was on safety. 'The great Rover 2000SC!'

shouted one advertisement. 'It boasts deep-built safety even when your foot's down hard.'

Other advertisements covered the whole range. Longevity was the focus in an advertisement that showed a new 2000 in front of piles of scrapped cars under the strapline: 'In an age of mass-production, thank goodness a Rover is still a Rover.' To stress comfort, there was an advertisement headed by a picture of an elegant lady in the back seat of a P6; and for safety, there were 'Nine things to remember about safety. (Or why the Rover 2000 is the safest car on the road.)'

The marketing value of safety was seen in other Rover promotional activities, too, and in February 1968 the dealer Morsmith Motors of Cardiff displayed a 2000 that had been crash-tested at MIRA to illustrate how well the P6 stood up to a serious collision. However, this was an initiative that seems not to have been followed up elsewhere.

Transmission (2000 Automatic and 2000SC Automatic)
Gearbox: Three-speed Borg Warner Type 35 automatic
Ratios
  1st: 2.39:1
  2nd: 1.45:1
  3rd: 1.00:1
  Reverse: 2.09:1
Axle ratio: 3.54:1

Suspension
Front: Independent suspension with transverse bottom links and leading upper links acting on coil springs mounted horizontally to the bulkhead; anti-roll bar; hydraulic telescopic dampers
Rear: Suspension with lower links and coil springs; De Dion tube incorporating sliding joint, with transverse location by fixed-length driveshafts and fore-and-aft location by Watts linkage; hydraulic telescopic dampers
Steering: Adamant Marles worm-and-roller type
Tyres: 165 SR 14 radial
Wheels: Five-stud steel disc wheels with 14in diameter; optional wire-spoked wheels with 14in diameter (TC only)
Rim width: 5in

Brakes
Type: Disc brakes on all four wheels, mounted inboard at the rear; handbrake acting on rear discs; servo assistance standard; Dunlop discs and callipers 1964–66, Girling discs and callipers 1966–73
Size: 10.75in front, 10.25in rear (Dunlop); 10.31in front, 10.69in rear (Girling)

Dimensions
Wheelbase: 103.375in (2,626mm)
Overall length: 178.5in (4,534mm)
Overall width: 66in (1,676mm)
Overall height: 54.75in (1,390mm)
Track, front: 53.375in (1,356mm)
Track, rear: 52.5in (1,333mm)
Running weight: 2,770lb (1,256kg), 2000 and 2000SC manual 2,793lb (1,267kg), 2000 Automatic and 2000SC Automatic 2,827lb (1,282kg), 2000TC

Performance
Max speed: 100mph (161.3km/h), 2000 and 2000SC manual 100mph (161km/h), 2000 Automatic and 2000SC Automatic 112mph (180km/h), 2000TC
0–60mph: 13.9sec, 2000 and 2000SC manual 17.75sec, 2000 Automatic and 2000SC Automatic 11.45sec, 2000TC

PAINT AND TRIM OPTIONS

For details of paint and trim options in North America, *see* Chapter 9.

June 1966–January 1967

Five paint colours were available in place of the previous six. Wedgwood Blue and Willow Green were no longer offered, and City Grey was replaced by Burnt Grey. Venetian Red did not become available until August 1966. Four new trim colours replaced all five of the earlier ones, and all headlinings were now in Oatmeal. Carpets were in Mortlake Brown with all colours except Toledo Red, which came with matching Toledo Red carpets. The standard colour combinations were:

Arden Green	with trim in	Buckskin, Buffalo or Sandalwood
Burnt Grey		Buckskin, Buffalo, Sandalwood or Toledo Red
Venetian Red		Buckskin, Buffalo or Sandalwood
White		Buffalo, Sandalwood or Toledo Red
Zircon Blue		Buckskin, Buffalo or Sandalwood

February–September 1967

The paint colours remained unchanged, but Ebony was introduced as a fifth trim option. This was available with all standard colours.

October–December 1967

The five standard paint colours were again unchanged. Buffalo trim was discontinued, leaving the four options as Buckskin, Ebony, Sandalwood and Toledo Red.

January–June 1968

The total of standard paint colours went back up to six, as April Yellow (from the North American options) was added. Brigade Red replaced Venetian Red for all markets. The choice of four trim colours remained unchanged.

The standard combinations were:

April Yellow	with trim in	Buckskin or Ebony
Arden Green		Buckskin, Ebony or Sandalwood
Brigade Red		Buckskin, Ebony, Sandalwood or Toledo Red
Burnt Grey		Buckskin, Ebony, Sandalwood or Toledo Red
White		Ebony, Sandalwood or Toledo Red
Zircon Blue		Buckskin, Ebony or Sandalwood

July 1968–July 1969

Two new paint colours, Corsica Blue and Tobacco Leaf, made the total up to eight options. The four trim colours remained unchanged again, always in leather.

The colour combinations were:

April Yellow	with trim in	Buckskin or Ebony
Arden Green		Buckskin, Ebony or Sandalwood
Brigade Red		Buckskin, Ebony, Sandalwood or Toledo Red
Burnt Grey		Buckskin, Ebony, Sandalwood or Toledo Red
Corsica Blue		Buckskin, Ebony or Sandalwood
Tobacco Leaf		Buckskin, Ebony or Sandalwood
White		Ebony, Sandalwood or Toledo Red
Zircon Blue		Buckskin, Ebony or Sandalwood

August 1969–August 1970

Eight paint colours were available again, but Davos White replaced White and Sage Green replaced April Yellow. The four trim colours were again unchanged, and leather was standard.

The colour combinations were:

Arden Green	with trim in	Buckskin, Ebony or Sandalwood
Brigade Red		Buckskin, Ebony, Sandalwood or Toledo Red
Burnt Grey		Buckskin, Ebony, Sandalwood or Toledo Red
Corsica Blue		Buckskin, Ebony or Sandalwood
Davos White		Ebony, Sandalwood or Toledo Red
Sage Green		Buckskin, Ebony or Sandalwood
Tobacco Leaf		Buckskin, Ebony or Sandalwood
Zircon Blue		Buckskin, Ebony or Sandalwood

RIGHT: **This 1968 advertisement reminded the public that despite the new performance image of the 2000TC, the traditional Rover qualities remained intact across the range. Note the British Leyland 'flying wheel' logo that was now associated with the Rover one.**

When you've moved on and left sports cars behind you'll thank goodness a Rover is still a Rover

When you love motoring. But you've learned to like a lot of comfort too. Then you'll be glad that Rover still build cars with a little extra.

Like a little extra performance. 0-50 in 8.5 seconds. And extra road holding. The Rover 2000's specially developed de Dion suspension is costly. But Rover think that having the best road-gripping system in the world makes it worth every penny. And the safety that goes with it is priceless.

Every Rover 2000 built gets all the extra time and care

that a high-performance car deserves. It has to. With each one we build our reputation is at stake.

The Rover Company Limited, Solihull, Warwickshire. Rover 2000 prices (inc. PT ex works): SC Manual £1,471.10.7; SC Automatic £1,567.7.3; TC Version £1,535.8.4.

ROVER

Rover 2000
SC/SC Automatic/TC

Some people buy this car for its name.

If you want a better reason, read on.

First we'll tell you what our car gives you. Then we'll tell you the name we gave it.

It gives you luxury.

Its scientifically designed seats are more comfortable than most armchairs. They certainly are better for you. On them is real leather where it matters most. On the floor is deep pile carpeting.

The engine is truly remarkable.

It has an advanced combustion chamber design and a racing-type overhead camshaft. You can have two versions. Quick. That's the single carburettor version. And quicker. That's the twin-carburettor model. Both sip petrol like misers. It is very quiet.

You'll soon get used to warning other cars

that you're passing them. We're tempted to say that you could hear the clock ticking. But we give you a very quiet clock.

The maximum speed is way above the U.K. limit. Don't worry. We give you four-wheel disc brakes to restrain it. And unique all-round suspension that just swallows bumps and curves.

We designed safety into this car before safety was fashionable. It was recently awarded a special AA Gold Medal for safety. You'll never have to pamper it.

After 3000 miles of torture-testing, the internationally famous "Car and Driver" motor magazine called it an "automotive milestone". Since then we've made some improvements.

So that may have been a bit extravagant.

It's too early to tell how long it will last you. But you could easily be still driving it in ten years' time.

In California it costs $4,198. And they're queueing for it. But don't let that scare you. Here it's only about £1,415. If that seems a fair price to you, we'll throw in its name free.

Rover 2000 T.C.

(Single Carburettor Manual or Automatic version available.)

The Rover Company Limited, Solihull, Warwickshire. London office: Devonshire House, Piccadilly. Makers of fine cars, gas turbines and the world-famous Land-Rover

Reasons for buying a 2000TC: by the time of this press advertisement, the Automatic models were available, too.

RIGHT: **Another 1968 advertisement, this time reassuring Rover buyers that their investment in a new Rover would not be undermined by seasonal updates that made it look old-fashioned.**

AUTOCAR, 17 October 1968

Your new car is about to become obsolete.

They're making the facelift that makes most models new and yours out of date.

At Rover we have a different philosophy. Instead of built-in obsolescence, we build in safety and performance features which do not date. And only make changes that actually improve the car. So your Rover 2000 will be the current model for years to come.

And, instead of just padding, a safety cage that surrounds and protects you and your passengers. Instead of brief checks, giving every engine a full bench test. And we drive every car round and round our test track until we're satisfied.

It's these standards, these features and the thinking behind them that make a Rover new. Year after year after year.

ROVER

In this age of mass production, a Rover is still a Rover.

PRICES AND RIVALS, 1966–70

The totals shown here were basic UK showroom prices for 4-cylinder models without extras. Also shown are the basic ex-factory cost and the purchase tax payable. Prices for the Three Thousand Five are shown in Chapter 7.

September 1966

	Total	Ex-factory	Purchase tax
2000	£1,357 9s 10d	£1,073	£254 9s 10d
2000TC	£1,415 5s 2d	£1,150	£265 5s 2d
2000 Automatic	£1,452 2s 8d	£1,180	£272 2s 8d

November 1967

	Total	Ex-factory	Purchase tax
2000	£1,357 9s 10d	£1,073	£254 9s 10d
2000TC	£1,415 5s 3d	£1,150	£265 5s 3d
2000 Automatic	£1,452 2s 9d	£1,180	£272 2s 9d

The November 1967 prices were the same as those for September 1966 except for a recalculation of purchase tax that put the prices of the TC and Automatic up by 1d each.

June 1968

	Total	Ex-factory	Purchase tax
2000SC	£1,471 10s 7d	£1,150	£321 10s 7d
2000TC	£1,535 8s 4d	£1,200	£335 8s 4d
2000 SC Auto	£1,567 7s 3d	£1,225	£342 7s 3d

December 1968

	Total	Ex-factory	Purchase tax
2000SC	£1,503 13s 7d	£1,150	£353 13s 7d
2000TC	£1,568 19s 2d	£1,200	£368 19s 2d
2000 SC Auto	£1,601 11s 11d	£1,225	£376 11s 11d

October 1969

	Total	Ex-factory	Purchase tax
2000SC (Ambla)	£1,499 15s 3d	£1,147	£352 15s 3d
2000SC (Leather)	£1,514 2s 6d	£1,158	£356 2s 6d
2000TC	£1,598 19s 9d	£1,223	£375 19s 9d
2000 SC Auto	£1,631 12s 6d	£1,248	£383 12s 6d

February 1970

	Total	Ex-factory	Purchase tax
2000SC (Ambla)	£1,537 12s 6d	£1,176	£361 12s 6d
2000SC (Leather)	£1,551 19s 9d	£1,187	£364 19s 9d
2000TC	£1,639 9s 2d	£1,254	£385 9s 2d
2000 SC Auto	£1,673 8s 1d	£1,280	£393 8s 1d

July 1970

	Total	Ex-factory	Purchase tax
2000SC (Ambla)	£1,614 13s 1d	£1,235	£379 13s 1d
2000SC (Leather)	£1,629 0s 3d	£1,246	£383 0s 3d
2000TC	£1,721 14s 2d	£1,317	£404 14s 2d
2000 SC Auto	£1,756 19s 2d	£1,344	£412 19s 2d

Rivals

The strongest competition for the 2000 models still came from the Triumph 2000 and, after 1968, from its high-performance 2.5 PI derivative. From 1969, that competition intensified even further when the attractively facelifted Mk II Triumph range arrived. Throughout the second half of the decade, the two 2000 ranges jockeyed for position as Britain's best-selling 2.0-litre saloon. On overall sales, the less expensive Triumph usually won, but press comparisons usually voted for the Rover.

For part of this period, the Jaguar 2.4-litre (and later 240), Citroën ID19 (and later D20 Super), Fiat 2300 and Peugeot 404 continued to compete with the Rovers. But new models were not long in coming: by the end of the decade, the BMW 2002, Audi 100LS, Volvo 144 and Ford Zodiac V6 were all competing for the same group of customers, while Peugeot's excellent new 504 probably presented the most serious threat of all.

CHAPTER FOUR

THE P7 INTERLUDE

If everything had gone according to plan, the P6 would have been followed in the mid-1960s by a high-performance 6-cylinder derivative that Rover knew as the P7 model. However, the original plan was disrupted quite early in the development programme, and the company's acquisition of the 3.5-litre V8 engine from General Motors soon provided a more cost-effective way of achieving the same end. The development story of the V8-engined car, known within the company as the P6B, is told in Chapter 6.

The P7 story is very far from being a linear one, and although the original P7 programme ground to a halt some time in 1964, the transition to the P6B programme was not a clean one. Even after P6B had been granted full project status within the Rover Engineering Department, the P7 designation persisted, being used for a series of development 'mules' associated with other projects.

In fact, there were three different groups of cars called P7. The first group of cars were development vehicles for the P7 project proper, which was intended to deliver that 6-cylinder derivative of the P6. The second group were then built to examine alternatives to the 6-cylinder engine, and the third group consisted of those development mules. There seem to have been eleven cars in all: four in the first group, three in the second and four in the third. But it was by no means as clear-cut as that breakdown suggests!

THE ORIGINS OF P7

It was only logical that a 6-cylinder derivative should have been considered from an early stage in the P6 project. The car was, after all, destined to replace the P4 range, which at the time had both 4-cylinder and 6-cylinder models. Surviving documents show that a 6-cylinder model was under consideration as early as 1957, but as Chapter 1 explains, a priority was put on the 4-cylinder car and no further work on the 6-cylinder was done until 1960.

Perhaps the main reason was that Rover were just about to introduce another new 6-cylinder model, the P5 3-litre that was announced in 1958. Although this was intended to sell at a higher price than the P4, Rover probably suspected that it would absorb many 6-cylinder sales from the P4 range. This would then leave the 4-cylinder P4s as the ones most in need of a replacement, so initial work on P6 focused on that 4-cylinder replacement model.

All this makes some sort of sense. However, the P6 was then designed around its new 4-cylinder ohc engine – with the same 2-litre capacity as the engine in the existing P4 Rover 60 – apparently without any thought for the later installation of a 6-cylinder engine. As a result, when Rover did eventually get around to working on a 6-cylinder derivative of P6, they came up against a major problem: the new engine was going to be too long for the engine bay.

It seems very likely that the idea of a 6-cylinder P6 was resurrected after Rover learned of Triumph's plans to launch their rival 2000 with a 6-cylinder engine. Once the design stage of the 4-cylinder P6 project was over, the New Vehicle Projects team under Spen King turned its attention to such a car. The project was formally given the green light on 12 December 1960, when an engineering policy meeting agreed to proceed with development of the 6-cylinder version of P6. However, there would still be a long gap between idea and execution, and serious work on the 6-cylinder P6 did not begin until the 4-cylinder car was about to be signed off for production at the end of 1962.

The first trace of what would become a full-scale development project dates from October 1962, when the executive directors' meeting learned that the company was considering a 6-cylinder version of the P6 with the 2.6-litre IOE engine then used in the P4 range. However, this seems to have been a short-lived idea and, some time over the next few months, thoughts focused instead on a new 6-cylinder engine that would be a development of the Rover 2000's ohc 4-cylinder type. The idea of making such an engine was

```
                    Engine

The engine will be an overhead camshaft type of
three litres capacity, installed in car inclined
to R.H. side 10°, with the following specification:-

     Firing order          1.5.3.6.2.4.
     Bore                  3⅝"  as P.6.
     Stroke                3⅝"  as P.6.
     No. of cylinders      6 in line.
     Swept volume          2969 c.c.s.  181-16 cu.ins.
     Cylinder head         Aluminium Alloy with
                           integerally cast, water
                           heated inlet manifold on
                           exhaust port side.
     Combustion chamber    In piston crown.  As P.6.
     No. of valves         2 per cylinder vertical in
                           line.  As P.6.
     Valve operation       As P.6.
     Cam shaft drive       As P.6.
     Camshaft              Monikrom 8 bearings.
     Camshaft bearing block  Cast Iron.
     Cylinder block        Cast Iron.
```

These pages from Gordon Bashford's technical brochure show the anticipated production specification of the P7 6-cylinder engine.

```
                Engine (Continued)

     Carburetter           Single S.U. type HD8 or HS8.
     Crankshaft            EN16T steel 7 bearings.
     Crankshaft bearings
     Main & Big End.       Lead Indian Vandervell VP2.
     Con Rods.             Forged Steel.  As P.6.
     Pistons               As P.6.
     Compression Ratio     9 : 1.   As P.6.

Performance:-

     Maximum BHP Bare        -    165 at 5000 r.p.m.
     Maximum BHP Installed   =    152 at 5000 r.p.m.
     Maximum BMEP Lbs/Ins"
                      Bare   -    154 at 4000 r.p.m.
     Maximum BMEP Lbs/Ins"
                 Installed   =    142 at 3500 r.p.m.
     Maximum Torque Lbs/Ft.
                      Bare   -    185 at 4000 r.p.m.
     Maximum Torque Lbs/Ft.
                 Installed   -    170.5 at 3500 r.p.m.
     Maximum Speed           =    6000 r.p.m.

     Weight:  500-lbs complete with flywheel,
              engine feet, fan and dynamo -
              excluding clutch, oil, water and
              air cleaner.
```

```
              Facia and Controls

A visually new facia panel will be fitted
obtained by locating circular instruments:-
Speedometer, rev-counter, fuel gauge, oil
pressure gauge, ammeter, water temperature
gauge and clock, plus warning lights,
beneath a completely new screen rail.

All major injection moulded parts, as do
the centrally disposed switches, heater
control etc., remain exactly as P.6.

A new steering wheel finisher will be
fitted, carrying the 3000 motif.
```

Another page from the technical brochure shows the intention to use a different instrument panel. This appears to be the one also planned for the 2000S that eventually entered production for the Federal 3500S and the Series II models.

Gordon Bashford in New Vehicle Projects was now given the job of producing a full technical brochure for the projected new car. This brochure was probably completed in February or March 1963; certainly, the idea of the new ohc 6-cylinder engine was firmly embedded in Rover's thinking by April that year. Bashford's technical brochure made clear that the new 6-cylinder car was going to be a long-nose version of P6, the extra length being necessary to accommodate the longer engine. It was also going to be different enough from the production 4-cylinder P6 to merit a new designation, and so the 6-cylinder car took the next number in the Rover sequence and became known as P7. Nevertheless, development chief Rex Marvin remembered that the P7 prototypes were also known as 'P6/Six' types within the Engineering Department.

THE OHC 3-LITRE ENGINE

Central to the new model was to be that 6-cylinder engine, and Bashford's calculations obviously depended on the anticipated dimensions of this. Its length and weight would have been calculated easily enough from those of the parent 4-cylinder ohc engine. The bore and stroke dimensions

not entirely new: it had been discussed as long ago as July 1961, when it was considered as a possibility for the 129in (3,277mm) Land Rover that was then being developed (but never reached production).

would be unchanged, as would the overall architecture; there would simply be six cylinders instead of four. The advantages to this approach were speed of development, lower costs, and the ability to make the engine on existing P6 transfer-line tooling.

Jack Swaine's engines team may well have built the first of the new engines by the time Bashford completed his technical brochure. The 2-litre size had entered production by this stage, although the launch of the Rover P6 was still some months away. Using the bore and stroke dimensions of that engine gave the 6-cylinder a swept volume of 2968cc. The same 9:1 compression ratio allowed commonality of pistons, and a seven-bearing crankshaft ensured smooth running. The carburettor was a single 2in SU HD8, as used on the existing IOE 3-litre engine: Maurice Wilks had died a few months earlier, but he had been opposed to using multiple carburettors on Rover engines because they required regular tuning to give their best, and his influence still held sway.

The technical brochure can only be treated as a statement of intent, but it contains a number of useful details. It shows the installed power output of the new 6-cylinder engine as 152bhp at 5,000rpm with torque of 170.5lb ft at 3,500rpm. This may have been increased later: motoring journalist Ted Eves quoted a figure of 185lb ft at 4,000rpm in his article for *Autocar* dated 15 August 1968. 'About half a dozen P7 engines were built,' Jack Swaine remembered in 1981, 'but I think some

A surviving 6-cylinder engine from the P7 programme, pictured at the P6 twenty-fifth anniversary celebrations in 1988.

Rover had other plans for the 6-cylinder engine, too. Here it is in a mock-up buck for a 6-cylinder Land Rover, in April 1964.

were cannibalized to keep the others going. All were origi-nally single-carburettor engines with the manifold integral with the head, in keeping with the Maurice Wilks' policy.'

Bashford's technical brochure also shows that the engine was to be inclined to the right-hand-side of the car by 10 degrees and that a viscous-coupled fan would be fitted together with a cross-flow radiator in place of the fixed fan and vertical-flow radiator of the P6. Also under considera-tion were pneumatic accelerator controls, although work on these seems not to have been taken any further, perhaps because of their poor service record on the Hillman Imp that pioneered them in 1961.

The plan at the start of the project was that the four-speed P6 gearbox would be standard, but that a new five-speed manual box and a Borg Warner type 35 automatic transmission were to be offered as options. The manual gearchange lever might ultimately be integral with the gear-box – as indeed it would be much later in P6 production – rather than mounted remotely on the base unit. The final drive ratio was to be the same 3.54:1 as on the P6.

Suspension would also be the same as on the P6 except for stronger coil springs at the front to match the greater weight of the engine. Interestingly, though, a revised front suspension with triangular lower wishbones was also under consideration. Power-assisted steering, with a Burman or Hydrosteer box, would be an option. As for the brakes, there would be thicker discs, a 'muscle servo' and possibly an anti-lock device, by which Bashford probably meant a load-apportioning valve in the rear brake lines; ABS was still a long way in the future.

In line with its greater showroom cost, the P7 was to be a more luxurious car than its 4-cylinder sibling. The seats were to be a development of the P6 seat, but with height adjust-ment on the front pair and slightly more form to give a more luxurious appearance. From this description, these sound like the seats that later found a home in the 1965 P5 3-litre Mk III. The instrument panel was to be the new round-dial type already being looked at for the 2000S; a three-spoke steering wheel would replace the 2000's two-spoke type, and consideration was being given to using vacuum opera-tion of the main air and screen bar flaps in the heating and ventilating system. Lastly, there would be a 15-gallon (68ltr) fuel tank instead of the 12-gallon (54.5ltr) type planned for the 4-cylinder P6.

Further planning work on P7 was done in the first half of 1963. The production engineering team had a draft pro-gramme ready in June that year, which began that month

and led to the launch of the new car in October or Novem-ber 1965. David Bache's Styling Department had probably started on their part of the work even earlier, because they had a quarter-scale model of the new car ready by the end of July.

Then, on 1 August 1963, a meeting called by general man-ager A. B. Smith agreed on certain revisions to that pro-gramme. The meeting also called for a ³⁄₈-scale model to be made during that month, and this was presumably additional to the Styling Department's existing quarter-scale model. The programme now expected twelve prototype cars to be built, and that volume production would begin in August 1965 after a pre-production batch had been made in May and June that year. The public launch was rescheduled for the end of 1965. As Chapter 1 explains, if the P7 had ever reached the showrooms, it might well have been called the Rover 3000.

FIRST STEPS

What was probably the very first 6-cylinder ohc engine was tried out initially in an early P5 3-litre, registered 3030 AC. Meanwhile, work began in autumn 1963 to construct the first full P7 prototype, which was probably built up in the jig shop at Solihull and was somewhat crudely modified from a P6 base unit. A picture in the Rover archives, dated Octo-ber 1963, shows the car in a workshop that seems to have been used by the mileage drivers whose task was to put the car through several thousand miles of hard use to see what problems arose. This car was numbered P7/1 and had been given the registration number 17 EXK, which seems to have been allocated to Rover just over a year earlier, in August 1962.

That number may well have been obtained for a seven-teenth prototype of the P6 that was never actually built. The timing is right, and the figure 17 would tie in with Rover's practice of giving the P6 prototypes registrations that reflected their engineering prototype numbers; the last P6 prototype had been P6/16 (16 DYF), also registered in August 1962. Once diverted to P7/1, however, the number took on a different significance: to Rover, the figure 1 indi-cated the first prototype and the 7 indicated the P7 project. It was, of course, not a Warwickshire number; as with the P6 prototypes of the time, using London registrations was thought to be a useful way of disguising the origins of an unfamiliar-looking car!

This was P7/1 in October 1963, displaying the lashed-up front end that accommodated the extra length of the 6-cylinder engine. Under a magnifying glass, the chalk boards behind reveal driver allocations for the P6 prototypes and pre-production cars.

However, anybody who saw P7/1 would immediately have recognized it as a modified Rover P6. The obvious changes were all at the front end, where the original wings remained in place next to a crudely lengthened nose and bonnet. The result left no doubt that the car was a test hack. Although no list of the other modifications has been found, it would be reasonable to suppose that these were much the same as on the later P7 prototypes.

MORE PROTOTYPES

The plan was now to build four more prototypes, and the

original schedule called for the last car (which would have been numbered P7/5) to be built in April/May 1964. However, during 1964, Rover top management were becoming interested in the new V8 engine, and so the construction of that fifth prototype was delayed by several months.

It seems probable that P7/1 was built with a manual gearbox, so P7/2 was built to test the automatic option. There certainly was one of each, according to some notes made by development chief Rex Marvin many years later. P7/3 was also automatic, while P7/4, the last one, was another manual car. P7/1 and P7/2 both had the same crudely modified front end, but the fourth car (and possibly P7/3 as well) had an attractively redesigned front end with headlamps enclosed

P7/4 is the sole survivor, and was pictured here in the 1990s after sale to Ian Glass. The front end on the later prototypes was considerably tidied up. Also in the picture is Roger Harries of the Rover Sports Register. ROVER SPORTS REGISTER

behind Perspex and the number plate angled backwards to act as an air scoop for the radiator, just as David Bache's July 1963 quarter-scale model had anticipated. A broadly similar nose design would later appear on his P6-based Alvis GTS styling prototype.

We know relatively little about the other modifications that produced these first four prototypes, but they probably all had the battery moved to the right-hand side of the boot. This would have improved the weight balance with the heavier engine, and would also have left more room for it under the bonnet. The major modifications were of course at the front, where the base unit's front cross-member was moved forwards, and upwards a little to preserve the original approach angle. The grille support panel on the base unit was meanwhile bowed outwards to clear the fan. The falling bonnet line of the P6 combined with the relocation of the cross-member further upwards reduced the height available for the radiator, and so the one fitted was shallower than the P6 type. It was also supplemented by a header tank fitted at the rear of the engine.

Among the engineers who worked on this stage of the P7 programme was a young Mike Lewis, who would lead the engineering team on the Rover SD1 a decade or so later. There was also a young Jim Randle, fresh from a Rover apprenticeship, who would become director of vehicle engineering at Jaguar in the 1980s. And when P7/1 and

P7/2 went off to the Alps with a trailer to undergo some brake tests, the engineer in charge was Rover's braking expert, Jim Shaw. There are pictures of the two cars on the web site run by his son, James Shaw (www.jshawmsc.f2s.com/rover.htm).

As development continued during 1964, a higher final drive of 3.36:1 was introduced into the P7 specification, and a ZF five-speed manual gearbox was tried out; the ZF box was also under consideration for the planned 2000TC at the time, but was eventually ruled out because of delays in designing a version that met Rover's standards of refinement. One development car may also have had a Moss four-speeder of the type used in Jaguars at the time – probably because this could handle more torque than the standard Rover type – while P7/4 was eventually fitted with a modified four-speed P6 box, which had ordinary roller bearings in place of the standard needle-roller type.

There were engine developments, too. Jack Swaine later recalled: 'After William Martin-Hurst decided to have a 2000TC, one of the P7s was converted to three carburettors by cutting and welding two 2000TC heads and inlet manifolds. The result was excellent apart from a slight water leak at the welded joint on the head, which was never permanently cured.' With TC pistons to give a 10:1 compression ratio, the three-carburettor engine gave 183bhp at 5,250rpm.

In tandem with the 3.36:1 final drive, the three-carburettor engine gave the P7 a maximum speed of 149mph (240km/h) in the hands of Rover test drivers enthusiastically giving the car its head on an almost-deserted M6 motorway early one morning. Test engineer Lyn Thomas remembered that they tried hard to hit 150mph (241km/h) but could not quite make it! This was done quite legally, of course: the high-speed test track at MIRA was not available in those days, and so Rover obtained special permission from the police to use a straight section of motorway during a quiet time of day for maximum speed testing.

Prototype cars of course regularly deliver better performance than their production equivalents. One reason is that they are usually lighter, without the weight of whatever luxurious trim and extra equipment is agreed for production. Another is that their engines usually enter production in a lower state of tune in order to reduce stresses and improve engine life. Even so, it is worth comparing what we know about the P7 prototypes with figures for the contemporary Mercedes-Benz 300SE – a hugely respected car that completely eclipsed the performance of almost every other saloon available in 1963. With 160bhp at 5,000rpm (and later 170bhp) from its fuel-injected 3-litre 6-cylinder engine, the Mercedes had a maximum speed of 118mph (190km/h) and could reach 60mph from rest in 13 (later 12) seconds. So the P7 was right up there with the fastest saloons of the time.

The actual performance of the P7 prototypes inevitably depended on the combination of engine tune and gearbox and back axle ratios in use at the time, but testers remember them as very fast, with the heavier engine giving both better directional stability and better cornering than the standard 'four' in the P6. Engineer Rob Lyall remembers that 'The one I tried was much better at straight line running as the C of G was further forward than P6/P6Bs.' As for maximum speed, however, Ted Eves reported for *Autocar* that Rover settled on a design target of a 128mph (206km/h) top speed with the single-carburettor engine and 3.36:1 final drive. Gearing in this form was 21.8mph (35km/h) per 1,000rpm in direct top on 175 × 14 tyres, which were slightly fatter than those used on the 4-cylinder model.

So it was full steam ahead on the P7 project during the early months of 1964. The first prototypes were out on test, and a plan was drawn up to accommodate production of the new model within the North Block at Solihull, where P6s were also built. There was once again talk of using the new 6-cylinder engine in Land Rovers, and one was tried out in a Land Rover 109 mock-up in April 1964.

In the background, however, storm clouds were gathering. It became increasingly clear that the 6-cylinder P7 was going to be expensive to make. On top of the tooling costs for the new engine itself would be further tooling costs for the modified base unit and new front skin panels. And, as early as November 1963, Managing Director William Martin-Hurst had set himself against the 6-cylinder option, although it would take some time before this opposition filtered through the system and put a stop to the project.

An interesting transcript of a letter from Martin-Hurst to Bruce McWilliams, who was then running Rover's North American operation, supports Jack Swaine's 1981 contention that Martin-Hurst 'did not want the P7 engine'. The letter is dated 13 November 1963, and Martin-Hurst was holidaying in Mallorca after the autumn round of motor shows at which the P6 had been introduced. He reported various happenings at Rover, and added:

> I also drove the prototype of the 6-cylinder again and, with regret, made the decision to drop it in favour of a new car to take both 4- and 6- cylinder engines without major alterations... The reason for the decision is two-fold – firstly, the weight of the 6-cylinder engine upsets the weight distribution and spoils safe cornering to a marked degree. If you fling the car round corners it feels very front heavy, like a weight on a string, and, with the power of the six it would, I am convinced, be a death trap on wet roads.

This same letter also indicates that Martin-Hurst was intending to visit Carl Kiekhaefer of Mercury Marine at the beginning of December. It would be during this trip that he saw the Buick V8 for the first time, and realized that it would be an ideal engine for Rover if they could get agreement from General Motors to manufacture it. So the traditional idea that the V8 killed off the ohc 6-cylinder is incorrect: as far as top management was concerned, the 'six' was dead before the V8 entered the picture. Lower down the Rover hierarchy, of course, the engineers continued to work on the P7 programme for many months, and to them the V8 certainly did appear as the reason for the demise of the 6-cylinder project.

That 'new car to take both 4-and 6-cylinder engines' that Martin-Hurst mentioned in his November 1963 letter, incidentally, seems to have been theoretical at this stage. The idea did not become serious until 1964, when Spen King drew up the basic proposal for what would become the P8.

THE ORIGINAL P7 PROTOTYPES

P7/1   17 EXK   Temporary front end panels; probably had a manual gearbox. Completed by early October 1963.

P7/2   27 EXK   Temporary front end panels; probably had an automatic gearbox. Probably built November–December 1963.

P7/3   37 GYK   Possibly with restyled front end; automatic gearbox. Probably built February–March 1964.

P7/4   47 GYK   Restyled front end and manual gearbox. Probably built March–April 1964. Originally City Grey. Sold to Ted Eves of *Autocar* in 1968 and subsequently painted white. Survives.

All four of these prototypes carried London registrations, and in each case the first digit of that registration indicated the car's position in the prototype sequence.

TRANSITION: ALTERNATIVE ENGINES

By comparison with the complexities of its second stage, the first stage of the P7 story is relatively straightforward. The second stage began over the summer or autumn of 1964, after doubts had begun to surface about the viability of the 6-cylinder P7.

By spring 1964, William Martin-Hurst was sure that Rover should buy in the Buick V8 that he had seen in the USA in December 1963. He had even managed to get an example dropped into a P6 for some initial tests. However, it was far from clear that the deal to buy the V8's rights from Buick would go ahead. So with the 6-cylinder engine option in doubt the P7 team had to consider how to take the project forward so that they had some options in case the V8 deal fell through. They already knew that major modifications to the front end of the base unit would be seen as too expensive, so they had to find some way of putting a more powerful engine into the existing P6 base unit – or at least into one that was only lightly modified.

Two very different ideas were tried during 1964 and into early 1965. One of these was to use Rover's existing 6-cylinder engine, which, with determination, could just be squeezed into the P6 engine bay. The other was altogether more radical, and was to use a 5-cylinder version of the ohc engine, which would of course be shorter than the 6-cylinder ohc tried in the beginning and could also be fitted into the existing engine bay.

Neither of these ideas got very far, because by the early months of 1965 Rover had the rights to the V8 engine and were forging ahead with getting it into production. But in the meantime, some very interesting experimental cars were built, initially under the umbrella of the P7 programme.

The IOE Six

Build of the planned fifth P7 prototype had probably started before it became clear that the ohc 3-litre engine would not go ahead, and so it was completed as planned. The car was registered as DXC 11B on 19 October 1964 (although not taxed until 1 December). Most interesting is that its identity number was recorded as P7A/1; the new P7A designation is first recorded in September 1964, when Technical Director Peter Wilks reviewed progress at the executive directors' meeting. The extra letter was clearly intended to flag up a new feature not associated with the earlier P7 programme. That new feature was not the engine, because the local authority registration records confirm that it had a 2978cc engine, number P7-9/10. What, then, was it?

In fact, the new feature was a redesigned front suspension. Rover's engineers had wanted to change the P6 front suspension for some time, because the production type transmitted far too much road noise into the passenger cabin and compromised handling to a degree. This new suspension was a double-wishbone type carried on a rubber-mounted sub-frame – almost certainly the one previewed in Gordon Bashford's early 1963 P7 technical brochure. P7A/1 seems to have been the first car to which it was fitted, and pictures exist showing it being evaluated for noise transmission from the front end.

The chances are that the P7 6-cylinder engine did not remain in DXC 11B for long. During 1965, the car was rebuilt with a 6-cylinder IOE engine, and a surviving photograph by Lyn Thomas shows that engine was shoehorned into what was essentially a standard-length P6 engine bay. This, then, seems to have been option one for ensuring that there was a fallback plan if the V8 deal failed.

Rex Marvin's notes about the P7 cars (made many years

after the event) state that the engine in DXC 11B was a 2.6-litre type, and that aligns fully with the plan that was in the wind during 1962 to use this engine. One way or the other, the engine would have needed further development because the production version delivered only 123bhp – pretty much the same as the 2000TC was expected to deliver when it entered production. Rex Marvin also thought that more than one P7 was built with an IOE engine, but no evidence for this has yet come to light.

By using a standard-length engine bay, the cost of the front-end modifications that had been instrumental in bringing an end to the original P7 6-cylinder project would be avoided. Even so, the front end was by no means standard P6: the front panel had been moved forwards an inch or so to make room for a repositioned radiator. P7A/1 also seems to have been the first car with a redesigned front end that featured oblong headlamps, a reshaped front valance panel, and front wings that were cut short ahead of the wheels to allow a new wraparound bumper to fit between the valance and wing panels. Versions of this would appear on several later P7 experimental cars.

With the single SU carburettor in its standard position, there was a foul with the underside of the bonnet, and so an additional modification was a small 'blister' that was added to clear it. An under-bonnet picture of P7A/1 with its IOE engine also shows much wider inner-wing valances than on a standard P6, which is consistent with the new front suspension being retained after the engine transplant.

P7A/1 probably had its second 6-cylinder engine for only a few months during 1965, because it was later rebuilt with a third engine – this time a V8. The exact timing of this is not certain, but it would be logical to assume that it was around August 1965, when the P6B programme

P7A/1 had a 6-cylinder IOE engine with the front-end proposal favoured for the original 6-cylinder cars. The bonnet bulge over the carburettor is clear in this picture. LYN THOMAS

This is the 2.6-litre IOE engine squeezed into the engine bay of P7A/1. The shape of the inner wings shows clearly that this car also had the proposed new front suspension. LYN THOMAS

was getting under way and the engineers needed some V8-engined test cars.

The 5-Cylinder

The idea of the 5-cylinder engine came from the Research Department, where Mike Lewis suggested it 'almost as a joke' according to Eric Branson, who actually designed and patented it with Brian Silvester. Like the 6-cylinder ohc engine originally planned, the 5-cylinder could be fairly simply produced using existing components and tooling. The concept of a 5-cylinder engine was quite advanced for the early 1960s, although not quite as radical as it initially sounds: as early as 1959 there had been a proposal to make a 3-cylinder version of the ohc engine to power a new small Land Rover (called L4), which did not progress beyond the design stage.

Chief Engineer Robert Boyle agreed that the 5-cylinder engine was worth a try, and Brian Silvester was given the job of overseeing the project, although development and testing remained the responsibility of Jack Swaine's team. The earliest mention of it so far found is in the minutes of the executive directors' meeting for January 1964, when those present were told that management were investigating such an engine for the P6 – and also an 8-cylinder engine, which was of course the General Motors V8 although it was not identified as such.

Just two prototypes were eventually built, 'by cutting and welding P6 cylinder blocks and TC heads', remembered Swaine in 1981. 'The camshaft and crankshaft were, of course, purpose-made.' The resulting 2472cc engine was only 4in (100mm) longer and 100lb (45kg) heavier than the original 1978cc 4-cylinder, although its 125bhp was not particularly promising at a time when the twin-carburettor 4-cylinder in the 2000TC delivered 124bhp.

There was a brief flirtation with a 5-cylinder version of the P6's ohc engine. Just two prototypes were built, this one with three carburettors.

This close-up
of the surviving
5-cylinder engine
clearly shows the
weld line on the
cam cover, where
two standard
4-cylinder types
have been cut
and shut to make
one that was long
enough.

Swaine had reservations about the engine from the begin-ning, mainly because he envisaged carburation problems. Petrol injection would have overcome these difficulties, and Swaine acknowledged that it had been considered for the longer term. However, 'at that time we had not sufficient confidence to commit ourselves to any of the existing sys-tems available.'

On paper, a single carburettor had seemed unlikely to be satisfactory, and the first engine – which survives in the BMIHT collection at the British Motor Museum in Gaydon – used triple SUs, with one carburettor feeding a single cylinder while the other two fed a pair each. The second engine had a twin-SU installation, with the carburet-tors at each end of a gallery, one pointing backwards and the other forwards. As these were constant-depression carburettors, the installation had in effect an infinitely long balance pipe, and both mechanical and pneumatic links between the carburettors were designed to overcome the difficulty: such a system had shown promise when tried out on a P5 3-litre engine in the 1950s, remembered Jack Swaine, although it had not then gone beyond the experi-mental stage.

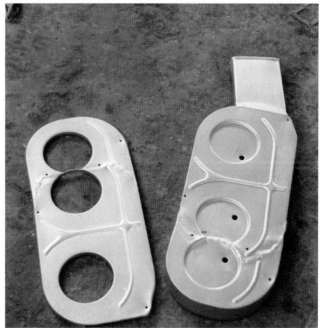

More cut and shut work: this is the air cleaner from the three-carburettor 5-cylinder engine, very obviously made from two 2000TC types.

This is the bottom end of the 5-cylinder engine, pictured when it was being rebuilt in the workshops of BL Heritage in 1980.

The first, triple-carburettor, engine was installed in a development car for work on the problem of engine mountings. The identity of this car is not known, and it is remembered as being either a white or a green P6 rather than a P7. Brian Silvester and Eric Branson decided to try an arrangement that allowed the out-of-balance forces to rock the engine back and forth rather than from side to side, as it seemed easier to control such motion when the engine was installed in the car.

Swaine remembered that the out-of-balance forces 'called for rather soft mountings… but such mountings aggravated "shake" on certain road surfaces and a satisfactory compromise was not reached'. The development engineers were sure that careful positioning and tuning of the engine mountings would do the trick, but they were never given the opportunity to find out. Work on the 5-cylinder engine was suspended when Rover committed to building the ex-Buick

V8 engine in early 1965, although it was still around at Rover as late as 1972.

THE FIRST V8s

While the P7 project inched forwards by looking at the viability of alternative engines and of a new front suspension, work was already under way on the new V8 engine. However, putting the new engine into the P6 was not the top priority; there was a lot of work to do in preparing this American-designed engine for manufacture in Britain, and the Rover board had decided to introduce it first in the older P5 model. As a lower-volume car, this would give time for production to build up while any unforeseen problems were sorted out.

So although work on the P7 programme gradually ground

Spotted at Solihull in 1970 was P7B/1, which also had a version of that proposed new front end, plus the double-wishbone suspension. ADRIAN MITCHELL

to a halt after January 1965, when Rover gained a licence to manufacture the Buick V8, there was a transitional period of several months before a formal programme to develop the V8-engined P6 as a P6B (P6-Buick) was established. In that period, some work was indeed done on V8-engined cars, but as there was no name for the V8-into-P6 programme yet, they were numbered as P7s.

The first of them was registered AXC 91B, and was given the very first V8 engine to arrive at Solihull; as Chapter 6 explains, this was the one that William Martin-Hurst had arranged to be shipped back from the USA

after he had seen it at the workshops of Mercury Marine. The Solihull local authority registration records clearly show it as a P7, even though none of the Rover records so far found show it with a number in the P7 prototype sequence. Logically, of course, it was indeed a P7: at that stage the P7 programme was primarily directed towards developing a high-performance derivative of P6, and AXC 91B was certainly that. There was also nothing else that it could be called: the P6B programme did not yet exist.

By the summer of 1965, it was clear that there would be

THE TRANSITIONAL CARS

'P7'   AXC 91B   P6-based, with chassis number 400-03535A. First V8-engined car; engine (number JN780) presumably the one shipped back from Mercury Marine by William Martin-Hurst. Described as P7 in Solihull authority registration records. Built May 1964.

P7A/1   DXC 11B   P6-based. Built with P7 3-litre ohc engine, later had a 6-cylinder IOE engine, and later still a V8. Experimental double-wishbone front suspension. Built December 1964.

P7B/1   HXC 21C   P6-based. V8 engine and experimental double-wishbone front suspension. First licensed August 1965.

All three of these cars had the oblong headlamps, but only the second two had the wraparound bumper and redesigned front wings and valance. All three started life as part of the P7 programme, but were later transferred to the P6B programme (see Chapter 5).

There was a fourth, unidentified car, which was used for trials of the ohc 5-cylinder engine. The likelihood is that this car was not part of the 'official' P7 programme, but was simply a modified P6.

a proper programme to develop a V8-engined P6, and two more V8-engined experimental cars were built in anticipation of the new programme. As already noted, one was converted from the long-suffering P7A/1. The second was called P7B/1, which was registered as HXC 21C on 27 August 1965. It had engine number 2158/14, which was one of several Buick engines shipped over to Solihull and renumbered in Rover's own prototype sequence. A photograph taken at Solihull in June 1970 shows that it had the oblong headlamps, wraparound bumper and redesigned valance of P7A/1.

Spen King remembered that this car also had the double-wishbone front suspension that had been seen on P7A/1. Although that suspension would never be used on a production P6 or P6B, it was by this stage intended for the P8, which was now being seen as the eventual replacement for the P6 range. It would also have a part to play in some later cars called P7s, but it did not become part of the P6B programme, which (as Chapter 6 explains) seems finally to have begun over the summer of 1965.

THE THIRD PHASE: P7 TEST HACKS

The P7 programme had originally been intended to find a new and more powerful engine for the P6. Now that new engine had been found in the shape of the V8 and the associated development programme had been named P6B, there should theoretically have been no more P7s. But there were: the difference was that these were mostly used for testing different types of suspension and other components for future new Rover models.

Even so, after P7B/1 was registered in August 1965, there was a break of around eighteen months before any more cars designated P7 were built. The P7 designation was then revived for a series of four experimental cars based on production-model Rovers that were used to test elements of the planned P8 and P10 models. They were what are now commonly called 'mules'.

The first of them was P7/C1, a V8-engined car that was

P7C/1 was comprehensively rolled on test at MIRA. In this picture, the V8 engine installation (with P5B-pattern air cleaner) and the hinges for the front-mounted bonnet are clear.

road-registered as OXC 831E in January 1967. This again had the double-wishbone front suspension proposed for the P8 and a new type of De Dion rear suspension also intended for that car. It had a pre-production or development Rover V8 engine (as distinct from a Buick block), and a bonnet that was hinged at the front, probably to test the arrangement that was planned for P8.

It also had an eventful career. For a time, it was used as a hack by the Range Rover development team, who mostly used it for journeys back and forth to the MIRA test ground near Nuneaton. The car was then rolled at the Lucas proving ground at Honiley during tests of low-profile tyres by Rex Marvin and Peter Storrie. It was subsequently rebuilt and was used for tests of Girling and Lockheed power-hydraulic braking systems – another feature that was to be in the P8 specification. Eventually, Peter Storrie himself bought it in early 1973 after its life as a development car was over.

The next P7 departed even from the original focus of the P7 programme. It was not based on a P6 of any kind, but rather on a V8-engined P5 3-litre! P7D (known simply by that name and not as P7D/I) was registered on 23 March 1966 and looked externally like an ordinary Mk III Coupé. However, it was used as a test mule for the combined heating and air-conditioning unit (made by Smith's) intended for P8. It also had the twin-wishbone front suspension used on the P7A, P7B and P7C cars. It was tested (by Eric Branson) in Rovaniemi (northern Finland) and in Italy.

The P7E car was also identified by that name only, and not much is known about it except that it was a V8-engined P6 with a single-scoop bonnet but otherwise standard P6 front end. (The bonnet scoop was a feature of the NADA 3500S; see Chapter 9.) When P7E was prepared for a barrier-crash test over the summer of 1970, its engine was dummied up as a fuel-injected type, with the plenum of an AE Brico injection system. However, it appears not to have been one of the petrol-injection test cars, so perhaps this plenum was necessary for crash-test purposes. The barrier crash, numbered J9, took place on 6 October that year.

The final P7 mule seems to have been known as P7F. The car had been built in summer 1966 as one of the P6B prototypes (see Chapter 5) and was originally numbered P6B/22. It was later fitted with the rear axle from a Vauxhall Ventora to test the feasibility of the proposed P10

This underside picture of P7C/I shows the experimental front suspension... BMIHT

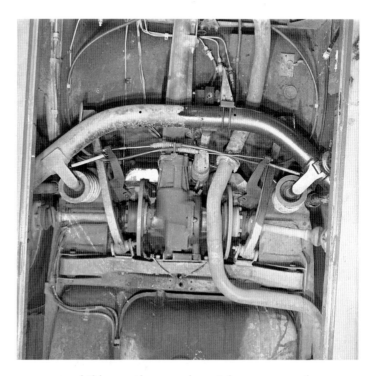

... and this was the experimental rear suspension, intended for the forthcoming P8 model. BMIHT

suspension layout. Most of its trim was removed to simulate the target P10 weight, and within the Engineering Department the car was known as 'The Lightweight Bomber'. It was tested in the UK and on the Stelvio Pass.

With that car, the P7s disappeared from the Solihull scene.

By 1970, P8 development was being carried out on full prototypes, and so the P7 mules with P8 features became redundant. During 1971, the P10 programme was given the green light by the Leyland board, but only as a joint project with input from Triumph. It became SD1.

THE LATER P7s

P7C/1   OXC 831E   P6-based. V8 engine, experimental double-wishbone front suspension and experimental P8-type De Dion rear suspension. January 1967.

P7D   KXC 963D   P5-based. V8 engine, experimental double-wishbone front suspension and experimental P8-type heating and air-conditioning unit. March 1966.

P7E   (Not known)   P6-based. V8 engine. Barrier crash test, October 1970.

P7F   JXC 820D   P6-based. Originally P6B prototype number P6B/22. Fitted with live rear axle to simulate P10 suspension arrangement. Probably became P7F in late 1969 or 1970.

At first sight, it appears illogical that P7C/1 should have a later date than P7D. The likely explanation is that KXC 963D spent some time on the engineering fleet as a V8-engined P5B test car before being fitted with the P8 heater, and only then became known as P7D. If this event occurred after January 1967, which is entirely likely, the converted car then took on the next available number in the P7 sequence, which by then was P7D.

The P7E prototype met its end against a concrete wall at MIRA. It was fitted with a prototype (or dummied-up) fuel-injected V8 for the purpose.
BMIHT

CHAPTER FIVE

ROVER P6 IN MOTOR SPORT

Rover as a company had no involvement in motor sport between 1945 and 1961. Although the company certainly had supported entries at Brooklands in the 1920s, and although it had also entered some of the more genteel domestic rallies during the 1930s, these events had all largely been forgotten by the 1950s. It was also undeniable that the Rovers of the 1940s and 1950s were simply not the kind of cars that encouraged competitive driving.

THE WORKS 2000s

It has often been said that Rover's re-entry into motor sport in the early 1960s was all down to the enthusiasm and efforts of its managing director of the time, William Martin-Hurst. Martin-Hurst certainly was an enthusiastic promoter of Rovers in competition, and he certainly was the man behind the development of the Rover-BRM gas turbine racing car of 1963. In his position on the Rover board, he was also well placed to put his weight behind the company's motor sport activities. However, the initiative behind Rover's first competition efforts came from engineer Dan Clayton, who ran the P5 project in the late 1950s and early 1960s. This was in 1961, when Martin-Hurst was still production director; he did not actually become managing director until after Maurice Wilks' death in 1962.

Some thirty-five years later, Clayton remembered it like this:

> Rover was a very gentlemanly company at the time and I was looking at the P6 – which wasn't my project – and thinking that it was an entirely different animal. But nothing was happening to make any awareness in the public that Rover can be exciting. I thought, 'the image really surely needs to be changed. One way could be to use present models in a very restricted way to make people's concept of Rover change.'

By this time, Clayton had been to Kenya several times with 3-litre P5s on rough-road and hot-climate proving tests, and he knew that the cars were immensely rugged. Despite some shortcomings in the performance department, 'I had the belief that we could enter a thing like the East African Safari Rally, where it was toughness rather than out-and-

Rover quickly realized that success in rallies generated useful publicity. This advertisement from *Autocar* magazine celebrated the success of a Rover 3-litre (P5) in the 1963 East African Safari Rally.

out speed that could achieve something. It was a chance of making people sit up and think, "My goodness, Rover's got more than I realized.'"

Other events of the time might well have influenced Clayton's thinking. In his job as P5 project engineer, he would certainly have been keeping an eye on directly competitive products. One of those was the Humber Super Snipe, which had been appearing in international rallies since 1959, and in 1961 achieved a very creditable fourth place overall in the very East African rally that figured in Clayton's thinking. Humber had been doing their reputation for building solid, reliable cars a lot of good throughout the 1950s with regular entries in long-distance rallies, even though they had never again equalled Maurice Gatsonides' second place on the 1950 Monte Carlo event.

Knowledge of this success may well have persuaded top management to give favourable attention to Clayton's proposal that Rover should enter a team of P5 3-litres in the 1962 East African Safari Rally. He addressed that proposal initially to Dick Oxley, who was then Rover's chief engineer (cars), and senior management picked up on the idea almost immediately. 'I can almost say verbatim what my last paragraph was,' Clayton remembered. 'I said, "The cost of this I estimate would be around £5,000 to enter four cars, which is the equivalent roughly of one half-page advert in the *Sunday Express*."'

Rover lost no time in taking the idea forward. Clayton found himself appointed team manager, with engineering shop superintendent Ralph Nash as his deputy and the man in charge of preparing the cars. Neither of them had any experience whatsoever of international motor sport, and nor was either of them particularly interested in rallying, but there were plenty of motor sport enthusiasts within the company who were only too keen to lend a hand. There were some fitters on Nash's staff who had been actively involved in motor racing as a hobby, and the choice as team foreman of Toney Cox, a Rover engineer who had solid experience of rallying at club level in Britain, injected some very useful knowledge. Other people were drafted in from various other departments in Rover to help out as the word spread.

Even though Rover's initial motor sport efforts were inevitably rather amateurish, the results from the first works entries were encouraging. Rover entered teams of 3-litres in three events during 1962, and after the first entry had demonstrated that the whole idea was not futile, the company formally established a Competitions Department in

July to oversee the rest of the programme. Ralph Nash was put in charge, Dan Clayton bowed out and returned to his real job as P5 project engineer, and suddenly Rover had a serious, credible, and not so amateurish works competition team. Needless to say, it had the whole-hearted support of William Martin-Hurst, especially after he became managing director – although he was never able to persuade his fellow directors to put very much money into it.

The 3-litres appeared in several more rallies during 1963 and 1964, never returning spectacular results but invariably doing far better than sceptical onlookers ever expected – and, more importantly, developing respect and a new and more vigorous image for Rover. This was exactly what Rover management wanted, because it prepared the way very well for the very different Rover 2000 that was launched during 1963, and continued to attract attention in the first year after that launch.

It should come as no surprise that a plan had been drawn up very early on to push the 2000 itself into motor sport as soon as practicable. The first 3-litre rally cars had been prepared in a corner of Ralph Nash's workshop, but when the Competitions Department was formally established, it was given a screened-off area within the newly built North Block where the first 2000s were already being built. The forward engineering programme for these cars included a more performance-oriented twin-carburettor model (which became the 2000TC), and Rover decided to use these as their rally cars as soon as examples became available. In practice, the earliest rallies in which the 2000TCs were entered were used as part of the proving programme for the twin-carburettor engine before it became available in production.

1964–65: 1 KUE TO 4 KUE (THE RED CARS)

The Competitions Department geared up for a four-event programme in the 1964 season, consisting of the Acropolis Rally in May, the Alpine Rally in July, the Liège–Sofia–Liège in August and the RAC Rally in November. The works P6s were not ready in time for the Acropolis event, and so Rover contested this with a team of 3-litres. The P6s then made their debut in the Alpine Rally, unaccompanied by the 3-litres; examples of both cars were entered for the Liège and thereafter the 3-litres faded from the scene and the P6s took over completely. Some of the old works rally 3-litres were retained as support and service vehicles for the new team.

There had been four 3-litres in each of the works rally teams before, and so four Rover 2000s were taken from the Despatch Department in two batches of two during January, registered at Solihull as 1 KUE to 4 KUE, and handed over to the Competitions Department for preparation. That 'preparation' was fairly minimal: although Rover drew on their experience with the rally 3-litres, Rover company policy remained unchanged: the minimum of modifications consistent with reliability were to be made.

Roger Clark, the best known of the drivers on the Rover team that year, recalled this well in his autobiography, *Sideways... to Victory*, written some years later with the aid of motoring author Graham Robson. 'The only changes Toney Cox and his mechanics made to the suspension', he wrote, 'were to stiffen up springs and dampers (I honestly think they did this just by upgrading a certain amount – there was no scientific testing involved) and to make sure that everything else was absolutely just so.'

TOP: **The first team of works P6 cars ran early events in a livery of all-over Copperleaf Red. This is 3 KUE on the 1964 Alpine Rally, when it was crewed by Peter and Ann Riley.**

BOTTOM: **The full Rover team lines up before the start of the 1964 Alpine Rally.**

Also on the 1964 Rover team was Anne Hall, who confirmed this attitude in an interview with P6 enthusiast Terry Foley during the 1980s. 'They did a bit to the suspension; very little else. They were too gentlemanly at Rover's.'

Of course, that 'very little else' was relative. As compared with the standard production cars, the works 2000s had special tyres, instrumentation and lighting; they also had duralumin sump guards, reinforcements to the rear suspension and boot floor leading edge – which was rounded off to reduce the risk of damage – a skid plate from the rear jack pad to the boot floor, and protective wire coils for the brake hoses. Yet the gearboxes remained standard and so did the engines in two of the four cars.

The other two cars, which were 1 KUE and 2 KUE, were given experimental twin-carburettor installations. Work on the twin-carburettor engine that would eventually deliver the 2000TC model was well under way by the start of 1964, and the opportunity to use a pair of rally cars for some very severe testing was very welcome to the engines team at Rover. This was not in any sense an attempt to cheat the rally regulations. The single-carburettor cars would run as Group 1 (Production) cars, and the twin-carburettor cars would run in the Group 3 (Modified) class. Interestingly, Rover was clearly keen not to let news of the planned twin-carburettor engine leak out to the public, and remained rather coy about what they simply called 'various modifications' in their own in-house newspaper, Rover News, for July 1964.

The small modifications that Rover allowed – all, of course, permitted under the regulations then in force – did make the 2000s more effective rally machines, but they were not yet really competitive. 'They were nice cars to drive,' recalled Anne Hall, but they were 'a bit heavy at times and [it was] difficult to unstick the back end when needed'. Roger Clark admitted in his autobiography that:

The cars weren't really competitive… but that didn't mean that we didn't try; I certainly drove my car flat out the whole time.

Nevertheless… I fell for the Rover right from the start… though it was very heavy and underpowered, it was fantastically strong and very forgiving… it had lots of wheel travel… and excellent steering… [but] the Competitions Department never modified their engines very much, so it was always a struggle to keep up the pace, which meant that we had to drive the cars even harder than usual.

Until I really got used to the Rover, and found out what tremendous handling it had, I didn't know just what liberties I could take with it. I'd never driven a car flat out for so long; you could go so far sideways and stay in control it was almost ridiculous, but it was essential… Being so tremendously strong and with such good handling and brakes, the cars gave us great confidence. Of course, something had to give from time to time, and I have to admit that we could break the gearboxes, while my cornering methods, more than other people's perhaps, could do nasty things to the chassis-mounted differentials, especially as I would insist on leaning the back wheels on things at the outside of corners.

Works rally cars take an inordinate amount of punishment and are often more or less write-offs by the end of a season's rallies. Well aware of this, Rover anticipated that their cars would survive four rallies before needing complete replacement. That is why this first team of cars ended up being entered for the Monte Carlo Rally in January 1965; this was to be their fourth event, as they had missed the first one of the 1964 season.

Those first three rallies with the 2000s had taught Rover a lot about the cars' strengths and weaknesses, and by the time of the Monte the standard of preparation was distinctly more professional. The Birmingham Evening Post newspaper 'adopted' the works 2000s for this event, and reported on their preparation in its issue of 13 January 1965. Their account of a conducted tour of the Competitions Department noted that:

Fitters were installing such diverse items as special disc brake pads [actually hard DS11-type pads] and a flange to direct air to the brake plates for cooling; an electrical fuel pump in the boot instead of a mechanical one on the engine; larger shock absorbers of the type fitted on the 2000 colonial models; rally-type front seats [probably just seat covers with built-in side bolsters] and an extra spare-wheel mounting in the boot, with a quick-release fitting [the quick-release fitting was actually fitted to both spare wheel mountings].

Navigation instruments were going in, an extra screen washer and headlamp washers. In addition to normal lighting, two spots and two foglamps [these latter being the showroom option Notek lamps] and *an extra reversing light were being fitted and the headlights were being equipped with quartz-iodine bulbs, which give much more power.*

An 'elapsed time' clock was being fitted, a time and average speed recorder [ie a Halda Speed Pilot], ammeter, engine oil and temperature gauges, a rev-counter, electrically heated elements for front and rear screens and a larger battery to take the increased load. Out came the 12.5-gallon [57ltr] fuel tank in favour of one with 15-gallon [68ltr] capacity, with a special cap for fast filling. Under the bonnet an inspection light was fitted and, in the boot, a first-aid kit and quick-release clips for special tools.

One additional modification that Rover had tried was a low-ratio 4.3:1 differential, which gave sharper acceleration at the expense of maximum speed and was therefore well suited to rallying. This had originally been developed for the planned 2000 Automatic, but seems to have been prone to failures and may never have been used in anger. Nevertheless, with all the extra equipment that the cars carried on the 1965 Monte Carlo Rally, it was no surprise that they should turn in a better result than they had in any of the 1964 events.

Not that the 2000s performed badly in the three 1964 rallies they entered. No rally car, however well-prepared, performs faultlessly on its first few outings, and manufacturers tend to treat these as shakedown exercises that allow them to discover the cars' weaknesses. The early problems with the 2000s were mostly associated with their engines; some were over-revved as their drivers tried to get the most from them, and others suffered from oil leaks, particularly between the cylinder block and the spin-on filter.

The 1965 Monte Carlo event nevertheless proved the highlight of the Rovers' competitions career. Roger Clark, driving 4 KUE with Jim Porter as co-driver, finished in sixth place, won his class, and also won the Touring Car category. It was a stupendous achievement, and a huge testimony to Clark's ability, not least because 4 KUE was of

course one of the lower-powered single-carburettor cars, and not one of the 'experimental' twin-carburettor types running in the Modified category.

Clark recalled in *Sideways… to Victory* that:

Jim and I did a lot of practice for that year's Monte, something I had never had to do before. At first I could grin and bear it, but before long I found it a great bore… We must have spent a week doing nothing else but driving up and over the Turini, correcting the notes, then driving up and over again (the test was used both ways, as usual), correcting the other notes, and so on.

Conditions for the actual rally were among the worst on record.

Everything was straightforward on the trundle round France, but soon after we reached St Claude the snow really began to bucket down. From there to the end of the rally, conditions couldn't have been more ideal for us. All that snow and very little grip meant that

Ken James and Mike Hughes with 1 KUE on the 1965 Monte Carlo Rally. By this time, the team cars all had white roofs with their Copperleaf Red paint. The Triplex heated windscreen that was tested on the rally cars is clear in this picture.

This was the drive that made Roger Clark a star: the 1965 Monte Carlo, when he and Jim Porter took 4 KUE to sixth place overall, coming first in class, and first in the Touring Car category.

the Rover didn't have its usual handicaps, and I really began to enjoy it.

By the time they reached Monte Carlo, Clark and Porter were lying seventh overall, and were the only Rover crew still in the running.

All that remained was the final Mountain Circuit, with another snow-covered 380 miles [612km] and half-a-dozen special stages. I had all Rover's attention as their only runner. What happened that night really does read like a good fairy-tale. I felt good, the car couldn't have been better, and by seemingly going sideways from the minute we left the parc fermé to

the minute we finished, we had a completely faultless run. The fairy-tale was that in the fabulous excitement of that night, two of the factory Citroëns disappeared [and] there was a bit of reshuffling.

It was that drive that both made Clark an overnight star and convinced him of his own abilities as a rally driver. 'After that,' he wrote, 'I never had any doubts about my own abilities – it was just up to me to put them to best effect in the future.' Within weeks he was demonstrating his abilities again, with the same car. Around a fortnight after the Monte, the pair of them were shipped out to Sweden for BBC TV *Grandstand*'s 'Swedish Monte', which was an ice-race held on and around a frozen lake. He finished third – an excellent result against local drivers who were used to driving in such conditions.

1965: 1 KUE TO 4 KUE (THE WHITE CARS)

As Roger Clark put it, there was another consequence of his success in the 1965 Monte Carlo Rally: 'Rover suddenly got all keen about their rallying.' Certainly, the second-generation works 2000s were far more professionally prepared than the first cars had been, and incorporated special fittings and purpose-built wiring harnesses.

The four new cars were taken off the assembly lines on 30 April 1965, registered with the old 1 KUE to 4 KUE numbers, and immediately passed on to the Competitions Department. In place of 1964's Copperleaf Red livery (latterly with White roofs), these cars were all-white in the beginning, although experience in the Acropolis Rally led to the addition of non-reflective black bonnets for the later events. Two of them (1 KUE and 2 KUE again) were prepared as twin-carburettor cars for the Group 3 Modified category, while 3 KUE and 4 KUE were single-carburettor cars for Group 1.

As the 1964 team cars had run in the Monte Carlo Rally and Rover had planned a four-event season for 1965, these team cars actually ran in only three events. These were the Acropolis, Alpine and RAC rallies. Logan Morrison, Anne Hall and Roger Clark all remained as works drivers from the previous season, and the fourth car was driven variously by Ken James, Andrew Cowan, and Peter Procter.

Although the four 2000s obtained some consistent results, there was nothing as spectacular as Clark's success in the Monte. A rash of accidents and sheer bad luck meant that the Rovers did not achieve anything new during the rest of 1965. Roger Clark's best result with 4 KUE was on the RAC Rally, where he came second in his class and fourteenth overall.

1966: JXC 5C TO JXC 8C

Rover campaigned a third team of four works rally cars for the 1966 season, and all of these were single-

The second team of cars were finished in all-over white. This is **2 KUE** on the 1965 Acropolis Rally, when it was driven by Anne Hall and Val Domleo.

The white **KUE** cars later acquired matt black bonnets. This is **1 KUE**, seen in restored condition on a show stand belonging to the **Historic Rally Car Register**.

ABOVE: **JXC 8C** has also been restored, and here represents the final Rover works team.

BOB GARDNER

Detail counts: JXC 8C shows its headlamp washer jets – a valuable addition for rallies.

BOB GARDNER

JXC 8C had lost its heated windscreen before restoration, but there was one in the Panelcraft convertible prototype (which had once been owned by a director of Triplex) – and it is now in place in the rally car.

carburettor models. The 2000TC was due for release later in the year, and in theory it would have been possible to switch to a new team of cars once that became eligible for the Group 1 Production Cars category. Whether or not that was the intention, it did not happen, because Rover's 1966 rally season was cut short.

Once again the works cars were painted white with matt black bonnets, and this time all four were taken from the assembly lines in November 1965. This year's drivers included Anne Hall and Logan Morrison again, but Roger Clark had been tempted away by bigger money to drive for Ford. Clark's partner Jim Porter remained, now paired with new driver Geoff Mabbs and acting as Rover's competitions secretary. The fourth driver was Sobieslaw Zasada, a Polish national who would go on to win the 1966 European Rally Championship with the tiny Steyr-Puch 650 car.

Rover's 1966 season began, as usual, with the Monte Carlo Rally in January. Mabbs and Porter finished a creditable tenth overall, but the other three cars were eliminated by accidents. This was the year of the great controversy: the winning BMC Mini Coopers and Roger Clark's fourth-placed Ford Cortina were disqualified at the end of the rally on a technicality concerning their headlamp bulbs, thus leaving the works Citroëns as the winners. There was a great outcry, not least because everybody was convinced that the Citroën team had been blatantly cheating, and several teams decided to boycott the rest of the season's rallies. Rover

did not join them, perhaps feeling it was ungentlemanly to complain just because you had not won.

In fact, the Rover team followed the 1966 Monte with some serious preparation for the East African Safari. Anne Hall recalled in her interview with Terry Foley:

Rover thought they might be able to do well in the Safari Rally that year if they prepared properly for it. Soon after the Monte, Logan Morrison and myself with about sixteen Rover engineers were shipped out to Africa to do some testing. Ralph Nash came too.

The Rover mechanics couldn't understand why the suspension kept breaking when I was driving and it was always all right when they drove. Eventually it came to light that they were driving around all the potholes and gullies and things. I had to explain to them that when you're driving in a rally, you have to go over or through all hazards like that; there just isn't time to go swerving round things!

We stayed out there six weeks. They worked really hard on those cars. They got them right. Logan and myself were absolutely certain they were ready for the rally. For my part, I was convinced the P6s were better than the Mercedes I had driven in the Safari in 1965. The cars were taken to Mombasa to be stored until needed for the rally. We were flown home. Very soon after that, Rover announced the end of the Competitions Department activities and the cars were flown home too. If only…!

The statement that Rover issued to the press read: 'Having demonstrated in numerous rallies the mechanical reliability of the Rover 2000 and 3-litre cars, the Rover Company has temporarily withdrawn from this form of competition in order to concentrate on current engineering commitments. It is the company's intention, in due course, to return to rallying.'

They never did return; and that diplomatically worded statement undoubtedly concealed the real reasons. The fact was that the new Group 1 homologation rules for 1966 had allowed many faster cars to compete against the 2000s, such as the Ford Lotus Cortina and the Mini Cooper S, and this meant that the Rovers now stood very little chance of spectacular success. Not even the 2000TC would compensate when it came on-stream. Rover management were not happy to let the Competitions Department continue in those circumstances, and so they closed it down.

1964–1965: THE FIRST TEAM CARS

These cars were painted in Copperleaf Red; White roofs were added during the season.

1 KUE

Car number: 400-00518
Engine number: Not known; it was an experimental twin-carburettor type.

Events:
1964 Alpine Rally (July)
Crewed by Ken James and Mike Hughes
Car number 91
Third in class and ninth in the Grand Touring category

1964 Liège (August)
Crewed by Logan Morrison and Johnstone Syer
Car number 5
DNF (retired)

1964 RAC Rally (November)
Crewed by Ken James and Mike Hughes
Car number 29
DNF (broken half-shaft)

1965 Monte Carlo Rally (January)
Crewed by Ken James and Mike Hughes
Car number 177
DNF (engine failure)

Re-registered as DXC 6B on 26 February 1965; 1 KUE was transferred to a new team car. DXC 6B was subsequently scrapped by Rover at Solihull.

2 KUE

Car number: 400-00801
Engine number: Not known; it was an experimental twin-carburettor type.

Events:
1964 Alpine Rally (July)
Crewed by Anne Hall and Denise McCluggage
Car number not known
DNF (engine failure)

1964 Liège (August)
Crewed by Anne Hall and Denise McCluggage
Car number 32
DNF (engine failure)

1964 RAC Rally (November)
Crewed by Anne Hall and Pat Spencer
Car number 45
Third in Ladies' section and sixteenth overall

1965 Monte Carlo Rally (January)
Crewed by Anne Hall and Val Domleo
Car number 209
DNF (electrical failure)

Re-registered as DXC 7B on 26 February 1965; 2 KUE was transferred to a new team car.

3 KUE

Car number: 400-00800
Engine number: Not known; it was a single-carburettor type.

Events:
1964 Alpine Rally (July)
Crewed by Peter and Ann Riley
Car number 43
Third in class and fifth in the Production Touring Cars category

1964 Liège (August)
Not used on this event

1964 RAC Rally (November)
Crewed by Ken James and Mike Hughes
Car number 48
DNF (engine failure)

1965 Monte Carlo Rally (January)
Crewed by Ken James and Mike Hughes
Car number 126
DNF (accident)

Re-registered as DXC 8B on 3 March 1965; 3 KUE was transferred to a new team car. Logan Morrison and Johnstone Syer borrowed DXC 8B for the 1965 Scottish International Rally, where they claimed a remarkable third place – the highest placing ever achieved by a 2000 in an international rally. Sadly, Rover could not make publicity capital out of this because the car had been privately entered. DXC 8B was later scrapped by Rover at Solihull.

4 KUE

Car number: 400-00805
Engine number: Not known; it was a single-carburettor type.

Events:
1964 Alpine Rally (July)
Crewed by Roger Clark and Johnstone Syer
Car number 44
DNF (axle or engine failure)

1964 Liège (August)
Crewed by Roger Clark and Brian Culcheth
Car number 24
DNF (engine failure)

1964 RAC Rally (November)
Crewed by Roger Clark and Jim Porter
Car number 66
DNF (engine failure)

1965 Monte Carlo Rally (January)
Crewed by Roger Clark and Jim Porter
Car number 136
First in class, first in Touring Car category, sixth overall

Re-registered as DXC 9B on 8 April 1965; 4 KUE was transferred to a new team car. DXC 9B was sold (or given) to King Hussain of Jordan. The *Rover and Alvis News* of November 1966 reported that 'His Majesty is a car enthusiast and plans to use the rally vehicle for competing in hill climbs and local motor rallies.'

1965: THE SECOND TEAM CARS

These cars were painted in all-over White for the Acropolis Rally, and gained non-reflective black bonnets thereafter.

1 KUE

Car number: 400-14262B
Engine number: 400-00799 was in the car when it was sold in August 1967. This was a single-carburettor type; the car had originally had an experimental twin-carburettor engine, of which no details are available.

Events:
1965 Acropolis Rally (May)
Crewed by Logan Morrison and Johnstone Syer
Car number 6
DNF (accident)

1965 Alpine Rally (July)
Crewed by Logan Morrison and Johnstone Syer
Car number 96
Fifth in engine capacity class and sixteenth in the Touring category

1965 RAC Rally (November)
Crewed by Logan Morrison and Johnstone Syer
Car number 50
Third in class and seventeenth overall

1 KUE ran again in the 1966 Monte Carlo Rally as a BBC-sponsored entry, bearing number 99 and crewed by motoring writer Michael Frostick with the BBC's motoring correspondent, Maxwell Boyd. They did not finish the event.

The car was then used for some publicity events. In August 1967 it was re-registered as JXC 226C and was borrowed for several events by Rover test engineer Brian Terry. At some point, it acquired an experimental 2000TC engine (number X14 TC 69/0). Terry left Rover in 1968 but was able to buy the car from Rover in July 1969. He painted the rear quarter-panels in red, and used the car on a number of events.

In the early 1970s, JXC 226C passed into the ownership of Gerald Dare, who then sold it again to Sandy Forbes. Re-registered as 1 AKF, it was used in club rallies for a further two and a half years approximately. The axle broke some time around 1973, and the car was then put into storage. In 1989, it was bought by enthusiast Bob Gardner, who restored it to original Rover rally condition. It now carries the registration number 1 KUE again.

2 KUE

Car number: presumed 400-14263B
Engine number: not known. This engine was an experimental twin-carburettor type.

Events:
1965 Acropolis Rally (May)
Crewed by Anne Hall and Val Domleo
Car number 1
DNF (accident)

1965 Alpine Rally (July)
Crewed by Anne Hall and Pat Spencer
Car number 97
Sixth in the Touring category and twenty-second overall

1965 RAC Rally (November)
Crewed by Anne Hall and Pat Spencer
Car number 34
DNF (accident)

The subsequent history of this car is unknown.

3 KUE

Car number: presumed 400-14264B
Engine number: not known. This was a single-carburettor engine.

Events:
1965 Acropolis Rally (May)
Crewed by Andrew Cowan and Bill Syer
Car number 47
DNF (De Dion tube failure)

1965 Alpine Rally (July)
Crewed by Andrew Cowan and Brian Coyle
Car number 124
First in class and third in Grand Touring category

1965 RAC Rally (November)
Crewed by Peter Procter and David Mabbs
Car number 64
DNF (accident)

The subsequent history of this car is unknown.

4 KUE

Car number: presumed 400-14265B
Engine number: not known. This was a single-carburettor engine.

Events:
1965 Acropolis Rally (May)
Crewed by Roger Clark and Jim Porter
Car number 48
DNF (accident)

1965 Alpine Rally (July)
Crewed by Roger Clark and Jim Porter
Car number 95
Fourth in class and tenth in Touring category

1965 RAC Rally (November)
Crewed by Roger Clark and Jim Porter
Car number 33
Second in class and fourteenth overall

4 KUE (the second) passed into the hands of Richard Martin-Hurst, son of Rover's managing director. He drove it on the Scottish International Rally in 1966, but rolled the car on the Eppynt special stage in Wales. This was probably the car's final outing and it seems likely that it was then broken up.

1966: THE THIRD TEAM CARS

These cars were painted in all-over White and always had non-reflective black bonnets.

JXC 5C

Car number: 400-25092
Engine number: 400-34644 (single carburettor)

Event:
1966 Monte Carlo Rally (January)
Crewed by Logan Morrison and Johnstone Syer
Car number 167
DNF (accident)

The car was subsequently entered in the 1968 London–Sydney Marathon by the British Army International Rally Team. It was crewed by Major John Hemsley and Warrant Officer Frank Webber. On this event, where it ran as car no. 54, it had a twin-carburettor engine, detuned to take low-octane fuel. It finished in thirty-seventh place overall. The car was then left with the Rover main dealership in Sydney and was subsequently moved to a museum, where it could still be found in the late 1980s. However, at the time of writing, its whereabouts are not known.

JXC 5C subsequently ran in the 1968 London–Sydney Marathon, crewed by John Hemsley and Frank Webber.

JXC 6C

Car number: 400-25093
Engine number: 400-33687 (single carburettor)

Event:
1966 Monte Carlo Rally (January)
Crewed by Jim Porter and Geoff Mabbs
Car number 177
Tenth overall.

The subsequent history of this car is unknown.

JXC 7C

Car number: 400-25094
Engine number: 400-34349 (single carburettor)

Event:
1966 Monte Carlo Rally (January)
Crewed by Anne Hall and Pat Spencer
Car number 178
DNF (accident)

JXC 7C was subsequently entered in the 1968 London–Sydney Marathon by the British Army International Rally Team. It was crewed by Major Freddie Preston and Major Mike Bailey. On this event, where it ran as car no. 44, it had a twin-carburettor engine, detuned to take low-octane fuel. Its final placing is not known. Like JXC 5C, the car was left with the Rover main dealership in Sydney. It was then supposedly used for towing boats on the beach at Sydney.

A car claimed to have been JXC 7C was restored in 1991 and given the registration number DBR 937D. It was used in historic rally events in 1991–92, was last taxed for the road in October 1991, and still existed in spring 2000. Its subsequent history is not known.

JXC 8C

Car number: 400-25095
Engine number: 400-33093 (single carburettor)

Event:
1966 Monte Carlo Rally (January)
Crewed by Sobieslaw Zasada and Adam Wedrychowski
Car number 217
DNF (accident)

JXC 8C then seems to have been used as a development car at Rover. By 1978 it belonged to Ralph Nash and had a prototype 2200 engine (number 22L/6), a Hollandia electric sunroof, box-pleated Ambla front seats and 1971-season bootlid badges. Most of its skin panels had been replaced, although various reinforcements to the base unit still bore witness to its rallying past. In 1978 it was bought by Anne Hall's husband, and then in 1984 it passed to Rover enthusiast Terry Foley. Anne Hall told him that, 'My children used to call this my cotton-wool car because I was so careful with it!' Nevertheless, by 1984 the car was in very poor condition, and in 1988 it passed into the ownership of enthusiast Bob Gardner, who restored it to original 1966 works team condition.

THEY ALSO SERVED

During the production life of the P6, a small number of other cars were actively campaigned in motor sport.

Perhaps the best known was 151 FLK, which was one of the 1963 launch cars (400-00051A). This became a service support vehicle for the rally team in 1964–65 and was maintained and prepared in the Competitions Department. Foreman Toney Cox then bought it and campaigned it as a privateer in a number of events. The car was subsequently re-shelled and fitted with a V8 engine; re-shelled a second time some years later, it was also given a five-speed LT77 gearbox (as used in the Rover SD1 from 1976). It has been used competitively right through to the present day in historic rally events. Like the proverbial grandfather's broom, it probably retains nothing of the original now but nevertheless has a documented history that demonstrates its pedigree.

151 FLK has had a long rallying history, and one that continues today. Here it is in action on the Gallaher Circuit of Ireland in 1966.

ABOVE: **This is 151 FLK in action again, on the December 2000 Land's End to John O'Groats Reliability and Touring Trial, run by the Historic Endurance Rallying Organisation. By this time, the car had a V8 engine.**

Old rally cars never die – they just get re-engined and re-shelled. This is the V8 engine in 151 FLK.

THE V8 RACING SALOONS

After the British Leyland merger in 1967, the former BMC Competitions Department at Abingdon became the British Leyland Competitions Department, but its achievements over the next couple of years were disappointing after the successes of the Minis in the mid-1960s. Leyland chairman Lord Stokes made clear to the department's manager, Peter Browning, that he expected better. So Browning combed through the existing and planned British Leyland catalogue in search of a car he could develop for competition, and chose the Rover 3500. As he put it himself in a 1980 article, 'We knew that with Traco or Repco versions of the engine we could easily double the power output and, although the car had a Rover reputation of a bit of a "gentlemen's carriage", one could obviously reduce the weight enormously and hopefully improve the handling.'

The Competitions Department decided on a four-stage programme. The first stage was to make an instant evaluation of the Rover's potential by entering a car in one of the popular televised rallycross events. If it was successful, they hoped this would gain the interest of British Leyland top management. The second stage would be to build a club racer so that they could evaluate the car's tarmac performance. The knowledge gained from this would go into the third stage, which was to build a proper works prototype to be tried out on selected rally and racing events. Then the fourth stage was to persuade Leyland to fund a limited production run, perhaps of 1,000 or so high-performance

models with special equipment, so that the racing Rover could be homologated for Group 2 events.

However, when Browning explained his plan to Rover's top management, he found them distinctly unenthusiastic about the whole idea. Their view was that the 3500 did not need any additional promotion, and that using it in motor sport would present completely the wrong image. But Browning persisted, seeking out Ralph Nash, who had earlier headed Rover's own Competitions Department, and persuading him to help. As a result, he was able to obtain a V8-engined car to start his project. It was JXC 808D, better known as P6B-8 and one of the now redundant 1966 P6B development cars.

The First Car

'Without doing too much to the car,' wrote Browning later, 'we whisked it off to a rallycross meeting where it was driven with great verve by Geoff Mabbs who could not resist placing a bowler hat, furled umbrella and a copy of the *Financial Times* on the rear parcel shelf!' This was in March 1968; the car ran in a second similar event in April and, although the car was unplaced in both events (which were televised by ITV), the second stage of the plan began very soon afterwards.

Browning decided to have the club racer built away from the Abingdon works, partly to preserve secrecy but also to avoid conflict with Rover. So he handed the whole project

Pictured during the 1970 racing season, JXC 808D was used to try out ideas for a racing Rover.

Almost a Rover V8: this was the 4.5-litre Traco-Oldsmobile engine in JXC 808D.

over to Bill Shaw Racing, and appointed Roy Pierpoint (who had been the British Saloon Car champion in 1965) as driver. The actual build was done in Pierpoint's garage at Walton-on-Thames by Jim Morgan and Jim Rose, who had been with Alan Mann Racing when that company prepared the European racing Fords.

JXC 808D was stripped right down and built up again with a lightweight racing body incorporating flared wings and wheel arches to cover 10in-wide Minilite wheels wearing Dunlop racing tyres. Jim Morgan had worked on John Coombs' McLaren M1B with its Traco-Oldsmobile engine, an enlarged and race-tuned version of the Rover V8's GM ancestor, and he suggested using such an engine in the Rover. So the Rover development engine was replaced by a 4.3-litre Traco-Oldsmobile V8 taken from John Coundley's McLaren-Oldsmobile sports racing car, and this was bored out to 4.5

litres for good measure and fitted with four Weber carburettors. The standard Rover gearbox was retained because that was all that was available, but it was quite obviously not going to last for long with an engine that put out 360bhp at 6,800rpm.

The standard Rover differential was replaced by one from a Jaguar E-type, and the front suspension was modified with fabricated lower wishbones. PTFE bushes were used throughout the suspension, and ventilated disc brakes were added front and rear.

In this guise, and in the colours of the old BMC Competitions Department (red with a white roof), JXC 808D made its debut at Mallory Park in April 1970, with Roy Pierpoint driving and in front of a gathering of expectant Rover directors. It did not cover itself in glory, either wrecking its gearbox (Browning's recollection) or going out with a

JXC 808D as it now survives, wearing the racing colours of British Leyland.

puncture (according to a contemporary press report). In its very next race at Castle Combe, however, it won. Of the eight races it entered that season, most of which were in the BRSCC Hepolite-Glacier Special Saloon series, it won one more, which was the Silverstone 100 Mile Saloon Car Race. Unsurprisingly, the gearbox had failed several times during the season, and by the end it had been replaced by an American-made Muncie racing box.

These results were good enough for Browning to proceed to the third stage of his plan, which was to build a Group 6 prototype. JXC 808D was withdrawn from active service and its Traco-Oldsmobile engine was removed to become a spare for the Group 6 car. In its place was fitted a Weber-equipped Rover V8. The car was then shipped out to the USA in support of Rover's flagging attempts to sell P6s there. On return to the UK, it was bought by Alec Poole, who raced it with some success in Ireland. Then in the late 1970s it went to a collector and was carefully restored. The car survives today, now in the British Leyland racing colours of blue and white.

The Group 6 Prototype

Bill Shaw Racing were again commissioned to build this second car. This time, they started with another redundant P6B prototype obtained from Rover, which was P6B-6 (JXC 806D). Out went its modified-2000 base unit, which was replaced by a new production 3500 type, suitably modified to save weight. With alloy inner panels, glass-fibre wings and Plexiglass windows, the weight was drastically

reduced, ending up at around 2,095lb (950kg) as compared with the 2,861lb (1,298kg) of the standard production Rover 3500.

In went another Traco-Oldsmobile engine with a large bonnet air scoop to improve engine bay cooling, plus a Muncie racing gearbox. The rear suspension was completely changed, for the independent rear end from a Jaguar E-type, and some Ford Boss Mustang parts were also incorporated, mainly to help locate the rear axle and suspension. The front suspension retained the standard P6 configuration but, like the rear, was rose-jointed. All brakes were McLaren ventilated discs, with type M10B on the front and type M10A at the rear. The dashboard area was stripped out and refitted with only essential instruments, and lightweight glass-fibre bucket seats were added. Nevertheless, the car retained its standard rear seats and door trim panels, and even kept its winding windows. Final touches were a full roll-cage and a leather-trimmed alloy steering wheel. The car was then returned to Abingdon and was completed in British Leyland's racing colours of blue and white. It was said to be capable of 176mph (283km/h).

This second car was ready by September, and the Competitions Department decided to enter it for the Marathon de la Route, an 84-hour endurance race held at the Nürburgring in Germany that was distantly descended from the Liège–Sofia–Liège endurance rally of earlier times. Abingdon had some experience of this event, and this would be an opportunity to see how the Rover performed against the European works racing teams, which would all be there. So JXC 806D was fitted with a 25-gallon (114ltr) fuel tank, and after some limited testing at Goodwood, the team set off for Germany with Bill Price (Browning's assistant) as team manager and a team of three drivers – Roy Pierpoint, Clive Baker and Roger Enever.

The event was to be run over both the north and south loops of the Nürburgring, which gave a lap distance of nearly 19 miles (31km). During practice – strictly limited in order to preserve the car – a propshaft vibration showed up but everything looked very promising. Clive Baker took the wheel of car number 21 for the start at 1am in the morning, under instructions not to exceed 4,500rpm in order to preserve the engine. Nevertheless, the Rover shot away from the rest of the field on the first lap of the Nürburgring and stayed in the lead for sixteen hours. Unfortunately, that propshaft vibration became worse and the car was then withdrawn for fear of a catastrophic failure or an accident. But it had delivered a sensational performance, and retired

JXC 806D ended up in Australia, and is seen here in its original Camel cigarettes colours at Adelaide International Race Track in 1974. At this stage, it had a 5-litre Repco engine. ROB HARRISON

while a full three laps (nearly 57 miles/92km) ahead of its nearest competitors, which were the works Porsche 914/6 racers.

Sadly, this great potential was never tapped further because BL withdrew from motor sport and closed the Abingdon Competitions Department as a cost-saving measure soon afterwards.

Once the closure of the Competitions Department had been announced, BL's Australian subsidiary was approached by Geoff Sykes, promoter of the Warwick Farm racing circuit, with a view to bringing one of the racers to Australia with Roy Pierpoint for some promotional appearances. Sykes' request was turned down, but Melbourne racing

driver James Smith persuaded BL Australia to give him financial support in purchasing the car, and it was shipped out to Australia in April 1971. With it went many spares, including the second racing engine taken from JXC 808D.

On arrival, the car was repainted in Leyland Australia's colours of blue with a white stripe. It was shown to the press in June and then settled down to a season of racing in Marathon trim. It did well enough to earn the affectionate nickname of 'Rover the Wonder Dog' from race fans, took a first place at Hume Weir in November 1971 and, during a brief visit to New Zealand, came second and third against Mustangs and Camaros in races at Bay Park.

Meanwhile, the spare engine had been sent to Repco

The engine bay of JXC 806D shows the later sponsorship stickers; the front wing carries the name of James Smith. ROB HARRISON

BELOW: As finally modified, JXC 806D had its Traco-Oldsmobile engine set further back in the structure to improve weight distribution. ROB HARRISON

for further development. The intention then was to go for another 50–80bhp by using fuel injection, and Repco were also to install a dry-sump lubrication system. However, the Australian racing regulations changed for 1972, and with them so did Smith's plans. He took the car off the circuits for a major rebuild in order to make it competitive under the 1973 regulations for modified sports sedans. It was during this period that Smith and Leyland Australia parted company; Smith kept the car and Leyland Australia kept the engine, from which it hoped to develop a racing version of its own 4.4-litre V8 – itself based on the Rover V8 engine – that was due to appear shortly in the Leyland P76 saloon.

The rebuild therefore went ahead with a 5-litre Repco-Holden F5000 engine, and the front bulkhead was removed to allow the engine to be located about 2ft (60cm) further back in the car than standard. The Muncie gearbox and E-type rear end remained, but a Lola F5000 coil-and-wishbone front suspension was fitted. New body panels were also made up, with lengthened lightweight rear wings in place of the rear doors, and it may have been at this time that the original laminated windscreen was replaced by a Perspex type. As Smith had now secured backing from Camel cigarettes, the car was painted in their bright yellow livery for the 1973 season.

The Rover had another successful season during 1973 and, as a result, Smith secured further sponsorship from Camel. However, for 1974 he decided to campaign a Chevrolet Camaro, and sold the Rover to a Leyland dealer in Adelaide. It was then raced for a time by David Jarrett under Shell sponsorship, though still wearing its Camel livery, but was later painted blue and white once again. In the late 1970s it was put into storage. Stripped of its Repco-Holden engine, it then lay derelict for a time until it was bought in the early 1980s by Rob Harrison, a Sydney enthusiast. Harrison was able to locate the car's original Traco-Oldsmobile engine and subsequently rebuilt JXC 806D with that engine in the mid-position, the bulkhead modifications and others having proved irreversible.

CHAPTER SIX

THE NEW V8

Despite exhaustive research over the years, many of the details about how the V8 engine found its way into the P6 are still not known for certain. However, the most important parts of the story are clear.

After Maurice Wilks died in 1962, William (Bill) Martin-Hurst moved from his post as production director to become Rover's managing director. He was a particularly dynamic and enthusiastic individual – and was also Maurice Wilks' brother-in-law – and he quickly made it a personal objective to improve Rover and Land Rover sales in the

William Martin-Hurst (standing) and Bruce McWilliams (seated) got on very well, and between them were responsible for Rover seeking a US V8 engine.

USA. To that end, he brought in a new management team to run the Rover Company of North America (RCNA), headed by American Bruce McWilliams, who had most recently been at Studebaker. The two men got along extremely well. McWilliams swiftly identified that a lack of power and performance was holding back Rover's sales in the USA, and in January 1963 he formally proposed to Martin-Hurst that he should look for a US-built V8 engine to put into Land Rovers sold there in order to give them the sort of performance that Americans expected. Martin-Hurst agreed; this was a step in the right direction.

So, over the next few months, McWilliams looked around for an engine that might be suitable, and the one he identified was built by Chrysler. Exactly which Chrysler engine this was is not clear (and McWilliams himself could not remember when asked many years later), but it is likely to have been one of the small-block A-series engines, either the 313 (5.1-litre) or the much more common 318 (5.2-litre). Whichever it was, it was very much a current production engine, and the Rover people had severe doubts about whether Chrysler would be prepared to sell any to them. In the event, no formal approach was ever made because events took a very different turn.

Meanwhile, as Chapter 4 explains, Martin-Hurst was having misgivings about the 6-cylinder ohc engine that Rover was developing to create a high-performance derivative of the P6. The letter he wrote to McWilliams in November 1963 that is quoted in that chapter shows that he was by then opposed to going ahead with the engine. When he went to visit Mercury Marine in December (primarily to discuss the use of Land Rover diesel engines in boats), he would have had two things on his mind. One was that Rover still needed a V8 engine to boost Land Rover sales in the USA, and the other was that they had no clear alternative to the ohc 6-cylinder that he believed should be abandoned.

It was during that visit to Mercury Marine that Martin-Hurst spotted a small-block V8 engine sitting on the workshop floor. He asked Mercury's owner, Carl Kiekhaefer, what it was, and learned that this was a Buick 215, a light-weight all-alloy engine developed for the General Motors' 'compact' cars of the early 1960s, and that this particular example had just been taken out of a Buick Skylark. Mercury intended to try it out as a power boat engine – which some individual owners had apparently already done.

Kiekhaefer added that General Motors had just taken the engine out of production. Intrigued, and no doubt quite excited at the same time, Martin-Hurst measured it up and discovered that it would not only fit into Land Rovers but would also fit very neatly into the engine bay of the

Rover 2000. Better yet: it would also fit into the engine bay of the P5 3-litre, which Martin-Hurst knew would soon become uncompetitive against newer rivals. So he asked for the engine to be crated up and shipped to Solihull, where it probably arrived some time during January 1964.

However, as Chapter 4 explains, when he returned to Solihull himself, he found that the Rover engineers were less than enthusiastic about it. Peter Wilks, the technical director, told him that they were just too busy to do anything with it. The Engineering Department had indeed just built the first of the 6-cylinder P7 prototypes and was about to embark on a test programme for the car. They had enough

This was the engine that Martin-Hurst found – the General Motors 215cu in (3,523cc), all-aluminium V8. This picture may be of the actual engine that Martin-Hurst saw in the Mercury Marine workshops. It had come from a Buick Skylark.

The 215 V8 was used in other compact cars from GM as well as the Buick. This is a 1962 Oldsmobile Jetfire sport coupé, which had a 215bhp turbocharged version of the engine.

It was American practice to change details of their models every year, to keep them fresh and appealing. This is a 1961 Buick Skylark sport coupé, which had a 185bhp version of the GM V8 engine; the one that Martin-Hurst saw had supposedly come from one of these cars. CHARKLES 01/ WIKIMEDIA COMMONS

on their plate already. Spen King was also not keen on the idea, believing that it made better sense to pursue the existing policy of developing a 6-cylinder from the existing 4-cylinder ohc engine.

Not one to be deterred that easily, Martin-Hurst found another way of taking his idea forward. He discovered that Rover's Competitions Department was under-employed because this was a lull between rallies – the last one had been the RAC Rally in December 1963 and the next one would be the Alpine Rally in July 1964, which would mark the rally debut of the P6 and for which the cars had been prepared early. So he persuaded the Competitions Department (which was then run by Ralph Nash) to install his Buick engine into a car so that he would have something more tangible that he could use to convince his colleagues that this engine would solve several of Rover's problems at a stroke.

The car that Martin-Hurst obtained for the job was a white 2000, with car number 400-03535A; built (as a 2000) on 23 April 1964, it went to the Engineering Department on 29 April. The main conversion work must then have taken place in early May, because the car was registered with a V8 engine on 22 May as AXC 91B. Its Buick engine was numbered JN 780, which indicates that it was a 1963 high-compression variant with the four-barrel Rochester carburettor and 185bhp.

As there was still no formal development programme, there were no engineers allocated to testing the car, and so Martin-Hurst had to continue to plough his rather lonely furrow without any proper engineering support. Nevertheless, he clearly had the bit between his teeth, and somehow managed to get his hands on a few more Buick V8 engines – almost certainly with the help of Bruce McWilliams at the Rover Company of North America. He had one of them stripped down at Rover during August, and engineer C. E. Field reported at the start of September on likely manufacturing costs and problems.

Meanwhile, as the next stage in his campaign, Martin-Hurst managed to get a second V8 engine installed in a car. This time, it was a P5 3-litre Saloon (number 775-03433B, a 1964-model automatic) that became BXC 620B on 12 August; interestingly, the engine in this car was numbered JN 776, which is remarkably close to the number of the one that had been imported from Mercury Marine. That coincidence, if coincidence it was, is unexplained.

Now that Martin-Hurst was able to demonstrate to his colleagues that the engine would fit both the existing Rover

If it looks like a lash-up, that's because it is! The first Buick V8 was fitted into a Rover 2000 that was then sent out on long-distance road test. Here it is on return to Solihull, looking rather the worse for wear. The grille and headlamp design is the one that was then being tried on some of the P7 experimental cars.

car ranges, he seems to have had another two examples put into P6s. In a memo dated 28 October 1964, he claimed that there was one engine in a P5 (which would have been BXC 620B) and that there were three in P6s. The three P6s would have included AXC 91B, but the other two have not yet been identified. Realistically, they may not have existed, and Martin-Hurst may have been expressing an intention rather than a reality in that October 1964 memo. However, in November 1964, a V8 engine with air-conditioning pump was pictured in a P6, and this may well have been one of the two unidentified cars.

During this period, Martin-Hurst's ideas seem to have been evolving quite rapidly. The original idea had been to find a V8 engine to boost US Land Rover sales, but that intention seems to have been forgotten in a rush of enthusiasm to use it for Rover cars. During 1964, BMC launched the Vanden Plas 4-litre R, with a 6-cylinder Rolls-Royce engine, and this newcomer represented a very clear threat to sales of Rover's P5 3-litre. Its arrival probably persuaded Martin-Hurst that the P5 range had now become the top priority for the new V8 engine. The P6 installation could follow later, as the planned 2000TC would meet demand for a high-performance model in the medium term.

All these plans were of course dependent on General Motors agreeing to let Rover have the Buick 215 engine, and throughout most of 1964, Martin-Hurst shuttled back and forth between Solihull and the USA to persuade the American manufacturer that Rover really were interested in taking on their redundant V8. He also spent a lot of time persuading his colleagues at Solihull of the wisdom of taking the engine on, and before the year's end he had cracked the most important nut of all: engineering director Peter Wilks agreed that the V8 was the ideal solution for Rover's needs. In January 1965, Rover signed a contract with General Motors for the licence manufacture of the engine, and the rest of that year would be taken up with tests, experiments, and working out how to get the new engine manufactured in Britain.

One of the first things to happen after the contract was signed was that GM agreed to provide Rover with a quantity of complete V8 engines; that quantity has been reported (by Graham Robson) as thirty-nine, which seems an odd number unless it represented all those that GM could lay their hands on quickly in the corporate spares store. These must have begun to arrive at Rover in early 1965, and it seems that Rover almost immediately began to strip the US ancillaries from them and to fit British-made carburettors, alternators and other items. These engines were then given new numbers, all with a 2158 prefix; that stood for '215 cubic inches, 8 cylinders', and during May 1965 Martin-Hurst issued an instruction that all departments were to refer to the new engine as the '2158'.

By July 1965, the programme to fit the V8 into the P6 was formally known as P6B ('P6 Buick'), and the earliest of the renumbered engines known to have gone into a car was 2158/19, which went into a 2000 numbered 400-00382A, which became HXC 104C that summer. Another one went into HXC 105C, which was formally numbered P6B/5, or the fifth P6B prototype.

That begs the question of which cars were considered to be the first four P6B prototypes. They did not of course have P6B numbers because they had been built before the P6B programme had been named. However, it seems likely that the first one was considered to be AXC 91B. The second and third cars were created by pulling two of the P7 experimental cars over to the P6B programme; and the fourth was HXC 104C. This is probably easiest to understand in tabular form – see below.

AN ENGINEERING SPECIFICATION

Those early prototypes demonstrated that the basic concept of a V8-powered P6 was viable, and further design work led to a provisional specification being ready by the end of 1965. Rover's aim was obviously to minimize differences from the 4-cylinder cars, but it was already clear that there would have to be some quite major changes and that there was much more to creating the P6B than squeezing a V8 engine into the existing base unit.

P7 MORPHS INTO P6B

When the P6B programme got under way in summer 1965, an early priority must have been to get some experimental cars on the road. It took several months to build the eighteen prototypes (twenty were probably planned) that became JXC 806D to JXC 823D in January 1966 and were identified as P6B/6 to P6B/23.

Very noticeable here is that this batch of prototypes began with number 6. While they were being built, the P6B project engineers would have needed something to be working with, and it seems logical that they treated the three 'transitional' P7s as P6B prototypes. Research by Chris Wilson has revealed the probable details of the first five P6B experimental cars.

Identity	Reg. no	Date	Remarks
P6B no. 1	AXC 91B	22 May 1964	First V8-engined P6, initially known as a P7 (see Chapter 4).
P6B no. 2	DXC 11B	19 Oct 1964	Originally P7A/1. Later re-engined with a V8 (see Chapter 4).
P6B no. 3	HXC 21C	27 Aug 1965	Originally P7B/1; built with a V8 (see Chapter 4).
P6B no. 4	HXC 104C	27 Aug 1965	Shown as a P6B in local authority records, but with a Rover 2000 commission number, 400-00382A. Engine number 2158/19.
P6B/5	HXC 105C	2 Dec 1965	Shown as P6B/5 in local authority records. Engine number 2158/23.

The changes obviously began with the engine itself, which was installed with a slight rearward tilt. This made it necessary to realign the final drive assembly, and the high torque of the V8 needed a stronger differential with a larger final drive casing that held a greater quantity of oil. Rover took the opportunity of this redesign to locate the final drive's oil filler more accessibly. They also raised the final drive gearing to 3.08:1, which allowed a comfortably high cruising speed, reasonable fuel consumption and good acceleration.

The general layout of the final drive and rear suspension remained the same as on the 2000, but some changes were made to reduce the transmission of road noise. The front cross-member was modified so that it was rubber-mounted to the sills rather than directly to the propshaft tunnel, and the forward ends of the bottom links were flexibly mounted to it instead of to the body. Larger and more compliant rubber bushes were drawn up for the top links of the Watts linkage, and the bottom link bushes were stiffened to compensate. Spring rates were also increased by around 15 per cent and larger-bore telescopic dampers were fitted, with improved rubber mountings.

At the front of the car, there were detail changes to the suspension's bottom links in order to clear the engine, plus slightly higher spring rates to cope with the additional weight, while the leak settings on the dampers were changed to give better control. Front wheel castor was also increased over that of the 2000 in order to maintain directional stability, and slightly higher-geared steering was later found necessary to offset an effect of all these changes.

Then, of course, the V8-engined car's higher performance demanded bigger brakes, so larger-diameter front discs were specified (although the rears were unchanged from the 2000), and there was an 8in servo instead of the 2000's 7in size. The exhaust system had some similarities to the 2000 type but of course needed a Y-section at the front where the downpipes from the two exhaust manifolds met behind the engine. Behind that, a single pipe led to a modified 2000-type front silencer, and then standard 2000-type pipes ran back to a new tailpipe with a 0.125in greater diameter – enough, supposedly, to release an extra 1bhp of power.

THE JXC-D CARS

This specification was further developed on a batch of eighteen more P6B prototypes. These cars had engines from the batch supplied by General Motors, but all of them were

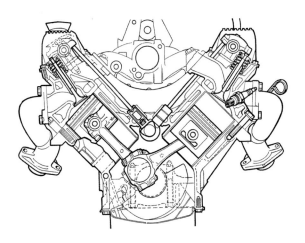

The **V8** engine had a classically simple design, with a single central camshaft operating overhead valves on both banks of cylinders through pushrods. Valve clearances were maintained automatically by hydraulic tappets at the camshaft end. This is a cross-section of the engine as it went into production at Rover.

Rover undertook some serious testing with the JXC-D cars. JXC 813D went to the USA, where testing was undertaken in conjunction with the RCNA engineers, notably Dick Green who was RCNA's product development manager, based on the West Coast. Here it is during that testing, disguised as a 2000TC. MIKE GREEN/RICHARD GREEN COLLECTION

The JXC-D cars were not all identified in the same way. This was the identity tag on JXC 822D, which described it simply as 'P6B'. NICK DUNNING

JXC 813D was identified more fully, if rather less formally. ANDRIES GRIEDE

'Roverized' and renumbered with 2158-prefix identities. Build probably began towards the end of 1965, and the first of the new cars was completed in January 1966. It became P6B/6 on the Engineering fleet, and records show that it had engine number 23, which must have been removed from HXC 105C (P6B/5).

The rest of the eighteen P6B prototype cars were completed over the next few months at the start of 1966, and all of them were registered in the sequence JXC 806D to JXC 823D. Most probably had right-hand drive, but there were some left-hand-drive cars, too; bizarrely, however, the development car for the US federal specification had right-hand drive.

The test programme for these cars was quite intensive, and led to further changes that were incorporated into the production specification. Among other things, they demonstrated that the P6B developed very high underbonnet temperatures, even with the enlarged radiator that was fitted right from the beginning. By autumn 1966, it was clear that more space was needed in the engine bay. So in September the inner front wings were redesigned with a scallop at the front, which both made more room for fitting some components (notably the brake servo) and helped air to circulate to reduce heat build-up in the engine bay. Some of the JXC-D cars were modified with the new design, but others appear not to have been.

The problem of heat build-up was nevertheless never really cured, and even adding bonnet louvres 'had no beneficial effect' on a car used for testing on the multiple hairpin bends of the Stelvio Pass in Italy during 1967. Rover added a spill-return fuel system, which did minimize vapour locks, but production V8-engined P6s often suffered from fuel starvation problems if hot weather and heavy traffic

conspired together. The same problem affected V8-engined P5s, too. Other cooling problems became apparent during testing, one being that the heater remained cool while the engine overheated. This was traced to air pockets created because the low-mounted filler cap prevented full bleeding of the system. It was impossible to fit the filler any higher, so the problem was cured by adding a bleed pipe between the inlet manifold water jacket and the radiator tank below the filler cap side so that the air could be expelled by running the engine up to operating temperature with the filler cap off. Still, purging air from the cooling system always would be a problem on production cars.

Wider tyres were a known requirement at the start of the JXC-D test programme, and of course 175 × 14s had been used on the P7 6-cylinder cars. These were tried again, together with 185 × 14s and a low-profile 190-section size, which was then new technology in the tyre business. After many miles of high-speed testing on Italian *autostrade*, the 185s were chosen for production cars, although the low-profile tyres proved quite satisfactory and it seems that the choice of 185s was partly dictated by their compliance with German regulations. The wider tyres of course needed new 5.5in wheel rims, and Rover took the opportunity to specify wheels with the latest safety-ledge rim. The wheels were offset an extra 0.375in to give enough clearance for all-weather tyres at the rear, and the front hubs were modified to maintain the original track with the new wheels.

BUICK V8 BECOMES ROVER V8

Information gathered during testing of those twenty V8-engined cars was fed back into the V8 development programme run by Jack Swaine's engines team at Solihull. Their job was to adapt the engine to suit European motoring expectations, and to suit British manufacturing conditions – and there was a lot of work to do in a fairly short time. Rover had deliberately chosen not to buy any of the Buick tooling

for the V8 engine, in order to leave the development team free to modify the design as they saw fit.

Two Rover engineers, Dave Wall and Gerry Boucher, led the development work on the engine. To assist them, William Martin-Hurst persuaded GM to release to Rover

THE JXC-D PROTOTYPES

The information in this table is based on written records and on the memories of several individuals. It was compiled with considerable input from Chris Wilson and Andries Griede.

Note that JXC 812D took an out-of-sequence prototype number, although it does not appear to have been completed late. JXC 823D was put on the road five months after the last of the other cars, and appears to have been given a Rover-built prototype engine.

	Engine no.	Reg. no	Reg. date	Remarks
P6B/6	2158/23	JXC 806D	11 Jan 66	RHD. Engine development. Later became racer; see Chapter 5.
P6B/7	2158/24	JXC 807D	01 Feb 66	RHD. Use not known. Later a competition car as WPX 3.
P6B/8	2158/25	JXC 808D	01 Mar 66	RHD. Use not known. Later became racer; see Chapter 5.
P68/9	2158/26	JXC 809D	01 Mar 66	To Goodyear, presumably for tyre work.
P6B/10	2158/27	JXC 810D	10 Mar 66	Probably transmission development car. Later to AE Brico for fuel injection development.
P6B/11	2158/28	JXC 811D	10 Mar 66	LHD. To Pirelli, presumably for tyre work. Later RHD and with ZF 5-speed gearbox.
P6B/12	2158/30	JXC 813D	01 Apr 66	LHD. For tests in USA. Survives.
P6B/13	2158/31	JXC 814D	01 Apr 66	No information.
P6B/14	2158/32	JXC 815D	28 Apr 66	Engine development car.
P6B/15	2158/33	JXC 816D	28 Apr 66	No information.
P6B/16	2158/34	JXC 817D	28 Apr 66	Possibly transmission development car.
P6B/17	No record found.			
P6B/18	2158/35	JXC 818D	01 Jun 66	No information.
P6B/19	No record found.			
P6B/20	2158/36	JXC 819D	01 Jun 66	No information
P6B/21	2158/37	JXC 812D	01 Apr 66	No information. Record shows same engine number as P6B/22; possibly should be 2158/29.
P6B/22	2158/37	JXC 820D	03 Jun 66	See also P6B/21. Later became P7F and used for P10 rear suspension trials; see Chapter 4.
P6B/23	2158/38	JXC 821D	03 Jun 66	No information.
P6B/24	2158/39	JXC 822D	29 Jul 66	RHD. Federal 3500S development car. Survives.
P6B/25	2158/108	JXC 823D	19 Dec 66	Rollover accident on test track in June 1967.

The main test programme was over by spring 1968, when the P6B entered production, and many of the JXC-D cars were sold off in the next few years. Others were simply scrapped. Two went to the BL Competitions Department at Abingdon and became track racers, as Chapter 5 explains.

Once Rover were serious about going ahead with the V8, they engaged Buick's Joe Turlay as a consultant. Turlay had been in at the start of the all-aluminium V8 story in the 1950s and knew the engine inside out.

Dave Wall was one of the Rover engines team who worked on the V8. In this picture, he has on his desk a prototype cylinder head from the slant-four derivative of the P6's ohc engine – a design that eventually delivered the 2.2-litre size in 1973.

Gerry Boucher was the other key engines man on the Rover team. Here he is pictured some four decades afterwards, during an interview with the author.

the man who knew more about the 215 V8 than anybody else. This was Joe Turlay, who had been one of the engine's principal designers in the 1950s, and had also overseen its production at GM. Now eighteen months from retirement, 'Aluminum Joe', as his colleagues called him, was seconded to Rover as an adviser on a US-sized salary. His detailed knowledge of the engine proved invaluable.

Wall and Boucher got to grips with the original design by sectioning some engines, by studying the GM drawings, and by consulting Joe Turlay when the actual engines deviated from the drawings. The next stage was to make the engine meet European expectations, which for a start meant translating its dimensions into metric measurements. So its 215cu in became 3528cc, retaining the original bore and stroke. The engines team also had to prepare the V8 for a higher rev limit than it had in American form. This demanded changes to the breathing, and at the same time they strengthened the block with additional webbing and with extra metal around the main bearings. Stronger crankshaft bearings were also specified to take the higher loadings that came with the higher rev limit.

In addition to making these changes, the Solihull engineers had to arrange manufacture of the V8 in the UK. No foundry in Britain was then able to make the cylinder block in the American way, using gravity die-casting with the iron

Rover proudly prepared this demonstration cutaway of their new engine. This picture clearly shows the valves, their rockers and pushrods, and the hydraulic tappets.

liners held in place during the casting process. So Wall and Boucher worked with Birmal (Birmingham Aluminium) at Smethwick to redesign the block so that it could be sand-cast and the liners could be press-fitted afterwards. They also introduced several changes of material specification right through the engine to make it fit for its new job.

Even then, not every engine component could be manufactured in Britain, and so Rover settled for importing several items from the original supplier, which was the GM-owned Diesel Equipment Company of Grand Rapids, Michigan. These included the self-adjusting hydraulic tappets, camshaft blanks, valve cotters, timing gears and timing chain, and it would be many years before manufacture of these items in Britain was achieved. British ancillaries also had to be found, so Lucas electrical equipment and SU carburettors replaced the American-made originals. Using SU carburettors demanded a new design of inlet manifold, and that task fell to Dave Wall, who told author David Hardcastle (for the book *Rover V8 Engine*) that he had taken inspiration from the manifold design of the contemporary Rolls-Royce V8 engine.

Rover allocated production of the new engine to their Acocks Green engine plant, and the very first Rover-built V8 was on test by April 1966. Production volumes would be very slow

The P6B version of the engine had a cylindrical air cleaner, and the oil filter projected forwards, as on the Buick original. Both features were different on the P5B engines, to suit the different underbonnet layout. The tips of the fan blades on early engines were bent over, a design that supposedly reduced fan noise.

to increase, however, and in the meantime the Engineering Department was faced with a shortage of engines. As a result, engines were swapped from one car to another, and this practice continued for some time past the actual introduction of the P5B and P6B models, when the V8 was in full production at Rover. As late as summer 1969, for example, engine 2158/19 was hauled out of HXC 104C (the fourth P6B prototype) to be put into Range Rover prototype 100/4, which promptly went off to the Sahara for hot-weather testing.

THE SEARCH FOR A MANUAL GEARBOX

In the beginning, Rover had every intention of offering the V8-engined P6 model with a choice of manual and automatic gearboxes. Tests with the Borg Warner Type 35 three-speed automatic proved satisfactory (although the gearbox was close to the limit of its torque capacity with the V8 engine). However, finding the right manual gearbox was not so easy.

The existing four-speed manual gearbox in the 2000 was not strong enough to handle the torque of the V8 engine, but, as Chapters 3 and 4 explain, the Rover engineers were already looking at a five-speed gearbox made by ZF in Germany. As supplied to BMW for their 'performance' 1800 TI/SA saloon, this had an unusual dog-leg gate with first gear out on its own, but it also had enough torque capacity to cope with the V8 and its fifth gear would be an additional attraction when the car reached Rover showrooms. So it was a natural choice for the P6B programme, and examples were probably fitted to prototypes JXC 810D, JXC 811D and JXC 817D.

By October 1966, Rover intended to go ahead with the ZF five-speed gearbox, provided that the German company was able to eliminate a rattle at idle. A further drawback was difficult gear engagement when the gearbox was cold, but Rover did not regard this as a deterrent. ZF did manage to reduce the noise by using special oil, but there was still a discernible rattle and by April 1967 Rover were talking about ways of warning buyers that this rattle was normal. Just a month later, though, Solihull's engineers had started to look at other options, and there was talk of using an uprated Rover gearbox or an uprated Triumph gearbox. ZF, keen to secure the Rover business, quickly came up with the offer of a newly designed manual gearbox.

Other options were in the air over summer and autumn

1967. There was an urgent need for a new Land Rover gearbox, which was known as the Mk III type and was intended initially for the new 101 Forward Control military model, and there was some discussion about building a five-speed version of this for the P6B. However, by October thoughts had focused on a Rover four-speed gearbox with modified bearings, and trials of a prototype were under way. This proved promising, and by January 1968 a batch of fifty had been built for assessment. By this stage, it was quite clear that a manual gearbox model could not be ready in time for the planned launch of the P6B, and so Rover decided that it should be introduced as a follow-up model when it was ready.

ZF kept their promise and had a new gearbox ready by April 1968, which was fitted to a car that Rover sent over to Friedrichshafen for the purpose. Back at Solihull, the British Leyland merger was beginning to provide some useful contacts, and the Rover engineers became aware of a new five-speed Jaguar gearbox that Harry Mundy had designed and which, by all accounts, was the sort of thing they needed. However, the negative side of the British Leyland merger now became apparent as well, as Jaguar were not granted the funds to progress with this gearbox beyond prototype form. It therefore never became a serious contender for use in the P6B.

Even though the new ZF gearbox was reported to be performing well in Rover's test car, the decision was eventually taken not to go with this but rather to settle for a further modified Rover four-speed gearbox. Perhaps cost was the reason; perhaps ZF could not get the new gearbox into production soon enough for Rover. One way or the other, it would still be three years before a manual-gearbox P6B entered production as an alternative to the automatic model.

STYLING THE P6B

Right from the start, it had been clear that the V8 engine would need a larger radiator than the one in the 2000, and the first V8-engined test car (AXC 91B) had an additional air intake below the bumper that anticipated the eventual production type. However, it was not until summer 1965 that David Bache's Styling Department became involved with the forthcoming V8 models; it had until that point been busy with the 2000TC and its North American variant, and with the Mk III versions of the P5 3-litre.

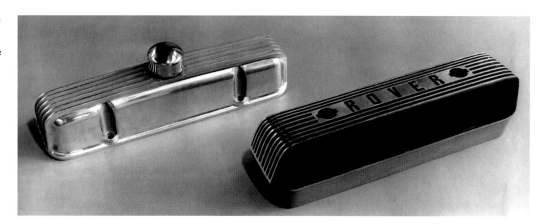

'Roverizing' the engine also called for some cosmetic changes. One of the Rover proposals for the rocker cover is seen here with an American original.

Bache's team focused on two main areas. One was the new engine itself, and the other was the front end of the car. From mid-July 1965, a series of proposals for rocker covers bearing the Rover name were prepared, quite probably by Tony Poole. That same month, a first front end mock-up was also produced, on a real car in the workshop rather than on a mock-up in the styling studio. This featured the larger one-piece headlight units that had already been used on some of the P7 prototypes, plus a production-ready version of the front valance with its additional air intake. This mock-up also had one of the grille badges with red and white sails (see Chapter 2), although that may not have reflected any real plan to use such a badge on the car. More likely is that one was conveniently lying around in the studio when a badge was needed.

Over the next few months, some variations on this front end design were tried in the styling studio, but the last one was pictured towards the end of November and it seems probable that the production front end styling with its chunky bright strip under the front edge of the bonnet was chosen soon after that. Quite possibly, this was selected because it was a simple cosmetic modification that minimized additional manufacturing costs.

THREE THOUSAND FIVE, 1968–1970

Even though Rover saw very clearly how important the new P6B model could be for their sales, there was a problem. The V8 engine was also intended to go into the P5 3-litre model, to turn it into a P5B 3.5-litre, which meant that a quite high volume of new engines would be needed very soon after production began. It would take some time to build up production to the required levels, and Rover recognized the impossibility of launching the two new models at the same time.

So the decision was made to launch the new engine in the P5B first. Not only was the older car very much in need of a performance increase, but it was also expected to sell in smaller quantities. So the P5B would get the V8 engine as production was building up, and the P6B would be introduced around six months later, by which time V8 engine production would be running at the necessary levels to feed the production lines for both cars. As a result, Rover's new V8 engine broke cover first in the P5B models in October 1967 – and an additional benefit was that its arrival aroused intense interest in the likelihood of a V8-engined P6 eventually becoming available as well.

Meanwhile, the final cosmetic details for the P6B cars were being settled at Solihull, and a production specification had probably been agreed by the early part of the year. Visual changes from the 4-cylinder models were to be quite limited, but David Bache's team had ensured that there would be no mistaking one of the new V8-engined models, even from a distance. A thick, anodized aluminium 'eyebrow' on the bonnet edge, a big under-bumper air intake to cover the deeper radiator, and fatter tyres were all immediately

Top priority for the new engine was Rover's P5 range, which became a P5B when it was announced with the V8 in autumn 1967.

obvious. Closer to, heavier-section bumpers and the squat rubber-faced overriders seen earlier on the NADA 2000TC (see Chapter 9) were distinguishing features, and overall the car looked more powerful – and even aggressive.

It took sharp eyes to spot that the bright surround for the grille badge was thinner than on the 4-cylinder cars, and that there was a new lashing ring protruding through the lower air intake. The twin-ring wheel trims, introduced on 4-cylinder cars at about the same time, were not immediately obvious either. Completely invisible unless the bonnet was open was the different stiffening frame that it needed to clear the V8's repositioned front cross-member. Then, to confirm that this was indeed the V8-engined model, there were bright metal V8 badges on bonnet and bootlid, and plate badges carrying the 3500 designation on the wings, the grille and the bootlid.

Those badges made good sense: the four-figure 3500 number linked the V8 model to the 4-cylinder 2000 range, and by December 1967 the initial service literature and the first edition of the owner's handbook were being printed, describing the car as a Rover 3500. Not long after that, however, Rover began to worry whether the name was too similar to the '3.5-litre' name applied to the P5B. It was managing director William Martin-

This front view of the Three Thousand Five shows the car's most obvious recognition features – an aluminium 'eyebrow' on the bonnet edge, plus **V8** and **3500** badges.

Many of the early cars were white, including **XXC 554F** (425-00045A). This car was registered in February 1968 and was another that went to the Publicity Department. The fatter tyres and substantial under-bumper air intake gave the Three Thousand Five a satisfyingly solid look.

Hurst who suggested calling the P6B a 'Three Thousand Five', and that name was chosen for the launch. It was too late for the printed literature, though, and although launch publicity material and sales brochures called the car a Three Thousand Five, the 3500 name remained on handbooks and service literature until reprints were required around

summer 1969! Ironically, perhaps, the Three Thousand Five name never caught on, and Rover would revert to the 3500 name after 1970. Meanwhile, the general public remained confused about which car was which for ever more, and the motor trade compromised by describing the P6B as 'the 2000 shape' and the P5B as 'the big old one'.

Rover remained characteristically discreet with the badges for the Three Thousand Five. The new plate badges had the model number and frame cast into them, and the new V8 badge was quite small, even though it was chrome plated.

There was a V8 badge on the radio speaker grille, too, perhaps to impress the passengers! The first cars had a D1-D2 automatic selector gate, as seen here.

On the inside, the cars were very much the same as the existing 4-cylinder models. However, the strip-type speedometer now read to 140mph (225km/h) and had a black bezel instead of a chromed one, while a V8 badge was fitted to the radio speaker panel, and the steering wheel crossbar bore a 3500 motif in place of the 2000 motif on the 4-cylinders. The dashboard anti-skid mat that was optional on the 4-cylinder cars was also standard here. Invisibly, of course, they had 15-gallon (68ltr) fuel tanks instead of the 12-gallon (55ltr) 2000 type, and they had the battery mounted on the right of the boot, recessed into the horizontal sidemember.

THE FIRST CARS

Pilot production began very slowly; the first two cars were built in July 1967 and then registered (as TXC 730F and TXC 731F) on 3 August. Two more were built in August, half a dozen with right-hand drive and the first two with left-hand drive in September, and then production gradually ramped up. Most of these early cars were white or red, and many were registered in the YXC-F series, although there were others with UXC-F and VXC-F numbers. Several were distributed around various departments at Rover for testing and assessment, and some probably always ran on trade plates and were never registered. Some, including TXC 731F, which was used for mileage testing, were very simply disguised with 2000TC badges.

Four of the early cars registered in November 1967 were TXC 745F to TXC 748F (respectively numbers 21, 33, 23 and 24 in the 425-prefix sequence), and these featured in early press and publicity photographs, also doing duty on the press and dealer launches. The press fleet proper was made up of later cars, however, registered in the XXC-F series. Probably around 200 cars had been built by the time the press were invited to try out the new Rovers at a preview held in northern France during early April 1968, and the official embargo date and launch day was 17 April. These were actually the first Rovers to be announced with British Leyland branding, which had not been used at the launch of the P5B models the previous autumn.

As cars began to reach the showrooms in the spring of 1968, they were made available with two new paint colours – April Yellow and Brigade Red – which were actually previews of the colour range planned for the 1969 season that was to begin that autumn. Racing Red and Venetian Red were not made available on the V8 cars, although some early F-registered examples had in fact been painted in Racing Red, which was a current colour at the time they were built in 1967. There were no changes for the interior colours, though, and the same four colours already available on the 4-cylinder cars remained available for the V8s. Optional equipment that could be fitted on the assembly lines was listed as front and rear head restraints (with reading lights on the front pair as a further option), a heated rear window, a laminated windscreen, Sundym tinted glass, a rev-counter (similar to the one in the 2000TC) and the bootlid mounting kit for the spare wheel.

The early cars were not without their problems, and among the more worrying was a serious high-speed vibra-

TXC 748F was an early car that went to the Publicity Department and was extensively photographed. This picture shows it on a large showroom poster that was available to dealers in 1968. The car was registered in October 1967 and was number 425-00024A. Ironically, in view of the fact that it was also offered to magazines for road test (*Motor* was one that used it), the car was actually painted in Racing Red, a colour not available on production cars.

tion that proved very difficult to trace. Colin Elmer, who was superintendent of inspection on the P6 assembly lines, remembered that the problem was initially blamed on the new Avon tyres and that Solihull's Quality Control Department tried to deal with it by grinding down tyres to see if the vibration disappeared as the tyres became more worn and better bedded in. Rover eventually traced the problem by doing some high-speed testing on a 15-mile (24km) unopened section of the M6 motorway (between Junction 5 for Castle Bromwich and Junction 3 for the A444 to Corley Moor). After a spell of high-speed running, Elmer told the Rover Sports Register's Nick Dunning, a heavy vibration became apparent at an axle speed of 1,500rpm. Further investigation revealed that the cause lay in the differential, which was essentially unchanged from the one used in the 2000. The solution was to re-machine the differential casting.

PRESS REACTIONS

The first press reports on the 3500 began to appear soon after the launch in France. Interestingly, photographs accompanying these reports showed cars with the earlier type of wheel trim; the production twin-ring type had clearly not been available in time.

Rover were probably surprised to read that the car they had touted in the press release as having 'impressive liveliness and performance' was actually appreciated more for its refinement than its speed. *Autocar* magazine of 18 April described the 3500 as 'first and foremost a Rover rather than a sports saloon in the same class, as, say, Jaguar… The 2000TC… remains a much more eager car for the sporty driver.' The issue of *Motor* dated 20 April suggested that

The passenger compartment of the V8 models was exactly the same as its counterpart for the 4-cylinder cars. With the front seats carefully placed, as in this picture, rear legroom could be made to look quite good!

'the new model will appeal mainly to buyers who want the now well-known handling and handiness of the Rover 2000, plus the extra refinement and performance given by the light-alloy V8 engine'. Bill Boddy of *Motor Sport* published his impressions in that magazine's May 1968 issue and was actually 'disappointed with the performance of the Three Thousand Five. I had expected a punchy feel and very impressive acceleration... [but] I can only report that on ordinary English – well, Welsh – roads I needed far more space than is commonly available to get near an indicated 100mph.'

Nevertheless, the new V8 engine came in for plenty of praise. 'The 3500's greatest virtue is the completely smooth and quiet nature of its power unit,' said *Autocar*, and *Autosport* for 19 April agreed: 'The remarkable quietness and smoothness of the engine, coupled with the silent transmission, render this a most restful car to drive.' The familiar P6 virtues remained intact, as well, and *Autocar* reminded its readers that 'this must be one of the best braking systems on any car today'.

The press did have some detail criticisms, though. *Autosport* found the steering 'a little heavy at parking speeds' and *Autocar* thought the fuel consumption disappointing in comparison with the 4-cylinder models. The same magazine also had reservations about the automatic gearbox, considering the change-up speeds to be too low and highlighting 'an annoying delay before kickdown selection takes place... we would much prefer a D-2-1 selector system with provision for part-throttle downshifts.'

Autocar also included the Three Thousand Five in a four-car comparison in its issue of 4 September 1969. The cars were described as 'Quality Saloons under £2,000', and the other three were the Audi 100LS, Triumph 2.5PI and Vauxhall Ventora. At this time, the Rover actually cost a shade over £1,830 including purchase tax, whereas all the other cars were priced below £1,500. It was therefore no surprise that it did not emerge as the best buy.

THE THREE THOUSAND FIVE IN SERVICE

As *Autocar* had predicted, the new Rover soon found 'a whole new sector of owners among the motoring public', becoming 'a satisfying and compact gentleman's carriage for the upper set'. Generally speaking, the Three Thousand Five proved

to be trouble-free, too. *Autocar* magazine took one on long-term test and reported on fifteen months and 14,000 miles (22,500km) of use in the issue of 28 August 1969. 'It has proved entirely reliable and exceptionally trouble-free,' they reported, 'giving us much less to report than is usual after this initial "breaking-in" spell of service... The 3500 certainly upholds the Rover traditions of longevity and freedom from irritating troubles.'

The Three Thousand Five also attracted the attention of London's Metropolitan Police, which had taken delivery of its first few examples by October 1968. These initial deliveries, some in dark blue and some in white, were allocated to traffic control and area control duties, with one example going to the Police Driving School at Hendon. The Metropolitan Police followed up in June 1969 with an order for a further sixty-one cars, plus twenty-seven examples of the 2000TC; then by December they had ordered another eighty-four Three Thousand Five models. Nevertheless, other police forces were perhaps surprisingly slow to follow suit, and the 3500's heyday as a motorway patrol car in the high-visibility 'jam sandwich' livery of the time did not come until the 1970s, when the availability of the manual-transmission 3500S gave a spur to sales. (There is more about police models generally in Chapter 12.)

Although a detailed breakdown of sales figures is not currently available, it is quite obvious that the introduction of the Three Thousand Five had a big impact on Rover's sales performance. The *Rover & Alvis News*, the company's in-house newspaper, proudly reported in its April 1969 issue that during 1968 'the Rover Company broke all previous car production and sales records'. Car production, at 36,673 units, was 5 per cent up on the 1967 figure (itself a record); car exports were 11 per cent up over 1967 and were again an all-time record; and car registrations in the UK were also higher than ever before. Rover were clearly on a high: similar record figures were calculated for their Land Rovers during 1968 as well.

For 1969, there were more records. The Rover financial year now ran from 1 October to 30 September, and the *Rover & Alvis News* for December 1969 reported that car exports during the relevant period for 1968–9 had hit another new high. Of the Three Thousand Five specifically, the newspaper noted that nearly 9,500 examples had been sold world-wide, of which 31 per cent were exported. At the time, the P6 assembly lines were working to their maximum capacity, building 900 4-cylinder and V8 cars every week.

EXPORT MODELS OF THE THREE THOUSAND FIVE

As usual, Rover launched its new model in the UK some months earlier than in other countries. This was partly to prevent unforeseen teething problems causing difficulties abroad: it was always easier to deal with such things at home. However, the delay also allowed production to get into its stride before the complications of overseas specifications were introduced. So for most of Rover's export territories, sales began early in 1969, while the special Federal 3500S for North America (see Chapter 9) did not enter production until June 1969.

In earlier times, export models had been less of a headache. It was simply a question of building cars with the steering wheel on the opposite side, maybe adding heavy-duty suspension, and sometimes fitting different light lenses or number-plate holders. However, the Three Thousand Five was introduced at a time when exporting cars was becoming a more and more difficult business. The mid- and late 1960s saw countries all round the world starting to introduce new safety regulations and to tighten up on lighting and other requirements. Then there was pressure from Rover's import branches – only doing their job of course – to modify the basic specification to give it more local appeal.

The major export markets for the Three Thousand Five were much the same as those for the 4-cylinder P6s – Western Europe and the countries of the British Commonwealth. An example was shown at the Tokyo Trade Fair in late 1969, but it is doubtful whether regular sales were ever established in Japan. For West Germany the 'Drei Tausend Fünf Hundert' had to have special interior door and window winder handles to reduce injuries to occupants in a collision. The German cars also had to have shrouded exterior door handles, similar to the ones that would become standard on all P6s from 1970, to prevent injury to pedestrians.

German cars, and those for France, Switzerland and some Scandinavian countries, all came with thin stainless-steel trim strips along the body sides as standard, exactly like those used on the North American 2000TC. Some European countries (West Germany among them once again) also took their Three Thousand Fives with Rostyle wheels, which certainly gave a sporting flavour but also added to manufacturing complication. Up to this point, Rover were buying in these wheels in a 15in size for the P5B models and in a 14in size with 5in rims for the North American 2000TC.

For the Three Thousand Five, a 14in size with a 5.5in rim width had to be added to the orders.

Then of course there had to be Three Thousand Fives prepared in CKD form for assembly overseas. There are more details about these in Chapter 13, but the special requirements of some territories led to further complications at Solihull. South Africa, for example, wanted its V8

Overseas variation: this early Swiss-market car shows the narrow trim strip that was not present on cars for the home market. It also has a dipping rear-view mirror.

Calling the car a Three Thousand Five meant that the name had to be translated for several overseas markets. These are the sales brochures for France (left) and Germany (right). Both cars have a trim strip on the body side, and the French one has Rostyle wheels – although in this case, they have been airbrushed onto the original photograph.

engines with a low compression to suit the 90-octane petrol that was typically available in that country; European cars had high-compression engines that needed 100-octane fuel, and carried red stickers on the rear window near the filler cap to remind owners of the fact.

EVOLUTION, 1968–70

There were relatively few changes to the Three Thousand Five models in their production run of just over two years. The earliest cars had commission numbers with an A suffix, and this switched to a B suffix in September 1968 for the 1969 models. Like the contemporary 4-cylinders, the 1969 models had through-flow ventilation with fixed rear quarter-lights, and a nylon steering column nacelle. A very small number of 1969 cars were fitted with the optional Coenan sunroof, which is described in Chapter 3.

The 1970-model Three Thousand Five reverted to the original ventilation system with opening rear quarter-lights, a change that was also made to the 4-cylinder cars. At the same time, a modified gearbox was introduced, with both the higher upchange speeds and the D-2-1 control system that *Autocar* magazine had called for in its April 1968 review of the Three Thousand Five. The 1970 models also took on the modified front valance panel that had been designed for the Federal 3500S, with twin cutout sections – although there was still only a single tow-hook instead of the Federal

The 1970 models had higher upchange speeds for the automatic gearbox, plus a new selector gate that gave D-2-1 control options.

BXC 997G was registered in September 1968 and had identity number 425-02717A. Although this press picture theoretically represented the 1969 specification, the car is actually a 1968 model with opening rear quarter-lights.

By the time of the 1970 season, Rover had begun to play tricks with registration numbers. CXC 81H did not exist, so the real identity of this car is unknown. At some stage, one of the plastic stoneguards for the optional auxiliary Lucas Square 8 lights had gone missing.

cars' twin lashing eyes. The Triplex glass roof and Hollandia sunroof (*see* Chapter 3) became available as options on home market cars, but would always be rare.

SELLING THE THREE THOUSAND FIVE, 1968–70

Rover were clearly able to sell all the Three Thousand Five models that they were able to produce, because press advertising in the 1968–70 period was almost universally focused on the 4-cylinder cars. This was the case from the very beginning, and even the Rover advertisement in the catalogue of the 1968 Earls Court show – which was where many Britons would have seen the Three Thousand Five for the first time – merely reminded customers that Rovers did not date, 'so your Rover 2000 will be the current model for years to come'.

Motor Sport for June 1968 did contain a rare advertisement for the model, perhaps because of its appeal to readers who favoured high-performance cars. This advertisement described the new model as 'the first car to seriously

challenge the Rover 2000 in five years'. It stressed the car's combination of performance and refinement: 'Power flows from its new 3,500cc engine as effortlessly as from a tidal wave. The road-holding attains new heights of achievement. The whole car acquires a character previously associated only with truly exotic machinery and unattainable sums of money.'

It went on to claim that:

> *Driving the Rover THREE THOUSAND FIVE is an uncommon experience. The car absolutely refuses to intrude. Acceleration, cornering, braking… all can be indulged in to an incredible extreme. Yet the driver remains unaware that any effort has been made. No exertion is demanded. None is noticeable from the car itself.*

The advert concluded by pointing out that the Three Thousand Five had all the features that had earned the P6 range its reputation for being a safe car, engineered to high standards and designed with attention to detail. Just as it was for the 4-cylinder cars in the late 1960s, 'A Rover is still a Rover'.

PAINT AND TRIM OPTIONS AND OPTIONAL EXTRAS

Paint and trim options for the Three Thousand Five were the same as those for the contemporary 4-cylinder models, and will be found in Chapter 3.

Optional extras for the Three Thousand Five were broadly the same as those for the contemporary 4-cylinder models, and are also listed in Chapter 3.

PRICES AND RIVALS, 1968–70

The totals shown here were basic UK showroom prices for Three Thousand Five models without extras. Also shown are the basic ex-factory cost and the purchase tax payable. Prices for the contemporary 4-cylinder models are shown in Chapter 3.

Prices

June 1968

Total	Ex-factory	Purchase tax
£1,790 19s 5d	£1,400	£390 19s 5d

December 1968

Total	Ex-factory	Purchase tax
£1,830 1s 5d	£1,400	£430 1s 5d

October 1969

Total	Ex-factory	Purchase tax
£1,895 6s 11d	£1,450	£445 6s 11d

February 1970

Total	Ex-factory	Purchase tax
£1,943 13s 1d	£1,487	£456 13s 1d

July 1970

Total	Ex-factory	Purchase tax
£1,999 15s 10d	£1,530	£469 15s 10d

Rivals

Rivals for the Three Thousand Five were the Daimler V8-250 (£1,826 15s 10d with automatic gearbox in October 1968) and the 2.8-litre version of the new Jaguar XJ6 (£1,999 5s in automatic form). Slightly cheaper, although hardly competitive, were the Ford Executive Automatic (a better-equipped Zodiac) at £1,677 14s 5d and the Austin 3-litre Automatic at £1,576 18s 11d. Competitors from abroad were the French Citroën ID20 Confort at £1,699; the German BMW 1800 at £1,678 3s; and the Italian Alfa Romeo 1750 (£1,898 6s 2d) and Lancia Flavia (£1,871 9s 5d). None of these, with the possible exception of the Jaguar, sold anything like as well as the Rover in the UK.

ROVER THREE THOUSAND FIVE, 1968–70

Engine
Type: V8 with light alloy block and cylinder heads
Cylinders: 8
Capacity: 3528cc
Bore and stroke: 88.9mm × 71.1mm
Five-bearing crankshaft
Single central camshaft, overhead valves
Carburettor: Two SU carburettors, type HS6 with 1.75in throats
Compression ratio: 10.5:1
Max. power: 184bhp SAE at 5,200rpm (144bhp DIN at 5,000rpm)
Max. torque: 226lb ft SAE at 3,000rpm (197lb ft DIN at 2,700rpm)
or
Compression ratio: 8.5:1
Max. power: 162bhp SAE at 5,000rpm
Max. torque: 210lb ft SAE at 3,000rpm

Transmission
Gearbox: Three-speed Borg Warner Type 35 automatic
Ratios: 1st 2.39:1,
                Intermediate: 1.45:
                Top: 1.00:1
                Reverse: 2.09:1
Axle ratio: 3.54:1

Suspension and Steering
Front: Independent suspension with transverse bottom links and leading upper links acting on coil springs mounted horizontally to the bulkhead; anti-roll bar; hydraulic telescopic dampers

Rear: Suspension with lower links and coil springs; De Dion tube incorporating sliding joint, with transverse location by fixed-length driveshafts and fore-and-aft location by Watts linkage; hydraulic telescopic dampers
Steering: Burman recirculating ball, worm-and-nut type with variable ratio
Tyres: 185 HR 14 radial
Wheels: Five-stud steel disc wheels with 14in diameter
Rim width: 5.5in

Brakes
Type: Disc brakes on all four wheels, mounted inboard at the rear; Girling discs and callipers; handbrake acting on rear discs; servo assistance standard
Size: 10.82in front, 10.69in rear

Dimensions
Wheelbase: 103.375in (2,626mm)
Overall length: 179.75in (4,565mm)
Overall width: 66in (1,676mm)
Overall height: 55.75in (1,416mm)
Track, front: 53.375in (1,356mm)
Track, rear: 51.75in (1,345mm)
Weight: 2,862lb (1,298kg)

Performance
Max speed: 118mph (190km/h) with 10.5:1 compression engine
                110mph (177km/h) with 8.5:1 compression engine
                0–60mph: 9.5sec with 10.5:1 compression engine
                11.0sec with 8.5:1 compression engine

CHAPTER EIGHT

GREAT IDEAS, 1964–1971

Rover pursued a policy of constant improvement for the P6 range during the 1960s, which was also a time when the company was exploring new ideas like never before. Inevitably, some proposals were investigated but not pursued: this was a time long before computer modelling, when the only real way of investigating an idea was to try it out in the metal.

In addition, there were those outside the Rover Company who saw great potential for developing the P6. So there were several aftermarket conversions and modifications that still have their own special interest today.

T4, THE GAS TURBINE P6, 1957–62

Rover had been experimenting with gas turbine propulsion for road cars ever since the late 1940s, their interest deriving from involvement with the Whittle jet aircraft engine during World War II. The first gas turbine-powered Rover had appeared in 1950, and there had been a few subsequent experimental models, but most of the Gas Turbine Department's work had been focused on the development and production of small stationary engines for industrial, aeronautical and maritime use.

The most promising of the experimental gas turbine cars had been called T3. Completed in 1956, this was a purpose-built glass-fibre-bodied two-seater coupé with a rear-mounted engine, four-wheel drive, disc brakes on all four wheels and a De Dion rear axle. It was primarily the work of Spen King, who at that stage was running the Gas Turbine Department, and he was very keen to take gas turbine propulsion on to the next stage, which was a proper production car. So when Robert Boyle called the first meetings in 1957 to discuss what would become the P6 project, he invited King along to see whether gas turbine propulsion might be a viable longer-term aim for the new car. King was sure that it was, and as a result a gas turbine-powered version of the P6 became an integral part of the car's development programme from very early on. The requirements of the gas turbine car fundamentally influenced the design of P6: 'I

The tenth P6 base unit was diverted to become the gas turbine car T4 (and was officially recorded as T4/10 for that reason). The nose design was unique, but the car was recognizably P6-based. It is now part of the Heritage Collection at the British Motor Museum, where this picture was taken. MATTHIAS V. D. ELBE/ WIKIMEDIA COMMONS

knew we would need a wide engine bay and a special suspension to fit round it,' remembered King, some thirty years later, 'and Gordon Bashford picked up on those ideas when he started work on P6.'

A small team working under Noel Penny began work on a suitable gas turbine engine, and by 1959 they were ready with the 2S/140 – 2S for the twin shafts and 140 for its 140bhp power output. This engine consisted of a centrifugal compressor backed by an inward-flow compressor turbine, plus a free-running power turbine that was geared directly to the transmission. There was also an integrally mounted heat exchanger, a new development that made the 2S/140 far less thirsty than earlier Rover gas turbines. Though it was therefore an important step forward, it proved to be very expensive to make. 'The materials we used in the heat exchanger weren't exotic,' recalled King. 'It was actually made of very thin 18/8 stainless steel, but we got hammered for the cost of rolling it so thin.'

Gordon Bashford and his principal assistant, Joe Brown, now set about designing the installation of the gas turbine engine. This proved quite challenging even though the front of the base unit had been designed to accommodate it. The exhaust of a gas turbine engine emerges at much greater volume than that of a petrol engine (though at lower velocity and temperature), and this presented some problems. Rover's earlier gas turbine cars had coped in various ways, but the only one with a front-mounted engine had been the T2, and the solution of taking the exhaust out through greatly enlarged chassis side-members had made that car disastrously heavy.

For the P6-based car, the solution was to run the exhaust duct down the transmission tunnel, but this introduced several complications that made the car more different from the petrol-engined P6 than its designers would have liked. With no room for a propshaft to the rear wheels, the car had to be re-engineered for front-wheel drive and, as the exhaust could not easily be routed past the De Dion rear axle, it also needed a new rear suspension. In practice, a swing-axle design was chosen.

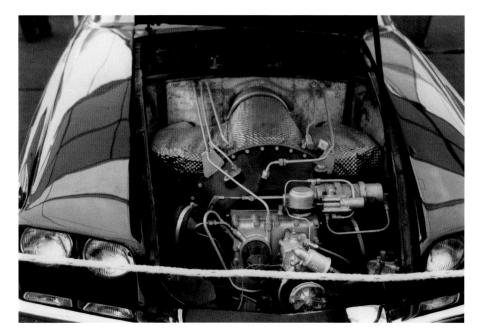

The wide engine bay needed to accommodate the gas turbine engine was the reason for the P6's unorthodox front suspension design. AUTHOR

The next problem was making room for a simple clutchless transaxle with a single forward and a reverse gear (there was no need for a clutch and multi-speed gearbox with the high-revving gas turbine engine). The engine had to be pushed forwards ahead of the front wheel centreline, and this in turn meant that the front of the base unit had to be rebuilt to accommodate the overhang. David Bache's stylists were asked to draw up a new front-end design, 'but the things they came up with were ridiculous,' remembered Spen King. 'In the end, I designed it myself.'

Mock-ups and models of the proposed styling for the gas turbine P6 were photographed for the record in February 1960, but it was not until 1961 that the Engineering Department allocated a prototype P6 base unit to the project. This was the tenth in the series, and the gas turbine P6 would be the fourth of Rover's gas turbine prototypes, which earned it the designation of T4. So the two figures were combined, and surviving records show the car recorded as T4/10.

T4 was completed in October 1961 and was registered on 1 November as 6427 WD, a Warwickshire number that made clear that Rover were not afraid to acknowledge parentage of this car when it went out on the roads. They even spelled the name Rover out in chromed letters across the blunt nose panel, and fitted hubcaps as used on the

P4 and P5 saloons of the day, complete with Viking ship logo in the centre. It was of no concern that the shape was close to that of the still secret P6; press and public had known for many years that Rover were experimenting with gas turbine propulsion, and would have assumed that this futuristic-looking car had been designed specifically with that in mind.

Early tests showed that T4 was capable of around 115mph (185km/h) and took about 8 seconds to reach 60mph from rest, although the latter was calculated from the time the car started moving; there were 3 seconds of turbine lag after pressing the accelerator, and this was a problem that would never be satisfactorily resolved. Fuel consumption was between 16 and 20mpg (14.2–17.7ltr/100km) overall, and was about 19mpg (14.9ltr100/km) at a steady 50mph (80km/h), running on the paraffin that would be the engine's normal diet.

Once Rover were happy that T4 was a viable prototype (not at all the same thing as a viable production model), they prepared to introduce it to the public. Meanwhile, Chrysler in the USA had been making progress with its own gas turbine engine, and in December 1961 had driven a 140bhp prototype installed in a Dodge Dart from New York to Los Angeles. This may well have been the reason that Rover chose to unveil T4 at the next available motor show in the USA.

So T4 was flown out to the USA in April 1962, accompanied by Rover's 1950 gas turbine car, JET 1, and the two were put on display at the New York Motor Show. T4 was also demonstrated to the press at the airport in Washington after its transatlantic journey. A month later, the car was taken to the Le Mans 24-hour race, where it did a demonstration lap of the 8-mile (13km) circuit before the race began, preceded by three motorcycle outriders. Then, in summer 1963, T4 did a demonstration run at Silverstone in the company of other Rover gas turbine cars, supposedly to celebrate the success of the Rover-BRM gas turbine racing car at Le Mans a few weeks earlier. And still there was no comment in print about the link between the gas turbine T4 and the forthcoming P6, even though several of the better-informed motoring writers must have been able to make the connection.

Rover's Publicity Department made optimistic noises to the press about how a gas turbine Rover might be in production within two to three years, and suggested that it might cost £3,000–£4,000 in the showrooms. That figure was roughly twice the cost of the company's own top-model 3-litre luxury saloon and more than half the cost of a £6,000 Rolls-Royce Silver Cloud II, which made the car far too expensive to be a realistic proposition. Besides, Rover were still struggling with development of the heat exchanger and with the need to reduce both fuel consumption and turbine lag.

Rover had other, higher priorities, and so the gas turbine P6 project lapsed. The prototype car still survives in the Heritage Collection at the British Motor Museum in Gaydon, and the 2S/140 engine was adapted to a variety of other uses that included early hovercraft, boats and the like. Rover built only one more gas turbine car, but the Rover-BRM first seen in 1963 was strictly a non-production vehicle built with the assistance of the BRM organization to demonstrate gas turbine power publicly at motor racing events. The Rover gas turbine expertise also went into a Leyland turbine truck prototype in 1970, but there was never any realistic chance of that becoming a production model.

THE TWO-DOOR SPORTS MODEL, 1958

As early as 1958, the Engineering Department was giving serious consideration to a two-door derivative of the P6 that would be built in parallel with the four-door saloon. No such car ever entered production, but the idea of a two-door P6 resurfaced several times over the next decade, and there may have been distant echoes of this original idea in the Rover TCZ and the Alvis GTS (see below).

Robert Boyle's progress report of 7 July 1958 informed the engineering board that the anticipated Sports P6 would be a two-door model, and that work on a quarter-scale model was expected to start immediately. Design and development would follow the saloon as closely as possible, but in view of the tight programme for the standard car it was extremely improbable that the Sports version would be ready for introduction at the same time as the saloon, which at that stage was expected to be ready for the 1961 Earls Court Motor Show.

In practice, the two-door Sports P6 seems to have disappeared from view soon after that brave statement of intent, and never became a formal development project. There is no evidence that a quarter-scale model was made either, and it is likely that the idea of a Sports model – two-door or otherwise – was absorbed into the plan for a high-performance P6 that led on to the 2000TC and the 6-cylinder P7.

The Styling Department did produce a sketch of a four-door 'P6/P7 sports model' in 1963, perhaps in pursuit of an idea for a four-door coupé along the lines of the P5 3-litre Coupé that had entered production about a year earlier. However, this was not taken any further.

PETROL INJECTION, 1964–71

From the middle of the 1960s, Rover put quite a lot of effort into work with petrol injection systems, focusing their efforts initially on the 2000's 4-cylinder engine and then switching to the 3.5-litre V8. A petrol-injected 3500 came close to production in 1971 but was cancelled a few months before production was expected to start.

There were several versions of the Brico injection system for the 4-cylinder cars. This one was pictured without its air cleaner to show the layout of the system. The car may be OXC 388D, which was run by Rover's David Bache.

Petrol injection systems were very uncommon at the start of the 1960s, and there were none in production for road cars in Britain, although Bosch in Germany and Bendix in the USA had viable systems. The Bosch system could even be bought in Britain, although it was confined to the top Mercedes-Benz models, where it delivered very worthwhile gains in power and responsiveness.

Rover were certainly aware of work being done on petrol injection in the UK during 1964, and Jack Swaine remembered in 1981 that petrol injection was considered as a longer-term option for the 5-cylinder engine at about that time. In fact, Lucas had a mechanical system that had been used in racing since the 1950s and was now being developed for road cars (it later appeared on the Triumph 2.5 PI). Much more interesting, from a technical point of view, was an electronic system that was under development by Associated Engineering of Leamington Spa.

Rover experimented with both types of system, beginning probably in 1965, but by the end of 1966 had discontinued work with the Lucas injection. They did pursue the AE system, however, development of which was transferred around this time to AE's Brico Engineering division – better known at the time as the makers of pistons, rings, valves and other components. Brico were based at Holbrook Lane in Coventry.

Gerry Beddoes was the AE engineer who led the petrol injection work, which was initially carried out at the company's Cawston R & D department near Rugby. He remembers that work had begun in early 1961, and that when an early mechanical system revealed insufficient accuracy of control, AE decided to develop their own solid-state electronic control system. He also remembers that they had some difficulty skirting around the very restrictive Bendix and Bosch patents.

Rover were of course not the only manufacturer to take an interest in the Brico injection work. When Associated Engineering arranged a press launch day for the new Brico injection system at Brands Hatch in October 1966, their injected Rover 2000 was accompanied by four other cars that had been developed by the R & D team at Cawston. Two were Ford Cortina GT models, one was a Jaguar Mk X saloon, and one was a Triumph 2000.

Rover had registered their 2000 as EXC 191C on 4 March 1965, and probably passed it straight on to Associated Engineering at Cawston. It was a Wedgwood Blue car with commission number 400-12389 and a single-carburettor engine that was numbered 400-16381. It became Cawston's primary Rover development car and, according to Mr A. Lowe, who worked for AE, was always known there as the 2000PI. He further remembered that Rover engineers designed the accelerator linkage but that the car was run by Associated Engineering as a development vehicle on Rover's behalf.

Over the next year or so, Rover's interest in the Brico injection system intensified. A further five development vehicles appeared, all of them based on 2000TC models because the different cylinder head gave better breathing than that of the single-carburettor engine.

Three of these five cars were built by Brico but run by Rover; one of them was allocated to Vic Rogers, who had oversight of the PI project at Rover, one went to E. G. (Ernie) Bacon, who was in charge of quality control, and the third went to chief styling engineer David Bache. This car was OXC 388D, painted bright red with Rostyle wheels and registered on 2 December 1966; it had commission number 415-01837B and engine number 415-05102A. The other two cars arrived a little later and were used by senior management at Associated Engineering. They were registered as LHP 397F and LHP 398F, 397 going to AE's chairman, Colin Hepworth, while 398 went to its chief engineer, John Rabson.

The AE system, meanwhile, was evolving. The original system had given an individually timed injection of fuel to each cylinder, but to work properly this required very precise manufacturing tolerances of the injectors, and there were problems in making up matched sets of injectors. So the

later system – probably used only on LHP 397F – had the injectors firing in pairs. The design of the injectors themselves and of the high-pressure fuel pump had also evolved, while the original design of trigger unit had been very complex, which made it hard to manufacture and sometimes unreliable, so a simpler one was developed.

The annual SMMT test day was held at the Goodwood racing circuit in 1967. It was then and still is an event where all the major manufacturers and importers in Britain make examples of their latest models available for invited members of the press to drive. Rover used it to draw press attention to their work with fuel injection, fielding examples of both Lucas and Brico injected cars for comparison with a standard 2000TC. The two injected cars proved to be much more tractable than the TC at low rpm but not significantly quicker.

A report in the Australian magazine *Modern Motor* suggests that examples of the injected 4-cylinder cars were still under development as late as January 1968, and Brico are known to have supplied workshop manuals for them to Rover in January 1969. However, during 1969, if not earlier, the focus of fuel injection development at Rover seems to have switched to the V8 engine. Brico were given or loaned several 1968-registered Three Thousand Five models, plus a pair of redundant P6B prototypes, JXC 807D and JXC 810D. JXC 807D arrived in 1968 with a four-speed manual gearbox, and Brico's Peter Wilson remembered in 2017 that, 'once equipped with the injection system it proved to be a real flyer and would wind its way up to and beyond the limit of the ribbon speedo – probably approaching 130mph [209km/h]!' JXC 810D followed in June 1969.

Meanwhile, Rover had started planning to introduce an injected P6B. When the question of a launch date surfaced at an executive directors' meeting on 27 May 1969, the aim was to introduce fuel injection as an option in spring 1970. In the

This was an early version of the injection system for the V8 engine. ROVER CO. LTD

late autumn of 1969 and over the winter, the favoured plan seems to be have been to introduce the manual gearbox and injected V8 engine together as a 'performance package'. This would be in addition to a manual-gearbox P6B with a carburettor V8 engine. There were delays, but then in March 1970 came a formal proposal to introduce the injected V8 model in spring 1971.

That plan remained intact for the rest of 1970, and at some point a decision was taken to call the new injected car a 3500EI, those letters presumably standing for Electronic Injection. It must have been around this time that the 'FI' cast into the inlet manifold of prototype engines was changed to 'EI'. In November 1970, photographs were taken of either mock-up or sample badges reading 3500EI, and documents in the Rover archives show that the model had been allocated its own commission number series: from 461... for home-market cars to 465... for left-hand-drive CKD export models.

Other Rover board papers of the time reveal that the intention was to produce a small run of cars for the UK market before rolling them out slowly to overseas markets as well. The USA is not specifically mentioned, but it is inconceivable that petrol injection would not have been planned for a market where other manufacturers were already using it to give the greater control of exhaust emissions that the latest regulations demanded.

There had now been a change in the programme. Whereas Brico had initially taken cars and converted them for Rover, they now began to supply injection systems that Rover themselves fitted to the cars. The first of these went into a batch of six cars in April and May 1970 that were numbered as 7035.PI.01A to 7035.PI.06 (the last four are recorded without a suffix letter). The prefix code suggests '1970, 3.5-litre, petrol injection', and John Carter, who was then in Rover engine development, remembers six injected cars of which some were lent to senior Rover managers for assessment.

These six cars were followed by a larger test batch with '999' identifying codes. The known examples were built between July and October 1970 and were numbered 999-00031M and 999-00042M, although Richard Twist, who was involved with the programme, suggested in 1987 that there were actually as many as fifty cars in all. At least one Brico injection system, plus some additional parts, also found their way to Morgan, where a Rover engineer was assisting with the engine installation of the Plus 8 model that was to use a Rover V8 engine.

One of the injected test cars achieved 135mph (217km/h) at MIRA, where it also burst a tyre on the high-speed banking and demolished twenty-four fence-posts and their railings – a feat which was a record at the time! Fortunately nobody was hurt, but the car (probably PXC 975J, with commission number 999-00035M) seems to have been written off. A rough estimate suggests that the engine would have been developing 175–180bhp to achieve that sort of speed in a P6B; standard cars had around 152bhp installed. It is not clear which gearbox was in use at the time.

Early and late V8 systems compared. The later system carried EI identification, in line with Rover's plans to produce a 3500EI model. ANDRIES GRIEDE

Pictured in July 1971, this injected V8 development car was being used at the time by A. B. Smith. NXC 22H was car number 7035.PI.03A and has the bonnet air scoops seen on the Federal 3500S. The sculpted wheels were also under consideration for a time. The picture dates from July 1971. ROVER CO. LTD

However, elsewhere, things had already started to go wrong. Aston Martin had boldly adopted the Brico injection system as an option for their DB6 Mk 2 cars in July 1969, but the system offered no additional top-end power and also proved troublesome in service. Many injected DB6s were converted to carburettors by the Aston Martin Service Department. By March 1971, Brico had decided to abandon their work with petrol injection, and sold it to Lucas, who would continue to develop it under their own name. Rover immediately entered talks with Lucas about the future of the injection project, but nothing further came of it.

So with the demise of the Brico project went the demise of Rover's plans for a petrol-injected P6B. It may well be that British Leyland was opposed to further work with Lucas, because Triumph were already using a Lucas petrol injection system and top management believed that the Rover did not need to spend resources on a similar development.

It seems reasonable to assume that Rover had been counting on the new 3500EI model to improve sales of the Federalized P6Bs in the USA. So the decision not to proceed with this model may well have been a factor in the decision implemented a few months later to withdraw Rover cars from North America altogether.

THE CONVERTIBLE PROTOTYPE, 1965

Even though Rover had not had an open model in production since 1948, there had been various experiments in the 1940s, 1950s and early 1960s with convertible versions of the P3, P4 and P5 saloons. It was therefore hardly surprising that the idea of a convertible P6 should also surface.

The train of events that led to the creation of a prototype had begun in April 1964, when technical director Peter Wilks received a visit from a proud Rover owner who had commissioned a London coachbuilder to turn his 3-litre saloon into a convertible. Wilks liked what he saw, and although a costing exercise showed that it would be too expensive for Rover to put a 3-litre convertible into production, he decided to look into the possibility of developing a convertible P6. It is not hard to see why: the sleek lines of the P6 were ideally suited to a convertible derivative.

As a first step, Wilks had the roof cut off a left-hand-drive 2000 saloon during June 1965. The rear doors were welded shut and the car was put through a series of torsional rig tests to assess the strength of the roofless structure. Presumably the results of these tests were encouraging, because Wilks then arranged for a 2000 from the Engineering Department fleet to be sent to the coachbuilder who had built the 3-litre convertible, FLM Panelcraft, for conversion into a feasibility prototype. The car chosen was a white right-hand-drive model with tan seats, numbered 400-10672B and registered as EXC 187C in July 1965.

Panelcraft removed the roof, relocated the B-pillars some 4in (10cm) further back to allow for longer front doors, and created a convertible top. Longer front doors were created by welding two door inners together and making up a new skin, and longer rear wings were made by welding an extension to the front end of the original panels. There were new front and rear side windows with special flat-topped quarter-lights, and the rear body sides were braced by diagonal struts concealed behind the side trim panels. Remarkably, there was no additional reinforcement of the base unit, although molten aluminium was poured into the windscreen pillars to reduce scuttle shake.

Panelcraft also modified all the seats. The front pair were mounted on new runners and now tipped forwards to give access to the rear. The rear seats were moved inwards to

LUCAS INJECTION

Did Rover take their interest in injection further with Lucas during 1971? No clear information is available, but a tantalizing hint surfaced in the mid-1990s when a derelict P6B was found in a field in Warwickshire. It was a real oddball – a Federal 3500S converted to RHD and manual gearbox that had originally been earmarked as a personal export for Canada. Most intriguing was a 3500S grille badge with it that had the words 'Lucas Injection' under the S.

The engine was a carburettor type, but had no identifying number. The car has been restored, but around a replacement base unit because the original had deteriorated so badly. Its full story – and that of any link to a Rover programme to use Lucas fuel injection – remains unknown.

make room for the hood mechanism in housings alongside the rear seat, and the rear centre armrest was made thinner to suit. A hood well replaced the rear parcel shelf, and a completely new fuel tank behind the seats made room for that hood well and extended back into the boot to restore the capacity lost in that operation. The hood itself was perhaps the least satisfactory of the changes. Although made of top-quality dark blue double-duck, lined with beige wool and provided with a matching dark blue hood bag, it had large blind rear quarters that seemed too heavy for the car.

EXC 187C was delivered back to Solihull in or around October 1965, and Peter Wilks took it on as his personal transport for a while. He seems to have racked up around 2,000 miles (3,200km) in it, but however much he may have liked it, he was not able to make a persuasive case for putting a convertible P6 into production. It would have been simply too expensive, and in any case Rover's production capacity was already at full stretch; the Engineering Department would be soon, too, as development began on the V8-engined P6.

So EXC 187C was sold, initially going to Anthony Cleminson, a director of the Triplex glass company. It was fitted with a heated windscreen (which Triplex had developed for the P6 rally cars), and was then repainted in Vauxhall Peacock Blue. The next owner, from 1972, was Chris Bramley, a Rover engineer who fitted a TC head to the car. He sold

it in 1976 to a Rover enthusiast who gave it the personal registration plate 666 HP and repainted it in Rover Corsica Blue. By 1980, it had deteriorated badly and, re-registered as CCN 346C, passed into the hands of the author. After a major structural rebuild, it then went to P6 enthusiast Bob Gardner in 1987, who returned it to near-original condition and added wire wheels. It still existed at the time of writing, in enthusiast ownership.

FLM Panelcraft built this convertible 2000 as a feasibility exercise for Rover. It is seen here in the ownership of a Triplex director, who had added a heated windscreen and a black sill stripe. TONY CLEMINSON

Extensively restored, the Panelcraft convertible now wears the wire wheels associated with the 2000TC models. The large and heavy convertible top was never one of its better features.
AUTHOR

THE DERRINGTON CONVERSION, c1965

The success of the Rover works 2000s in international rally events after summer 1964 (see Chapter 5) certainly inspired a number of privateers to try their hand at club level with tuned 2000s, and it is said that the British tuning company Derrington offered a bolt-on twin-carburettor conversion kit from around 1965 to aid their endeavours. Vic Derrington was among the first of the British tuners of the 1960s and provided power upgrades for many popular cars of the time from his premises at Kingston-on-Thames. However, details of the Rover conversion are lacking and, if it ever existed, it seems to have remained extremely rare.

THE GRABER CONVERSIONS, 1966–68

After Rover absorbed Alvis in 1965, a small number of P6s were turned into convertibles and coupés by the Swiss coachbuilder Hermann Graber, of Wichtrach. Graber had strong links with Alvis. He had made his reputation by building cabriolet bodies, and focused largely on British-built chassis after World War II. In the early 1950s he held an Alvis franchise and built a number of special bodies on the company's chassis. One of his designs became standard on the 3-litre Alvis models that were in production during 1965, although by this stage it was actually being built by Park Ward in Britain and not by Graber himself in Switzerland.

Graber had shown an interest in building on Rover chassis as well, and supposedly acquired distribution rights for the marque – although that is not borne out by any entries in Rover's published lists of dealers and distributors. In 1948, the coachbuilder had bodied a Rover P3 75 as a cabriolet, and in 1963 he had turned a 3-litre saloon into a convertible. Nevertheless, it seems probable that Graber's flurry of activity with Rover cars in the mid-1960s can be attributed to Rover's acquisition of Alvis.

One way or the other, Graber built at least six special cars based on P6 or P6B models between 1966 and 1968. The known examples were two convertibles on the 2000, three coupés based on the 2000TC, and one coupé based on the Three Thousand Five.

1966: the Convertibles

In the period 1964–65, Peter Wilks at Rover was taking an interest in the possibility of a Rover 2000 convertible, and it may well be that he commissioned Graber to build a pair of convertible cars as feasibility prototypes. The coincidence of timing with his commission of the convertible prototype from FLM Panelcraft in London seems too great not to be no more than that, but so far no clear evidence has come to light.

Swiss coachbuilders were always pre-eminent in the business of convertible coachwork, and the lines of this conversion by Hermann Graber – a cabriolet in the coachbuilder's description – make the point admirably.
JOHN DIVALL

EXPERIMENTAL DEVELOPMENT

Close-Ratio Gearbox
Rover were aware that the rival Triumph 2000 was slightly quicker than their own 2000 in standard form, and did some development work in the early years with close-ratio gearboxes, which had higher intermediate ratios.

Diesel Engine
One car – possibly one of the early FLK-registered 2000s – was given a Land Rover diesel engine. As the engine was too tall to fit into the standard engine bay, the bonnet was modified and sported a distinctive bulge. With only 62bhp, the car must have been slow – and it was probably noisy as well. Details of the project are sparse, but the minutes of an executive directors' meeting on 25 February 1964 reveal that the project was live at that stage and that managing director William Martin-Hurst wanted it to continue. The project was eventually dropped, and the car passed to Bill Wale, who was foreman of the Land Rover experimental shop.

Overdrive
Work was also done on an overdrive for the P6 in 1964–65. The probable impetus for this development was the fact that the rival Triumph 2000 came with an overdrive – although of course overdrive had been a feature of late Rover P4 models and was still available for the P5 3-litre at the time. A few scraps of information are available. At an executive directors' meeting on 16 October 1964, Peter Wilks said that work on an overdrive was in progress, and on 4 May 1965 the executive directors were told that Rover might need to use an AT overdrive unit at short notice. However, the Engineering Department was very busy in this period, not least with the arrival of the new V8 engine, and stretched resources probably led to overdrive becoming a casualty.

Former test engineer Brian Terry remembers one development car fitted with an overdrive gearbox, possibly in tandem with the 4.3:1 final drive that had been developed originally for the 2000 Automatic and the rally cars. Lyn Thomas recalls that the overdrive was a Laycock J-type, and that it was mounted to the differential rather than to the gearbox. He also remembers that vibration was a problem.

Safety Seats
In the mid-1960s, there were trials with proprietary Cox Safety Seats that had inertia-reel belts incorporated within them. They were fitted to development car FXC 534C (400-17412B), which was written off in crash testing, and were modified to take Rover's own 'ET' head restraints.

It is possible that the plan was to use these seats in a two-door car, such as the P6-based Alvis GTS (see below); it is also possible that they contributed to the development of the special seats for the Range Rover when it was under development in the later 1960s, as these had integral belts (although they were initially static types). One way or the other, the integral-belt system was not carried over to a production P6, and surviving pictures make clear that the seats were very bulky and would have rendered rear legroom almost non-existent.

Supercharging
Brian Terry also remembers that one development 2000 was fitted with a Shorrock supercharger, obviously in pursuit of more performance. The Shorrock supercharger was first developed in the 1930s and was a popular bolt-on performance conversion during the 1950s and 1960s. At the time of Rover's interest, the superchargers were distributed in Britain by the London-based Allard Motor Company.

Suspension Experiments
Around 1964, Rover were also experimenting with different front suspension layouts. A double-wishbone type was built into two of the P7 prototypes (see Chapter 4), and one 2000 development car was given adjustable front suspension links. This was 400-02549A (AXC 180B), which dated from April 1964 and seems to have been used for cosmetic development as well. It still survived in 2011, and had a number of optional extras as well as a non-standard two-tone colour scheme of White with a Copperleaf Red roof.

The lines of the P6 certainly lent themselves to open coachwork, and this view of the Graber cabriolet shows just how good such a car could look. JOHN DIVALL

Subtly different from the earlier 2000TC coupé, this car served as transport for Frau Graber for many years. UNKNOWN

Two left-hand-drive 1966-model Rover 2000s were shipped out to Switzerland on 19 October 1965, both having left the production lines on 12 October. They had chassis numbers 403-06713C and 403-06717C. Both were painted Zircon Blue, and were part of a batch of six (403-06712C to 403-06717C) that went to E. Fehlmann & Co. in Zurich, the main distributor for the German-speaking areas of Switzerland. They acquired job numbers 788 and 789 respectively when they went to Graber, who turned them into convertibles.

Pictured during setting-up for the Geneva Show, this was Graber's 2000TC coupé, another sleek and elegant piece of work from the Swiss coachbuilder. CLASSIC & SPORTS CAR ARCHIVE

Nothing is known of the fate of the second car, but 403-06713C appeared on the Graber stand at the 1966 Geneva Show. It was painted metallic green and had a tan hood and interior, as usual with Graber's characteristic fluted leather. It rated a brief mention and a picture in *Autocar* for 18 March 1966. In 1967, it was sold to a customer in Switzerland, and it remained in his family until 2004. The car was then bought by a Swiss enthusiast who has carried out a sympathetic restoration.

1967: the 2000TC Coupés

Graber's experience with the two convertible 2000s may well have inspired him to turn his hand to creating a coupé from the P6. He would certainly have become aware of Rover's experiment with the Zagato-bodied coupé, and quite possibly believed he could come up with a more cost-effective design that stood a better chance of entering volume production. So during 1967, the Swiss coachbuilder constructed three fixed-head coupés, in each case based on a Rover 2000TC, which at that stage was the performance model of the P6 range.

It is not clear which of these was built first, although it seems likely that the one shown on the Graber stand at the 1967 Geneva Show was the earliest. That car was probably numbered 418-01576A, which started out as a white example that was delivered to the importer Fehlmann; it was built on 5 July 1966 and left Solihull on 13 July. As shown

The design of the rear interior was very neat. This picture also shows the pleated seats characteristic of Graber at the time. UNKNOWN

This later Graber coupé had a distinctive notch in the bonnet. RICHARD LEZER

at Geneva, it was painted in Pearl Silver and upholstered in tan leather (according to *Autocar* for 16 March 1967); it also had wire wheels. The Swiss Car Register believes it has now been scrapped.

Possibly the second of the Graber 2000TC coupés was painted in dark metallic green, had standard steel wheels, and was used for many years by Graber's wife. After her death, it passed to a Dutch Rover dealer and then, supposedly in a dilapidated state, it went on to an enthusiast in Amsterdam towards the end of the 1990s. Another story says it passed to a German collector. At the time of writing, it still survives, in enthusiast ownership.

There was then a third car, again painted silver. This was 418-07300B, built as a Burnt Grey saloon in October 1967 and shipped to Graber's usual supplier, Fehlmann in Zurich.

This retained standard steel wheels but was distinguished by a modified bonnet. It was certainly displayed at an international motor show, possibly Geneva in March 1968. This car also survives in enthusiast hands, and at the time of writing was under restoration.

1968: the V8 Coupé

Graber's last known Rover conversion was another coupé, this time based on the V8-engined Three Thousand Five model. It was another left-hand-drive car, but the design had evolved from that of the coachbuilder's 2000TCs. The roof line was lower and flatter, there were different body-side trims, and the car had the Rostyle wheels available on export models but not in the UK.

Graber's 3500 coupé had a distinctive additional chrome strip above the model badge. UNKNOWN

There are pictures of this car at what appear to be the Paris and Turin motor shows, perhaps in the second half of 1968. It seems probable that Graber would have displayed it at the company's home show of Geneva in about March 1969, but there is no definite evidence of this. Unfortunately, no more information is available, and the car has disappeared without trace.

THE P6BS, 1967

In the mid-1960s, Rover's acquisition of the ex-Buick V8 engine opened up several new possibilities. Spen King and Gordon Bashford believed it would make an excellent basis for a high-performance sports car and, working without any official approval or budget, they drew one up in their spare time. With a V8 engine mounted amidships just behind the seats, a fixed roof and many mechanical elements from the production P6 saloons, the single prototype was a highly impressive machine. King and Bashford called it the BS (Buick Special).

No decision on its future had been made by the time the new P6B 3500 was due to be launched, but Rover lent it to some motoring magazines shortly before the launch. By this time, it had been renamed P6BS to link it more closely with the forthcoming new model and to whet the appetite of the public for the new V8-engined saloon. The car was also shipped over to the USA, where it was shown at the New York International Motor Show under the name of the Leyland GE, those letters standing for Group Experimental.

Reactions to the prototype persuaded Rover to think in terms of a production derivative, which they called the P9. David Bache designed a sleek new body for it, and although the full-size styling mock-up carried Rover badges, there was talk of releasing it with the badges of Rover's Alvis subsidiary, where production of the sporting 3-litre grand tourer had just ended.

However, Jaguar's Sir William Lyons feared it would harm sales of his E-type, while Triumph's George Turnbull had similar concerns about his company's forthcoming Stag grand tourer. So in 1969, Rover were instructed to stop work on it. The P6BS prototype and a one-eighth scale styling model for the P9 have both survived, and belong to the British Motor Museum at Gaydon.

One or two things gave away the P6BS's purpose as an experimental test-bed, and the transparent 'bubble' over the carburettors was one of them! BRUCE MCWILLIAMS

The P6BS had excellent proportions, even though it was only really an experimental try-out.

THE ESTATE CARS, 1967–75

Triumph's introduction of an estate version of its 2000 saloon in 1965 tapped into a waiting market, and this may well have been the inspiration behind FLM Panelcraft's idea of creating a Rover 2000 estate. This specialist London coachbuilder already had links with Rover through their work on the 2000 convertible, and asked for a car that they could turn into a prototype. So on 16 May 1967, an early left-hand-drive 2000TC (number 418-00050A) changed hands. It had been registered by Rover as KXC 142D on 16 February 1966.

By the time it emerged from the Panelcraft workshops towards the end of the year, it had been converted to right-hand drive and had become the prototype of what Panelcraft called the Rover Estoura (even though the first sales catalogue spelled the name as 'Estourer'). That name was presumably a combination of 'estate' and 'tourer', although it never really caught on. *Autocar* magazine of 21 December 1966 carried an article about it, and this was probably the first public announcement of the conversion.

This first prototype was not pretty. The roof line sloped too steeply towards the rear, giving the car a very odd appearance and restricting the height of the tailgate opening. David McMullan and Jeff Smith of Crayford, another specialist coachbuilder in the London area, were friendly with 'Nobby' (H. S.) Fry, one of the directors of Panelcraft, and took him to task about its lines. In an email to the author some years ago, McMullan recalled a long evening session with copious amounts of whisky, and that in the end, Fry conceded that the design was not ideal. Robin Wayne, who bought the car from Panelcraft, was in agreement with that. He recalled in a letter to *Thoroughbred & Classic Cars* magazine in November 1981 that, 'due to its added weight it was extremely heavy at the rear end; hence with four people on board the rear wheels would rub against the body... it also leaked where the conversion work had been carried out, but being the prototype one had to suffer such discomforts'.

So the estate was redesigned with a flatter roof that increased the height of the tailgate aperture by a couple of inches. Like the original car, it had a specially designed fuel tank that fitted under the floor and was filled from a filler in the left-hand rear wing; this allowed for a flat rear floor,

Early estates like this one had concealed hinges at the top of the tailgate. FLM PANELCRAFT

The prototype estate had a sharply sloping roof, which was not ideal. CRAYFORD CONVERTIBLE CAR CLUB

This was almost certainly the first 'production' Panelcraft estate, after the disastrously styled 2000TC prototype. It was based on a Three Thousand Five. FLM PANELCRAFT

The tailgate on the Panelcraft estates lifted to give access to a raised floor above the relocated fuel tank and spare wheel. FLM PANELCRAFT

and the rear seat back was arranged to fold forwards in typical estate-car fashion. The full load capacity was now claimed to be 49.5cu ft (1,400ltr). During 1968, Rover examined a car remembered as 'the prototype' (it was probably a 3500-based model registered as NHO 757F) and granted approval for the conversion, agreeing to honour the standard warranty for cars so converted. Panelcraft also secured approval from the Ministry of Transport.

This production design was rather attractive. It had a custom-made aluminium roof panel (which was always trimmed with vinyl) and a one-piece tailgate that was supported by a 'star wheel' prop when open. The top of the tailgate was made flush with the roof, so giving a little extra height to the aperture when it was open, and the hinges were concealed. By April 1969, production of the estates had begun, and at that year's Earls Court Motor Show, a Three Thousand Five estate conversion appeared on the Crayford stand. (The Panelcraft version of the story is that they had come to a marketing agreement with Crayford but, as explained later, there are other versions of the story!)

The first franchise holder was Hurst Park Automobiles, of East Molesey in Surrey – a Rover specialist appropriately sited in the heart of London's stockbroker belt, which was where Panelcraft probably thought most sales were likely to be made. Hurst Park charged customers £680 plus purchase tax for the conversion, which could be carried out on a new car or on a customer's existing vehicle. Then, not long after the Series II P6s went on sale, the prestigious London-based H. R. Owen dealership took on a franchise (or perhaps became the sole franchisee). Much against Panelcraft's wishes, Owen fitted all the estates they sold with an electric fuel pump to overcome problems with vapour locks in the fuel system.

Both franchisees offered a number of optional extras. One was a Coenan sliding metal sunroof – for which Panelcraft were the sole UK agents – although the alternative Webasto folding type was considerably cheaper. The estates could be ordered with electric window lifts, rear seatbelts, a dog guard and a rubber mat for the rear load area. The later Owen cars also had two door-mounted mirrors as standard, though these were proprietary round types and not the same as the ones Rover offered from 1973.

As time went on, so the design of the estate was further modified. The original concealed tailgate hinges were changed for a pair of externally-mounted hinges that allowed the tailgate to open even wider, and twin gas struts replaced the single manually operated type used on the first cars. Later cars also had a Triplex Hotline heated rear window and a rear wash-wipe, although it is not clear if these items were exclusive to the cars sold through H. R. Owen. There were undoubtedly some special orders, too, one being a 3500 with a specially raised roof line (this was registered as 2299 KM at one stage).

Unfortunately, the story of the Rover estates has been clouded over the years by a certain amount of disagreement about the facts. It is not at all clear whether Panelcraft redrew the original design or Crayford did it for them. Nobby Fry claimed in a 1980 letter to the author that 'the

Later estates were marketed as the **H. R. Owen** conversion, and the dealer's number plate was used on this publicity picture.

design was between myself and Mr John Trowell, our works manager'. However, Crayford's David McMullan insists (in his book *The Crayford Story*) that 'this was a Crayford design and built by FLM Panelcraft's Fulham based works'. He adds that the first 100 examples were sold as Crayfords.

Crayford certainly did give the impression that the design was theirs, and a very early sales leaflet that they issued contains pictures of the prototype KXC 142D – which they had definitely not designed – and makes no mention of Panelcraft at all. There is an uncorroborated story that the marketing agreement between Panelcraft and Crayford was cancelled when Panelcraft discovered that Crayford had been putting their own motifs on the cars they sold. All this may explain why Panelcraft began to add a plastic tailgate badge, probably around 1970, describing the car as an 'Estoura, by FLM Panelcraft, London'.

Whatever the truth of all this, it does appear that Crayford continued to build examples, probably in tandem with Panelcraft. A further complication is that H. R. Owen marketed the later cars as the Owen Conversion – which was perhaps stretching credibility a bit far.

Panelcraft's records for the construction of these estates were probably destroyed many years ago, and no exact production figures survive. 'We did about 160 of these on 2000 and 3500 vehicles,' claimed Nobby Fry in 1980, and the discovery of the number 157 chalked inside the panels of one car tends to support this. By contrast, David McMullan claims in his book that there were 400 examples of the Rover estate, while Rover enthusiasts claimed to have traced at least 184

Some estates carried a plastic badge claiming them as an FLM Panelcraft conversion, but these were far from universal. AUTHOR

cars by 2011. For the moment, a precise production figure remains elusive, but the relatively small number of survivors is a reminder that these cars were always rare.

THE TCZ COUPÉ, 1966

There were probably two factors that steered Rover towards looking at a two-door coupé based on the P6. The first was that the P6 was developing as a high-performance car, with the introduction of the TC (twin-carburettor) model in 1966 and the planned introduction of the 3.5-litre V8 engine in 1968. The second was Rover's 1965 purchase

By the time the TCZ was presented in public, it had been given Rostyle wheels that were painted to match the coachwork. ROVER CO. LTD

The dashboard of the TCZ was a mixture of Rover and Zagato elements, which worked well. AUTHOR

of Alvis and the associated need to develop a new model to replace the existing Alvis grand tourers.

Rover's first try at a coupé design was probably planned in late 1965. It appears to have been David Bache who proposed commissioning an outside design consultancy, and he settled on Carrozzeria Zagato of Milan. Zagato was an old-established Italian company, and Bache had met its current head, Gianni Zagato, at various motor shows and had admired his work.

The car shipped out to Zagato in 1966 was one of the redundant 2000S twin-carburettor pilot-build cars, number 410-00010A and registered FXC 206C. It probably returned to Solihull in 1967 and was certainly there by the beginning of October that year when Zagato himself visited Bache's styling studio.

Zagato constructed a new two-door fastback coupé body for the car, similar in many respects to his contemporary designs for Lancia and others. In order to get a lower bonnet line, he replaced the twin SU carburettors with less bulky Dellorto items mounted horizontally on a custom-made manifold. The body was 5in (127mm) lower than the P6 saloon type, and the car was 9in (229mm) shorter to suit its squared-off tail. The sloping tail window was designed as a hatchback with no outside handle but an electric motor operated from inside that raised it by a few inches to give access to a release handle inside – or to give through-flow ventilation while driving. As initially made, it had standard P6 steel wheels and carried no badges except for the Rover Viking motif on the grille. An attractive feature was blacked-out horizontal grille surfaces, which made the bright leading edges stand out more; it was an idea that Bache would later adapt for Rover.

Inside the car, Zagato had retained some P6 elements, such as the centre console, the drop-down oddments lockers and the neat dashboard switches, but had fitted a new cowled instrument binnacle with main dials by Smith's, as used in the contemporary Humber Sceptre. The seats, too, were of a special design.

If all had gone according to plan, the car would have appeared in a James Bond film that was in the planning stages. Tony Poole from the Styling Department at Solihull remembered that some sort of deal had been done with the film makers and that the film in question was to be *On Her Majesty's Secret Service*. The team's plan to make this had already been postponed once because of a dispute over the use of the rights to the story, and in the event *Thunderball* became the next 007 film in the series. *On Her Majesty's Secret Service* was rescheduled to follow that, but a warm winter in Switzerland, where the film was to be shot amid typical snow in early 1966, led to it being postponed yet again in favour of *You Only Live Twice*.

So the car never did appear in a film. Instead, it remained at Solihull and was not seen again until the October 1967 Earls Court Motor Show, when it appeared on the Carrozzeria Zagato stand. By this stage it had been slightly modified and was wearing Rostyle wheels with white-painted sections (to match the bodywork), Zagato's 'Z' logo on each front wing, and 'TCZ' badges front and rear. The car had worn one of the experimental grille badges with red and white sails (see Chapter 2) for many years, and this had almost certainly been fitted for the 1967 show stand as well.

However, any thoughts that Rover might have had of turning the design into a production car had clearly been abandoned. After the show, the car returned to the Zagato workshops in Italy, where its rear seat was modified. It then returned to Britain and went to Rover's Seagrave Road service depot in London for a thorough check-over. It was fitted with a new engine and other items were renewed or replaced, while some of the short cuts that Zagato had taken in carrying out the conversion (which was, after all, a design exercise) were rectified.

The job of turning it from a show car into a useable road car was given to Neil Murray, then a tester at Seagrave Road, who recalled the episode in a letter to *Sporting Cars* magazine that was published in their December 1982/January 1983 issue.

When it arrived, we soon found its beauty was only skin deep. It was a typical coachbuilder's exercise and not meant to be used… to shorten the base unit, the tail was cut off just behind the rear suspension upper radius arm mountings with what may have been a cold chisel and left unfinished… The fuel tank was a joke: it fitted into the wing space behind the rear wheel arch, and was twice as high as the standard one but fitted with standard sender unit which meant the gauge indicated 'full' with the tank half full… The

joints were butted instead of properly flanged and leaked like a sieve. We did our best with it.

Some time in 1968 or 1969, the TCZ was then sold to an Englishman. The asking price has been reported as £3,000, which compares with under £1,600 for a standard Rover 2000TC. The car was re-registered as PBC 2G, a number that made it appear newer than it really was; the G suffix was

This artwork for the TCZ was produced in early 1967 by Tony Poole in the Styling Department, and its purpose may have been to suggest how the car could be dressed up for motor shows later that year. The wire wheels and slatted front end with concealed headlamps were never transferred to the actual car. ROVER CO. LTD

The TCZ was an attractive car from all angles, although it embodied styling themes seen in several other Zagato cars of the period. AUTHOR

The TCZ as it survives today, reunited with its original registration number and carefully restored. The picture was taken at the prestigious Salon Privé event in 2014. NEWSPRESS

current in 1968–1969 and the car must have been declared new by Rover for such an allocation to be made. A change of ownership in the early 1970s brought another number (SNP 12), and then another change of ownership saw it re-registered as YNP 851G. At this stage, it was also given a late 2000TC engine with the smaller HIF6 carburettors. The car was fully restored in the early 1980s and still survives in the hands of a Zagato enthusiast, now reunited with its original registration number of FXC 206C.

THE ALVIS GTS, 1966–67

David Bache's own design for a two-door fastback coupé

David Bache's design for the Alvis GTS was built up as a full-size clay model in the Rover styling studio. ROVER CO. LTD

was probably in his head towards the end of 1965, and by January 1966 had been translated into a full-scale mock-up in the Rover styling studio. Renderings of the design and photographs of the mock-up make clear that this car was always intended to become the Alvis GTS.

Rover had bought out the old Alvis company during 1965, largely because its military vehicles promised a valuable synergy with the large number of Land Rovers that Solihull was selling to military users, but of course Alvis was also a long-standing maker of high-quality sporting cars. By 1965, its 3-litre TF range was nearing the end of its production, and Bache seems to have persuaded his fellow directors at Rover that he should design its replacement. At the back of his mind was the idea that his new coupé might enter production with the new V8 engine that was then in the planning stages at Solihull, and photographs of the mock-up were catalogued at Rover with the description of 'V8 P7'. (As Chapter 4 explains, the P7 designation was then being used fairly freely and was associated with the V8 engine before the P6B project designation was established.)

Bache's fastback coupé was very different indeed from the Zagato design, with several echoes of the P6 itself and a front end that incorporated rectangular headlamp units similar to those then under consideration for the eventual V8-engined saloon. The car was an imposing grand tourer rather than a lightweight sporting design like the Zagato coupé, and its heavy-skirted look earned it the nickname of 'Gladys' within the Rover Company.

The full-size mock-up was translated into a running proto-type in late 1966, and yet again one of the redundant 2000S pilot-production cars became the donor; this time it was 410-00012A, which seems not to have been registered when it was built in November 1965. At this stage, only Buick-built V8 engines were available at Rover and none could be spared for this project, so the car retained its original 4-cyl-inder twin-carburettor engine. Bache arranged for the new bodywork to be constructed by the Radford coachbuilding company in Hammersmith in London. By that stage, Radford were concentrating on customized Minis, although they had earlier been best known for 'Countryman' conversions of Rolls-Royce and Bentley saloons. The company was also going through a period of financial difficulty (it went into voluntary liquidation in September 1966 and was re-established in October 1967) so was probably very grateful for the business from Rover.

Bache took a keen interest in the construction of that prototype. Maureen Hill, who was his PA at the time, remembered many years later that, 'David was perhaps a bit naughty about that. He spent a lot of time down at Radford's and he was hardly ever in his office in that period.' The car that emerged was registered as PXC 200E on 25 January 1967, and the official entry in the Soli-hull borough registration records describes it as a Rover. Painted dark metallic grey and set off by wire wheels and chrome edg-ing on the lower body, it was an imposing-looking machine although from some angles there was an undeniable heaviness about its looks.

Unfortunately, it had arrived at an inauspicious time. Rover were just in the process of merging into the Leyland Group, and Spen King's BS mid-engined sports car concept had been grabbing all the attention as a likely Alvis product. So the GTS had probably been sidelined by summer 1967. David Bache's wife, Doreen, used it for a while and in the late 1980s Bache had some minor restoration work done on it. It subsequently passed to the collection of the British Motor Industry Heritage Trust (now the British Motor Museum),

The Alvis GTS, known as 'Gladys', was built by Radford in London from a redundant 2000S. It was pictured here in the Rover styling studio. ROVER CO. LTD

Some commentators have detected American influence on the shape of the Alvis GTS, which was registered for the road in January 1967. ROVER CO. LTD

**The Chapron landaulet was built several years
after the P6 went out of production, but is
nevertheless worthy of interest as a product
of one of France's great coachbuilders.**

and is displayed there with Rover badging on the tail – which
may have been added when Bache had that restoration work
done.

However, the GTS was not a complete dead end in the
story of the Rover P6. Several of its features later appeared
on production cars: the box-pleated seats, four-dial instrument panel and long armrests with stowage bins below them
would appear on the Federal 3500S in 1969; and the twin
power bulges in the bonnet would arrive on other P6 models
in 1970.

THE CHAPRON LANDAULET, 1985

The distinguished French coachbuilder Henri Chapron had
created an extremely elegant cabriolet from a Rover 3-litre
in 1961, but was not asked to work on a P6 until long after
the model had gone out of production. By this stage, the
company was being run by Chapron's widow and was near
the end of its existence, and the landaulet that it created in
1985 must have been among its last commissions.

The car was commissioned by Alain Bernardin, owner and
founder of the Crazy Horse Saloon on the Avenue George
V, the most famous striptease nightclub in Paris. It was based
on a 1971 Monza Red 3500 from which the rear window
and most of the roof were removed to create a landaulet
for Bernardin's marriage to one of his dancers. The car was
repainted in Jaguar Midnight Blue, and all Rover emblems and
badges were either removed or painted black. The original
seats, apparently in Sandalwood leather, were retained and
a white convertible top was installed.

This car was kept in storage after Bernardin's wedding and
was partly dismantled in preparation for a repaint. In practice, it remained in storage until 2007, when it was partly
reassembled for that year's big Rétromobile classic car show
in Paris. The plan then was for its new owner to carry out
a full restoration.

CHAPTER NINE

THE NADA AND FEDERAL CARS

Rover had never really become an established name in North America. Inspired by the flurry of interest there in British cars during the late 1940s, the company had begun to ship both cars and Land Rovers across the Atlantic in 1950, piggy-backing on the sales network set up by the Rootes Organisation. But sales were small; buying a Rover or a Land Rover was more of a statement than a mere choice of automobile, and the typical US buyer was likely to be an intellectual and an Anglophile. He or she also had to be prepared to live with a vehicle for which neither spare parts nor expertise were readily available. Rover franchised dealers were few and far between, and a breakdown on a long-distance journey could result in a recovery operation that involved hundreds of miles and was followed by a wait of several weeks for new parts.

Rover did try to get greater control of the situation from 1958, when they established their own North American operation – the Rover Company of North America – with headquarters in the Canadian city of Toronto and a branch office in New Jersey. RCNA was run by F. Gordon Munro, a Briton, but it struggled to improve Rover's sales and dealer network in North America. The country was simply too vast, and to establish an operation that could compete with those of the established domestic manufacturers like Ford and General Motors would have demanded an enormous investment. Rover had a few hundred dealers, who all sold other makes as well; a company like GM had nearer 5,000 dedicated outlets.

There was a secondary problem, too. Throughout most of the 1950s, British saloon cars of all types had sold in only penny numbers, and the real interest among American buyers lay in British sports cars. Rover did not have any sports cars in production, but only saloon models. The P4 saloons were staid and upright, without the interior space of the typical US domestic saloon, and the P5s that followed in 1958 were scarcely better, if a little more modern in approach. As for the Land Rover, most Americans would

automatically buy a Jeep if they wanted a small working vehicle.

After the death of Maurice Wilks in 1962, William Martin-Hurst became Rover's managing director, and he took a careful look at the company's performance in North America. Well aware that Rover were preparing the new P6 saloon for release in 1963, Martin-Hurst became convinced that this new model might provide a turnaround in Rover's North American fortunes. One thing that probably influenced his thinking was that the late 1950s had seen a surge of US interest in European saloon cars generally; in fact it had been so marked that the US domestic manufacturers had begun to build a number of 'downsized' or 'compact' models to compete with these European imports. Martin-Hurst must have reasoned that Rover could and should see if they could benefit from that.

It appears that Martin-Hurst and Munro did not get on well, and one of the new managing director's first moves was to replace Munro at RCNA. In his place came Bruce McWilliams, an Anglophile with an English wife who had spent time with both the American Mercedes-Benz operation and with domestic manufacturer Studebaker-Packard. The brief that McWilliams received from Martin-Hurst was simply to improve Rover's penetration of the US market in whatever way he could, bearing in mind that there would be an exciting new product coming off the lines very soon.

McWilliams eagerly accepted the challenge, and one of his earliest moves was to suggest that Rover should improve their sales of Land Rovers in the USA by fitting them with an American-made V8 engine to improve their performance. The end result of that suggestion was Rover's acquisition of the Buick V8 engine in 1965 – a story told in more detail in Chapter 6. Mrs McWilliams – 'Jimmy' to her friends – was meanwhile installed as the head of RCNA public relations, and quickly launched a highly imaginative publicity campaign that got the Rover name noticed far more than it ever had

Rover promoted the Icelert system quite heavily in North America, arguing that it made an important contribution to safety. This North American publicity picture probably shows a prototype installation, on a 'shark's-tooth' single-carburettor car; the first production type is pictured on the 2000TC sales brochure on p.148.

The first Rover 2000s shipped to North America were single-carburettor 2000s, with no differences from the standard left-hand-drive export specification. This postcard with its very English-looking background was an early promotional tool.

been before. RCNA moved its headquarters to New York to be nearer the action, but its sales organization was still scattered around a small number of regional centres.

THE FIRST 2000s

The Rover 2000 was previewed at the New York International Automobile Show that opened on 4 April 1964, when one of the gold cars and the white cutaway whetted customer appetites. It then went on sale in the USA in the late summer of 1964, with a minimum of changes from the standard specification. Nevertheless, those changes were enough to earn these cars the name of NADA models at Rover; the letters stood for North American Dollar Area.

The first cars had a dipping interior mirror and a foot-operated dipswitch to meet US expectations, but they also had the standard rectangular rear number-plate plinth; a squarer one to suit US-style licence plates did not appear until the summer of 1965. Optional extras included an Icelert warning device mounted ahead of the grille that was linked to controls and a light on the dashboard. Made by Findlay Irvine in Scotland, its purpose was to warn the driver of the risk of ice on the road. All those fitted to early 2000s were round, and most had the controls and lights in the corner fillet next to the speedometer. A few very early ones had a sensor design that resembled the Jodrell Bank radio telescope, and with these the controls and light were fitted into the facia rail. The Icelert was not at this stage made available outside North America.

It was also possible to order special overriders, which were manufactured from cast aluminium in France by a company called Sacred. Their extra height provided additional protection from low-speed parking accidents involving larger cars whose bumpers were mounted higher up. These remained unique to the NADA cars, and were not the same as the 'tall' (and almost equally rare) overriders introduced for the home market at the same time.

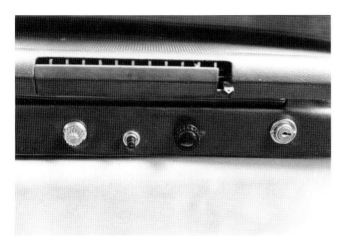

This is another North American publicity picture for the Icelert, showing that the controls and warning light on early cars were located on the dash rail ahead of the passenger.

The early pattern 'tall' overrider option is seen here. It was dropped when the 2000TC arrived with its neater standard overriders. AL WORSFOLD

The new 2000 made quite a splash in the USA. 'Can this car be the world's best?' wondered *Road Test* magazine for December 1964, rating the car a 'best buy' when compared with the Mercedes-Benz 220 SE, Jaguar 3.8-litre S-type, Lancia Flavia, Ford Thunderbird and an unidentified Humber. The magazine was not alone in its extravagant praise of the Rover, but the North American experts' enthusiasm for the car's technical advances and driving qualities did not persuade many of their fellow countrymen to part with $3,885 (or $3,985 on the West Coast) for a Rover 2000.

Probably, most Americans thought the car was too small. That it was a European import would only have impressed a small percentage of possible customers, even though such things were supposedly fashionable at the time; in those days, only around 1 per cent of all Americans had ever travelled abroad, and few took much interest in happenings outside the borders of the USA. Americans would certainly have been unimpressed by the fact that the Rover had only 4 cylinders, and there was no doubt that the car was more than a little under-powered for US driving conditions at a time when the muscle-car craze was at its height.

Figures from RCNA documents show that 1,092 examples of the 2000 were sold in its first year on sale, as a 1965 model. Sales then dropped to just 565 for 1966, although overall P6 sales were now higher and the lion's share went to the new 2000TC. Even then, RCNA were not selling enough cars to break even in the USA – although the management was eternally optimistic.

THE NADA 2000TC

As explained in Chapter 3, the 2000TC was released for some export markets before it reached showrooms in the UK, and among those markets that received it early was North America. The NADA 2000TC was announced in the early summer of 1966 to catch the start of the 1967 model year in the USA and Canada.

Rover had not only ensured that the car complied with the new regulations; they had also made some cosmetic changes that gave the NADA 2000TC a distinctive visual identity. To British eyes, the car was a rather garish creation that went against the Rover traditions of restraint and discretion, although with the passage of time it now appears a particularly attractive variant of the P6. The full treatment was reserved for white cars, which had a painted Solent Blue square as background to the 'TC' badges on the bonnet, front wings and bootlid. The same blue paint was used for the rear roof pillars. The NADA TCs also had a narrow stainless steel trim strip along the bodyside crease, as seen on versions for the European continent, and this was accompanied by a painted coach line. Special features common to all the NADA TCs were a racing-type rear-view mirror on the bonnet; a new style of overrider, still faced with a rubber buffer but squatter and neater than the earlier type (which was fitted to a few very early cars); and an Icelert warning system, initially with the circular sensor first seen as an option on single-carburettor 2000s in North America.

With the introduction of the 2000TC in 1966, Rover moved up a gear. This is a White car with Solent Blue rear pillars and badge backgrounds. It has the North American specification overriders and racing mirror, and an Icelert system.

This wheel may look like a Rostyle, but it is in fact an American-made Magnum 500 type. The North American 2000TC was the first production Rover to have styled and chromed wheels. They had a 14in size, like the standard ones; a 15in version followed later on the P5B 3.5-litre Saloon and Coupé.

The Magnum 500 and later Rostyle wheels were both steel, but the optional MagStar 500 made by Kelsey Hayes in the USA had an alloy centre. Narrow-band whitewall tyres on the early 2000TC added to the sporting air.

A few mock-up and pilot-production cars were built with the original 'shark's tooth' front valance panel, but the full-production NADA 2000TC had the later type. Optional equipment included Triplex Sundym glass, which reduced glare and cut down heat absorption in the passenger cabin; a Webasto fabric sunroof; the streamlined roof rack; and two different types of chromed and painted styled wheels. These were called the Magnum 500 and the MagStar, and both were manufactured in the USA. The MagStar, made by Kelsey Hayes, was the more extrovert of the two, and actually had an alloy centre that bolted directly to the standard Rover hubs. On the 2000TC, it was fitted with centre caps that carried the Rover Viking ship logo. The Magnum 500 required special hubs that were fitted (along with the wheels) on the assembly lines at Solihull. These wheels had a 4.5in PCD as compared with the 5in PCD of the standard Rover hub. When Rubery Owen in Britain began manufacture of their Rostyle wheels – visually hard to tell from the Magnum 500 – Rover understandably switched to the British wheel because it fitted the standard hubs. This was at the start of the 1968 model year, and the MagStar was dropped from the Rover options list at the same time.

Inside, the NADA cars had a TC badge on the radio console and a rev-counter rather crudely tacked onto the dashboard beside the instrument panel, just as home market cars would have. Other standard fittings were a wood-rim sports steering wheel with alloy spokes, a matching wooden gearshift grip, a dipping rear-view mirror and front seat belts. Rear belts, a radio, a heated rear window and air-conditioning were all optional; the last one being the newly developed factory-fit unit that had been developed jointly by Rover and Delanair and was installed in the centre console. Air-conditioned cars were always fitted with tinted glass.

The NADA 2000TC in fact lasted only for one season in its original form; in mid-1967 it was replaced by the so-called Federal model. It had nevertheless got off to a good start, selling 1,463 examples alongside just 565 single-carburettor models.

The 2000TC and the Press

Like the single-carburettor model that preceded it, the 2000TC was well received by the North American specialist press. In fact, the superlatives heaped upon it were so excessive that the car could not possibly have lived up to what these reviews led the public to expect. Good though

Inside a May 1966 2000TC at speed: the car has a wood-rim steering wheel and the early style of rev-counter housing. Just visible beyond the sticker on the windscreen is the racing-type mirror. TOM RYMES

the 2000TC was, RCNA's dealer network was wholly inadequate to provide the level of service back-up needed to maintain customer faith in a car that had been so comprehensively ballyhooed. So was the build quality coming out of Solihull, and the multiple reports of faults and component failures that were fired back and forth within RCNA make deeply depressing reading.

It was *Car and Driver* magazine that started the near-hysterical praise for the 2000TC in its May 1966 issue with a road test report that applauded the car's appearance, handling, comfort, build quality, performance and fuel economy. A few quotations give the flavour of this report: 'Driving any Rover 2000 is a pretty impressive experience, but driving the 2000TC is so good that it should be reserved for people of taste, breeding and documented automotive enthusiasm.' The road testers went on to say: 'We feel so strongly about the car that we have asked the Rover Motor Company to lend us one that we can take to Detroit and demonstrate to some of the enthusiastic young men who shape the country's automotive future. We figure that a strong injection of 2000TC wouldn't hurt the domestic car industry a bit.'

Predicting potential North American sales of 75,000 cars a year – which was actually more than twice Rover's total P6 production capacity at the time – *Car and Driver* summarized its views by describing the 2000TC as 'absolutely the best sedan that has ever been presented in the pages of this magazine. We think it's an automotive milestone.'

Other magazines had some difficulty in following that. *Road & Track* for June 1966, perhaps deliberately trying to be different, carried a fairly restrained appreciation of the new arrival's advantages over its single-carburettor stable-mate. Across the border, however, *Canada Track and Traffic* for the same month was equally bowled over by the car:

> *After reading a recent report which had nothing but praise for the Rover 2000TC sedan, we put in our minds that we would somehow find some small criticism of this latest model from the Rover Motor Company. Needless to say we failed in our assignment. This is a car which does everything just right and to say that the Rover 2000TC is a perfect piece of automotive engineering is certainly not exaggerating.*

After enumerating the car's many virtues in comfort, performance, handling, equipment levels and build quality, the magazine concluded that the TC:

This is a 2000TC engine bay on one of the Federal-specification cars introduced in autumn 1967. Note the special air cleaner and the York compressor for an air-conditioning system.

> *… has the class of a champion executing every move with excellence and even under the close eye of the most critical judge there are no flaws to be found. It just doesn't make any mistakes. The Rover Motor Company might even be tempted to use only the initials TC and call it 'The Car', which dares to be known by this name alone.*

More praise followed in the September 1966 *Road Test* magazine, which reported a marathon three-part test of an early 2000TC. The car in question, 418-00087A, was driven for four and a half days in low gears across rough terrain in Baja, California; it then raced the Santa Fe Super Chief express train from Los Angeles to Chicago and beat it by more than three and a half hours; and finally it did an economy run from Chicago to New York achieving averages of 53.45mph (86km/h) and 27.94mpg (US) for this final leg. After that, the car was put on display at the New York International Motor Show to reveal how well it had survived the ordeal.

It had indeed survived well. No servicing or adjustment had been required throughout the whole event, although it had been necessary to find a spare nut and bolt in a hurry when the propshaft support bracket had been ripped off by a rock during the first stage. The car itself had been modified only with factory-supplied extras in the shape of a long-range fuel tank and rally-specification springs and dampers, plus an additional auxiliary fuel tank and an aluminium sump guard. 'Never before has an automaker dared to give any new model a public testing of such severity,' concluded writer Bill Carroll, 'a testing that beyond a shadow of a doubt demonstrated durability, performance and economy of a car that can take the best, and the worst, a driver can dish out.'

THE FEDERAL 2000TC AND 2000 AUTOMATIC, 1967–70

It was in 1965 that Ralph Nader published his seminal book, *Unsafe at Any Speed*, which castigated the US automotive industry for its general reluctance to spend money on improving safety in the cars it designed. The book caused a sensation and, after a formal Senate enquiry, the US government created a new Department of Transportation and the predecessor agencies of the modern National Highway Traffic Safety Administration. That was in 1966, and it was quickly followed by a series of laws that demanded compliance with a number of newly crafted safety standards.

These new Federal Safety Standards differed in many respects from requirements in other markets around the world, and their introduction meant that any manufacturer intending to export cars to the USA had to develop special versions for that country. At Solihull, the cars that Rover built to meet them were known as Federal types, and one of the factory's main concerns was to make them meet Federal Standard 515, which was a detailed set of requirements relating to passenger safety in an accident.

When Rover had crash-tested a 2000 at the Road Research Laboratory for their own purposes, the car had emerged with flying colours. However, the new Federal regulations now demanded a properly monitored barrier-crash test, and so a 2000 was put through this at MIRA in late October 1966. Fortunately, the amount of thought that had gone into safety considerations when the car was being designed meant that no redesign of the structure was necessary for the P6 to meet the requirements. There were, however, a number of subsidiary requirements in the new US federal safety regulations, relating to such things as safety belts and interior protrusions, and the Rover designers set to work to produce modifications that would satisfy these.

Major changes were needed during 1968 to meet the new Federal Motor Vehicle Safety Standards. This is a 1969-season Federal 2000 Automatic, showing the additional lighting, reflectors, and all-amber front sidelight units. By this stage, the Icelert was on its third design, with a rectangular body.

The protective sheeting over the carpets of this 1969 2000 Automatic was probably added for shipping. Clear here are the foot-operated dipswitch required in the USA and the textured vinyl Amblair upholstery.

This Federal 2000 Automatic has the extra-cost Delanair air-conditioning system, which added to luxury but did nothing for the performance of an already slow car.

A second major concern in the USA in the mid-1960s was health problems attributable to polluted air, particularly in major cities like Los Angeles. One factor contributing to the build-up of smog in such areas was considered to be the large amount of exhaust gases pumped out by road vehicles and, with the introduction of the Clean Air Act in 1967, the US government acquired powers to limit by law the amounts of noxious gases – principally carbon monoxide and oxides of nitrogen – permissible in vehicle exhausts.

These new requirements prompted a flurry of activity at Solihull. A special team was set up to develop engines that met the new exhaust emissions rules and the fully 'Federalized' P6 models were able to enter production in July 1967, just in time for the start of the 1968 sales season in the USA. In the meantime, Rover decided to withdraw the basic 2000 from the North American market, and so only the 2000TC and 2000 Automatic were introduced in Federalized form. Both cars were also sold in Canada in that same form, even though that country had not yet followed the US lead and introduced its own safety and exhaust emissions regulations.

The new Federal models were sufficiently different from the regular left-hand-drive export cars for Rover to give them special commission number sequences, and all cars bore a label that their engines complied with federal exhaust emissions standards. The Rover engineers had achieved control of these emissions by altering the engine's carburation characteristics and by retarding the ignition in the lower speed range so that much weaker fuel/air mixtures could be used. Crankcase emissions were also controlled by a system of piping – actually standardized on 2000s for all markets at the beginning of 1967 – which drew crankcase fumes through the carburettor to be burned with the fuel/air mixture. These emissions-controlled engines tended to run hotter than the standard types, so they were fitted with larger cooling fans.

To meet new safety regulations it had also been necessary to modify the P6's lighting arrangements. All new cars sold in the USA now had to have side-marker reflectors, and these were added in the shape of rather ugly excrescences on the wings that did not nothing for the car's good looks; similarly, regulations governing the position of direction indicators had led to blanking off the Rover's front units and the addition of new indicator units slung below the bumpers. As running lights other than headlamps now had to be amber, the sidelight lenses were also changed from white to suit so that the front lamp lenses were now all amber.

Further regulations required the elimination of reflective surfaces within the car which might distract the driver. As a result, the Federal P6s had a non-reflective matt black finish to the inner surfaces of the chromed speedometer bezel, to the rear-view mirror's stem and fixings, and to the sun visor fixings. Modified wiper arms and blades were also designed to reduce reflections.

Safety considerations meant that the courtesy light integral with the rear-view mirror had to be deleted, and a single courtesy light in the centre of the roof was fitted instead. There were also anti-burst devices on the doors, a hazard warning system that would flash all four turn indicators at once, a new design of the front seat slide assembly with a more positive bar lock in place of the cable-operated type, front seatbelts as standard – though, oddly, head restraints were optional extras – and a brake servo with a tandem slave cylinder, one half operating the rear brakes and the other operating the fronts. A driver's door mirror and Icelert – the latter now a rectangular type in place of the original circular variety – became standard on both Federal 2000TCs and 2000 Automatics. The 2000TC was now distinguished by Pirelli Gold Band tyres, which had a thin decorative gold band on the sidewall and remained part of the standard specification until at least July 1970.

All these changes inevitably cost money, and Rover recognized that they could not pass the cost on to their North American customers. The Federal models did cost more than their predecessors, but showroom price rises were minimized by cost-cutting measures. So the Magnum 500 and MagStar wheel options disappeared, and were replaced by British-made Rostyles that looked exactly like the Magnum 500 type. Most important, perhaps, was the replacement of costly leather by Amblair vinyl upholstery with a basket-weave pattern for the centre panels. In the hotter regions of North America, it undoubtedly lasted longer than leather, which was prone to cracking; but it also robbed the Federal cars of one of their distinctive 'British' qualities and can have done nothing for sales.

This, then, was one of the penalties that Rover suffered as a result of their need to meet the new federal regulations. Yet these regulations had also obliged the company to use design features that went against their engineers' better judgment. Peter Wilks, then engineering director, had told *Motor* of his objections to dual-circuit braking systems in an interview published in that same magazine's 16 July 1966 issue. Wilks' view was that 'the driver who finds himself in an emergency with only two-wheel braking is likely to get into worse trouble than the driver with none – doubling up master cylinders doubles the chance of failure'. Rover, he went on to say, had also 'experimented with a 2000 with the alternative diagonal-split braking system, pioneered by Saab, which links each front-wheel brake with the rear brake on the opposite side, but found it unsatisfactory'.

There were further penalties, too. The emissions-control equipment damaged performance: the TC's 0–60mph time went up by around 1.5 seconds and its top speed came down by 6mph (10km/h). No figures are available for the 2000 Automatic, but what it did for that car's already sluggish performance can be imagined. Although no such conversion was ever approved by Solihull's engineers, at least one Federal 2000 Automatic (858-00231F) was given a twin-carburettor head, probably by the supplying Canadian dealer. It is not hard to understand why.

This loss of performance was only part of Rover's US troubles, however, because when the Federal models arrived, serious customer dissatisfaction with the P6 was beginning to surface in the USA. *Car and Driver* magazine, so enthusiastic about the P6 in 1966, said in its November 1969 issue that the cars had been:

> developed with features that would appeal to the American market but they were never tested here and, soon after they were put on the American market, problems caused by corrosion, vast temperature variations not found in England and the American driving style began to take a whack at Rover's new car warranty.

Why not combine the twin-carburettor engine with the automatic gearbox? The badges on the bootlid of this Canadian car show that it could be done.

In addition, the Rover dealerships were still ill-equipped to provide the necessary support for customers. Reports of poor servicing and of delays in obtaining spare parts became common, and some frantic discounting in the showrooms to get rid of old-stock cars in 1967 before the new regulations came into force cannot have helped. Not surprisingly, the new Federal models did nothing to overcome these problems.

The North American specification cars were also delivered to some other countries. This early one was pictured with its proud owner, a Rover and Land Rover salesman, in Venezuela in the early 1970s. ROGER CRATHORNE

By 1969, Rover were struggling in the USA. Sales of 2,000 cars per year were not enough to sustain the operation, and they were low at a time when other importers were enjoying increased successes: 1968 was the first year in which imports accounted for more than 10 per cent of all new cars registered in the USA, and that percentage would continue to rise steadily. Summer 1969 was crunch time – and it coincided most unhappily with the introduction of the 3500S model that had been confidently expected to rescue Rover sales.

In order not to flood their dealers with unsold cars, Rover stopped production of the 2000 Automatic models in mid-year and the only 4-cylinder P6s available in the USA for the 1970 season were 2000TC types, selling alongside the newly introduced 3500S. Even these were not doing well, and RCNA cancelled a deferred order for 500 2000TCs in autumn 1969. By the time production stopped in August 1970, just under 5,000 Federal TCs had been made; the Automatic had inevitably been much rarer, with just 940 examples built. Some of these cars, of course, had been sold in Canada.

Road & Track magazine highlighted Rover's problems in a survey it conducted of 100 owners of 2000TCs for its November 1970 issue:

> *It is now our somewhat painful duty to report that, of the fourteen different models we have surveyed so far, the Rover 2000TC unquestionably has caused its readers more problems than any other make … Getting into the troubles experienced by Rover owners is like opening Pandora's box. Once the lid is off, everything comes flying out. No make has been completely free of mechanical troubles but the Rover 2000TC has exceeded every other marque in numbers of problems reported … of our 100 owners, only one reported having no trouble with the car. And his was a 1969 model with only 8,000 miles [13,000km].*

The full catalogue of owners' woes made depressing reading, but the survey also revealed that a massive 32 per cent of owners considered the service available from their dealer to be poor, 'which puts Rover dealers well toward the bottom of the list, though not at the very bottom as that distinction is shared by Triumph, Jaguar and Corvette dealers'. Many owners stressed that they liked their cars in spite of these troubles, and the five best features were stated as handling, comfort, brakes, safety and economy, in that order. Most

THE 100,000TH P6

The 100,000th P6 was a North American 2000TC that was completed on 27 February 1968. It was collected at a short ceremony on the assembly lines by Professor John E. Dorn from Orinda, California, who was then in Britain on a lecture tour. By that stage, according to the *Rover and Alvis News*, 'nearly 10,000' P6s had been sold in North America – a figure that was quite clearly an exaggeration.

Professor Dorn was the 420th overseas customer to visit Solihull to take delivery of his car from the Personal Export Department, which opened for business in June 1967.

owners had no complaints about the car's overall concept or the standard of its build quality. The commonest complaints, however, concerned dealer service and servicing costs, gear selection problems, lack of power and reliability.

Road & Track commented that many of the niggling problems were common to other British cars of the time and were the result of poor quality control by parts suppliers; not for nothing did Joseph Lucas, founder of the electrical components company, earn the nickname 'Father of Darkness' in the USA during the 1960s. However, the magazine could not forgive Rover's lack of success in dealing with these issues: 'It is nowhere apparent that Rover has been able to correct these faults or to put its own house in order so far as its US dealers are concerned.' It was a terrible indictment of Rover's attempt to overreach themselves, of the state of the British motor industry in the late 1960s, and of how an excellent design could be let down by poor quality control and inadequate dealer support.

THE FEDERAL 3500S, 1969–71

Ever since 1966, Rover had been working on the development of a V8-engined P6 to suit the North American market. It seemed like an excellent idea: the model would give American customers both an automatic gearbox and more of the performance that they wanted, and there would be a host of special features to make it into a compact luxury car. Rover had initially hoped to have it ready for release in January 1968, but delays in the development programme set it back by some eighteen months, and the car was not actually announced in the USA and Canada until 10 October 1969. Production had begun at Solihull in June, and a launch stock of 500 cars was in place in US dealers' showrooms by that date.

The name of 3500S that was eventually adopted for production was not the only proposal. In August 1966, Bruce McWilliams put forward the idea of calling it the 437X8, which (he explained to the author in 2003) was derived from the way Ferrari named their models; 437 was the size of the combustion chamber in cubic centimetres, the X was for 'times', and the 8 was for the 8 cylinders of the V8 engine.

McWilliams also sent Solihull a rendering of the way he thought it should look, and David Bache's department translated this into a full-size mock-up in late 1966. What Bache himself thought of the exercise is not known, although it must be said that the front end styling with its prominent grille – suggesting a Lincoln more than anything else – was not altogether successful. The idea was not pursued.

Worse was to come, though. It is on record that British Leyland's chairman, Sir Donald Stokes, asked the Rover board at its meeting on 14 October 1968 to consider selling the P6B as a Jaguar in the USA because that name was better known than Rover. It is probably fortunate that the Rover board's views on the matter are not on record.

High equipment levels were what the 3500S was all about, as a quotation from a sales brochure explains:

Over at the Rover Company of North America, the V8-engined car was eagerly awaited. This sketch was produced in the USA to give the Styling Department an idea of what might sell well, and was labelled '437x8'. A full-size mock-up was also produced at Solihull.

The Rover 3500S with its V8 engine, power steering, factory designed and installed air-conditioning (optional) and electric windows has been built for America. To be sure, the European version, the 3500, is already a very great success in Europe, but it was developed and engineered in response to requests from this side of the Atlantic for the features Americans want in their automobiles of such a level of craftsmanship.

Here at last! This press picture of the 1970-model 3500S shows a Sage Green car – although most early deliveries were red. The three bonnet scoops, bolt-through wheel trims and front seat head restraints are very noticeable, as are the Pirelli Gold Band tyres.

This is a restored example now in the UK, again in Sage Green. It has head restraints of the early 'ET' type. The blacked-out horizontal surfaces of the grille and around the headlights are shown to good effect.

While trim and equipment development was done on prototype P6B/24 (JXC823D), which somewhat bizarrely was a right-hand-drive car, the emissions-control team in the engine development department worked out a Federal specification for the V8. By January 1967 they had it ready. By November 1967, a test car – prototype P6B/12 (JXC 813D) – had been out to the USA for proving trials and was back at Solihull for examination. Once the mainstream Three Thousand Five had been launched in April 1968, Rover were then able to focus on getting the Federal 3500S into production.

The Federal V8 engines retained the high 10.5:1 compression, but would also have multiple special features to meet the new emissions control regulations. Crankcase emissions were fed through the carburettors to be burned with the fuel-air mixture, and evaporative emissions from the engine and fuel tank were fed into a pair of charcoal-filled canisters to be absorbed before they reached the air outside. There was a special distributor with a vacuum switch that retarded the ignition under part-load conditions, and a damper slowed throttle closure to control fuel delivery on the overrun. In production, Rover quoted the same 184bhp at 5,200rpm and 226lb ft of torque at 3,000rpm for the Federal V8 as for the standard engine – a claim that was probably on the optimistic side.

To reduce emissions, rapid engine warm-up was important, and so the Rover engineers devised an air intake tem-

perature control system that was designed to achieve an intake temperature of 100°F (38°C) as quickly as possible and to maintain it while ambient temperatures were below 100°. The system consisted of a hot box surrounding the right-hand exhaust manifold, an air cleaner fed directly from a scoop on the bonnet, a temperature sensor in that air cleaner, and a thermostatically controlled flap valve that drew on hot air from around the exhaust when it was needed. To keep underbonnet temperatures within bounds, they also used a multi-blade nylon fan in place of the fixed metal type on other versions of the V8.

Air-conditioning was to be an option on the Federal 3500S model, and the best place for its belt-driven compressor was alongside the left-hand cylinder bank – where it would foul the mechanical fuel pump. So Rover installed a remote electric fuel pump to take care of that problem. The US engines also had an automatic choke, which Rover believed was necessary to meet US customer expectations. This was a fully automatic auxiliary carburettor that provided the necessary additional fuel-air mixture when the engine was below its working temperature. Made by Lucas, it was known to Rover as the AED or Automatic Enrichment Device. It was sealed for life, and theoretically required no adjustment. Unfortunately, it was also prone to jamming in the 'choke on' position. Engine test engineer Brian Terry remembered that it worked beautifully on the test bench but was an unqualified disaster in service.

The Federal 3500S pioneered several other new features. It was the first Rover to have the D-2-1 automatic gearbox selector instead of the earlier D2-D1-L type. It was the only Rover ever to have a 'sight glass' filler for the automatic gearbox. It became the first P6 variant to have Adwest Varamatic power-assisted steering as standard, and it was the first P6 to have brake pad wear indicators, which were fitted to the front wheels only as part of the Federal-standard dual-line braking system. It was also the first P6 variant to have a variable-delay windscreen wiper control.

A further special feature was a longitudinal tubular reinforcement bar inside each of the four doors. These were not side intrusion bars (as they are often wrongly called) but were designed to resist rearward movement of the car's frontal structure in an impact and so reduce steering column intrusion to meet federal safety regulations. (When the federal authorities proposed FMVSS 214 covering side impact provision, Pressed Steel Fisher carried out some appropriate tests for Rover at Cowley in August 1970, which showed that the tubular reinforcements did not meet the new safety standard for side impacts.)

Visually, there was absolutely no mistaking a Federal 3500S for any other version of the P6. The cars had heavier bumpers to suit US parking habits, and there were three air scoops on the bonnet – needed for the rapid warm-up system and also to keep an already cramped engine bay cool when the optional air-conditioning was fitted. These were the first P6s to have five-spoke bolt-through wheel trims, which were accompanied by Pirelli Gold Band tyres when the cars were new. They also had a thick trim strip along the bodyside crease, with a painted coach line above it. The horizontal surfaces of the radiator grille were blacked out, echoing Zagato's example on the 1966 TCZ show car, and the sill panels were also blacked out to make the car look lower. Then, of course, there were '3500S' plate badges, and both front and rear number-plate carriers were square to suit US-style licence plates.

There were twin door mirrors as standard, too, plus of course the side marker lights and reflectors required by US regulations. And sharp eyes would spot the two openings for lashing eyes in the front valance panel, where the Three Thousand Five had just one. The twin lashing eyes on the lower cross-member were needed to lash these vehicles securely during their long sea voyage across the Atlantic.

The passenger cabin was also very different from that of the mainstream P6s, and pioneered several features that would later migrate to the New Look models introduced in

The 3500S had engraved wing badges (later ones on the manual-gearbox 3500S were printed), a wider trim strip than the 4-cylinder cars, and a painted coach line above the strip rather than below it. PAUL SMITH

The coach line and rear side reflectors are clear in this picture. PAUL SMITH

1970. Box-pleated upholstery was new, possibly inspired by the Graber P6 cars of the mid-1960s, and came as standard in Ambla vinyl (a smooth type, not to be confused with basket-weave Amblair), although leather was available for extra cost. Both types had perforations in the recessed sections. Teardrop-shaped front head restraints were standard, and were the first use of this new shape. The transmission tunnel cover was upholstered in leather as standard, and the handbrake had a leather gaiter, both features intended for the 2000S back in 1962 that would never be seen on another P6 model. There was a leather-bound sports steering wheel,

THE NADA AND FEDERAL CARS

The steering wheel had a leather-trimmed rim and spokes, and a large '3500S' badge in the centre. The array of extra dashboard switches can be seen here.

The front seats on the Federal 3500S were upholstered in box-pleat Ambla, and the transmission tunnel cover was padded and upholstered as well.

Electric windows were essential for US buyers of luxury cars, and the main switch panel was set between the controls for the air-conditioning – the installation was much neater than the Delanair type used on the 4-cylinder cars. This car was used in the UK and has a UK-specification radio. PAUL SMITH

Extra switches for extra equipment: the heated rear window control is joined by air-conditioning and window master switches. PAUL SMITH

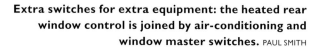

On the 3500S, the Icelert controls and warning light were tucked neatly out of the way below the windscreen pillar. PAUL SMITH

too, trimmed in black rather than to match the upholstery. This had a 16in (406mm) diameter rather than the 17in (432mm) of the standard P6 wheel, its smaller size feasible because of the lower effort needed to turn the wheels via the car's standard power-assisted steering.

The Federal 3500S also became the first P6 variant to have the marvellously clear four-dial instrument panel and revised switchgear that David Bache had developed some six years earlier for the P7 and the 2000S. That instrument panel was remarkable for being completely enclosed behind a non-reflective concave surface; for depending on the latest printed-circuit technology instead of wires for its electrical connections; and for illumination by glare-free green-tinted lighting. It would later become standard on the New Look models, too.

Even the door trims had unique features. Armrests and door pulls were combined in a single feature, and below them was a stowage bin. There were also turnwheel controls for the front quarter-lights, and these, like the armrests, had probably been inspired by a BMW design. On some early cars, the turnwheels had recessed or cupped faces, but most seem to have had the flat faces like their counterparts on the later Series II cars (see Chapter 10).

All cars had electric windows, their switches mounted centrally where the radio speaker panel normally went. When the optional air-conditioning system was fitted, its controls were in this same panel, and the displaced fuel reserve control was fitted lower down, alongside the speaker grille panel on the passenger's side; there was of course no choke control because the 3500S had an automatic choke. Air-conditioned cars also had an extra vent in the space above the radio mounting panel, together with extra switchgear on the facia rail. There was one slightly bizarre feature: the front ashtray was finished in black to eliminate reflections, although the rear ashtray was the standard chromed type!

Lastly, all the Federal 3500S cars came with the latest through-flow ventilation system, as introduced for all the

The armrest has either discoloured over time or is a later replacement, but this driver's door shows the standard map pocket and the turnwheel control for the quarter-light (later standardized). PAUL SMITH

Rear-seat passengers also had controls for their windows, located on the door trim. PAUL SMITH

Federal regulations required the car's identity number to be displayed on the driver's window sill, where it could be seen from outside the vehicle. PAUL SMITH

1969-model P6s (see Chapter 3). Although this system would be dropped on 1970 models for other markets, it remained standard on the Federal 3500S until production ended in 1971 – perhaps because there were overstocks of the bodyshells that needed to be used up.

The Federal 3500S and the Press

With all its extra equipment, Solihull was confident that the Federal 3500S would be a sales success, but it met with mixed reactions from the very start. Both *Car and Driver* and *Road & Track* road tested examples for their November 1969 issues, but the car tested by the former seems to have been down on engine performance, which may explain why the *Road & Track* report was more favourable.

Where *Road & Track* discovered a 117mph (188km/h) maximum speed and an average fuel consumption of 17.5 miles per US gallon (14.5 miles per Imperial gallon, or 19.5ltr/100km), *Car and Driver* could achieve no more than 105mph (169km/h) and a fuel consumption in the range of 12–16mpg (21.8–28.3ltr/100km). Curiously, however, *Car and Driver* recorded 10.8sec for the 0–60mph standing start, while Road & Track could not better 11.9sec. These figures may be compared with those claimed by Rover for a UK-specification car: a 118mph (190km/h) top speed and consumption of 21.6mpg (13.1ltr/100km) from the larger

Imperial gallon. On paper, the Federal model was thus both thirstier and slower than its UK-market counterpart, but those who have driven both varieties say that the Federal cars do not feel noticeably slower, and in any case very few owners of UK-specification Three Thousand Fives ever see much more than 18–19mpg (15.7/14.9ltr/100km) in practice.

Road & Track thought the 3500S was 'just about the nicest sedan we've come across this year', and found very little to criticize. Front end styling was a little busy for their taste, and the automatic transmission would have been better off with a part-throttle kickdown; the brakes on the test car were also a little slow to release but, overall: 'We don't know any car costing less that makes you feel you've got more.' The testers were well aware that 4-cylinder P6s had earned themselves a poor reputation, but thought that their test 3500S showed every sign of the durability that its stable-mates seemed to lack.

For *Car & Driver*, 'the advancements in the 3500S may not have been to significantly improve performance. Instead, the effort has been concentrated on providing automatic transmission, power steering, power brakes, air-conditioning, electric windows – all in a package labelled luxury and aimed directly at that discriminating segment of Buick/Oldsmobile/Chrysler market.' Their car suffered from a braking problem, which was diagnosed as servo lag. The body roll was found to be 'intimidating' and they were scathing about the Borg-Warner transmission: 'a device 1955-vintage in its operation and extremely reluctant to co-operate by being in the right gear at the right time'.

They thought the rear seats and the boot were too small compared with American luxury saloons; but the interior – which in their car had the optional leather trim – had considerable appeal: 'Except for its modest dimensions, we find it more satisfying than the Mercedes 250 or the Volvo 164 which are the logical competitors and it is with this feature that the 3500S will make most of its new friends.'

The Federal 3500S on Sale

In fact, the car made very few friends at all in the North American market. Sales got off to a bad start after the launch on 10 October 1969, when most of the first examples arriving in US showrooms did not have the air-conditioning that the dealers had been convinced would be essential. Most of the early examples were also supplied in red with a black interior, and US customers expected a wider choice to be readily available. By early 1970, the dealer network was beginning to despair of the 3500S, and in February or March British Leyland Motors, who oversaw US imports, actually asked Rover to suspend deliveries of the car. Although colour options and air-conditioning supplies improved later, it was too late to save the situation. All this was of course occurring at a time when there was widespread public perception that the quality of Rover dealer support was questionable.

Documents from RCNA show that stocks of unsold cars were building up. As at 31 May 1970, there were 900 in the USA, plus around ten more in Canada. Rover had no choice but to cut back production of the 3500S, diverting resources to meet continued strong demand for 2000 variants in other markets.

It was becoming increasingly clear that the Federal 3500S was a failure in its intended market. Worse was the fact that tougher new emissions-control regulations were scheduled for introduction in the near future, which meant that Rover would have to invest heavily in further redevelopment, and might have to resort once again to discounting in order to dispose of old stocks before the new regulations came into force. The fuel-injected version of the V8 then under development (see Chapter 8) would probably have been able to meet these regulations and improve performance as well, but by summer 1971 that project had come to an end.

So once again, Rover were left with no choice: they had to end production of the Federal 3500S. The last car was built in August 1971, the total of 2,043 built making for an annual average of just on 1,000 cars. It is no surprise that such poor sales persuaded Rover to pull out of the North American market altogether.

No important running changes were made on production, although there were some minor variations between cars (such as the use of recessed and flat quarter-light turn-wheels). Rover service literature claims that the exterior door handles changed to the 'shrouded' type introduced on the 1971-season New Look models for other markets at car number 433-01839. However, this may have expressed an intention rather than reality, as no cars have been found with the later type of door handle.

A few of these Federal cars never actually crossed the Atlantic at all but were sold off in Europe. The reason for this was probably that a number of cars went to dealerships in West Germany, which sold primarily to members of the US Forces stationed in Europe and were thus already on the Continent awaiting sale when Rover's North American operation was discontinued. As the company could not sell cars for which a service back-up would no longer be available if customers took them back to the USA, they were sold off in what looked like the best market, Belgium, which traditionally favoured American cars and was thus likely to respond favourably to Rovers that had been specifically designed to suit American tastes.

This picture has been turned sideways for clarity: it shows a Federal compliance plate attached to the passenger's side door pillar. LES VARNAI

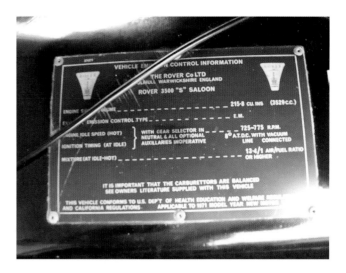

Yet another special sticker, this time offering tuning advice to ensure compliance with Federal emissions regulations. PAUL SMITH

NORTH AMERICAN PAINT AND TRIM OPTIONS

The paint and trim options for North American cars up to June 1966 were the same as for cars for other markets and are shown in Chapter 2.

June 1966–January 1967
Eight paint colours were available. The standard colour combinations were:

April Yellow	with trim in	Black
Arden Green		Buckskin, Buffalo or Sandalwood
Burnt Grey		Buckskin, Buffalo, Sandalwood or Red
Emerald Green		Not known
Racing Red		Black
Venetian Red		Buckskin, Buffalo or Sandalwood
White*		Buffalo, Sandalwood or Red
Zircon Blue		Buckskin, Buffalo or Sandalwood

* On the 2000TC only, White was always accompanied by Solent Blue for the rear quarter-panels and as a background for the TC badges.
Headlinings were available in Biscuit or Light Grey.

February–September 1967
The paint colours remained unchanged, but Ebony replaced Black as a fifth trim option. This was probably available with all standard colours. Headlinings were still available in Biscuit or Light Grey.

October–December 1967
Emerald Green was deleted from the North American options, reducing their number to seven. Buffalo trim was discontinued, leaving the four options as Buckskin, Ebony, Sandalwood and Toledo Red.
   The standard colour combinations were:

April Yellow	with trim in	Ebony
Arden Green		Buckskin or Sandalwood
Burnt Grey		Buckskin, Sandalwood or Red
Racing Red		Ebony
Venetian Red		Buckskin or Sandalwood
White*		Sandalwood or Red
Zircon Blue		Buckskin or Sandalwood

* On the 2000TC only, White was always accompanied by Solent Blue for the rear quarter-panels and as a background for the TC badges.
The Light Grey headlining option appears to have been dropped, leaving Biscuit as the only colour available.

January–June 1968
The total of standard paint colours remained at seven, although Brigade Red replaced Venetian Red. The choice of four trim colours remained unchanged.

The standard combinations were:

April Yellow	with trim in	Buckskin or Ebony
Arden Green		Buckskin, Ebony or Sandalwood
Brigade Red		Buckskin, Ebony, Sandalwood or Red
Burnt Grey		Buckskin, Ebony, Sandalwood or Red
White*		Ebony, Sandalwood or Red
Zircon Blue		Buckskin, Ebony o Sandalwood

* On the 2000TC only, White was always accompanied by Solent Blue for the rear quarter-panels and as a background for the TC badges.

July 1968–July 1969

The eight paint colour options were the same as for other markets and North America no longer had any special colours. North American cars had leather upholstery until February 1969, but from March 1969 they came with Amblair vinyl upholstery that was available in the four standard colours.

White was usually known as Rover White in North America during this (1969) season, and Ebony was no longer listed as an interior trim option for Burnt Grey. On the 2000TC only, White was accompanied by Corsica Blue for the rear quarter-panels only.

August 1969–August 1970

The eight paint colour options were again the same as for other markets, but the sills on the new 3500S were always painted black. The four trim colours were unchanged, and 4-cylinder cars again had Amblair upholstery, while there was Ambla for the 3500S, with a leather option.

September 1970–August 1971

The eight colour options were again the same as for other markets, five being carried over from before while three were new. Black vinyl rear quarter-panels were standard with all colours on 4-cylinder models, and sills were painted Satin Black on both 4-cylinder and V8 models.

Examples of the 3500S sold to US Forces, incidentally, had standard white lenses for the front sidelights; the amber lenses needed for the USA were packed neatly in the boot and the Owner's Manual contained a reminder that these should be substituted before the cars were used in the USA.

How seriously Rover considered producing a right-hand-drive version of the Federal 3500S as a sort of more upmarket Three Thousand Five is unclear. A commission number series was certainly reserved for such a car, and there have been reports that up to six examples were built. However, it is likely that the cars in question were actually left-hand-drive models converted at Solihull to right-hand drive: one such car, 433-00062A – originally registered ROV 1 and later re-registered OXC140H – was converted in the Engineering Department in October 1969 for Sir George Farmer, then Rover's chairman. Interestingly, this car also had no front passenger seat, to give more legroom in the rear, and it also had fabric rear door pulls that made it easier to close a door from inside the car.

The Federal Series II 2000TC was never a strong seller, and looked a lot less sporting than the earlier NADA and Federal variants.

FEDERAL 2000SC, FEDERAL 2000TC AND FEDERAL 3500S, 1968–71

North American cars generally had the same technical specifications as those for other markets before the 1968 season, which was when new Federal regulations came into force. The details below are for these Federal models.

Federal 2000SC Automatic (1967–69)
As for contemporary standard models, except:

Engine	Fitted with emissions-control equipment. Power and torque always quoted to SAE standards and claimed to be identical to standard models; DIN figures never quoted but undoubtedly substantially lower
Brakes	Dual hydraulic circuits standard
Running weight	2,767lb (1,255kg)
Performance	Max speed and 0–60mph figures not quoted in sales literature

Federal 2000TC (1967–69)
As for contemporary standard models, except:

Engine	Fitted with emissions-control equipment. Power and torque always quoted to SAE standards and claimed to be identical to standard models; DIN figures never quoted but undoubtedly substantially lower
Brakes	Dual hydraulic circuits standard
Running weight	2,810lb (1,275kg)
Performance	
Max speed	'About 108mph' (174km/h) according to RCNA salesman's guide; *Road & Track* magazine achieved 106mph (171km/h) in a February 1969 test
0–60mph	*Road & Track* magazine recorded a time of 13.2sec in their February 1969 test

Federal 3500S Automatic (1969–71)
As for contemporary Three Thousand Five or 3500 models, except:

Engine	Fitted with emissions-control equipment. Power and torque always quoted to SAE standards and claimed to be identical to standard models; DIN figures never quoted but undoubtedly substantially lower
Steering	Power assistance standard
Brakes	Dual hydraulic circuits standard
Dimensions	
Overall length	180in (4,597mm)
Running weight	3,195lb (1,449kg)
Performance	
Max speed	117mph (188km/h)
0–60mph	11.9sec

Federal 2000TC Series II (1970–71)
As for contemporary standard models, except:

Engine	Fitted with emissions-control equipment. Power and torque always quoted to SAE standards and claimed to be 106bhp at 5,500rpm and 119lb ft at 3,000rpm
Brakes	Dual hydraulic circuits standard
Running weight	2,840lb (1,275kg)
Performance	Max speed and 0–60mph figures not quoted in sales literature

A RARITY – THE SERIES II FEDERAL 2000TC, 1970–71

When the Federal 3500S was introduced, Rover stopped production of the Federal 2000 Automatic, and the last example of this model left Solihull in November 1969. This left the 2000TC and 3500S as the two Rover models on sale for the 1970 season. In the meantime, RCNA were reorganized as a branch of British Leyland in the USA, and although Bruce McWilliams retained a senior position in the new organization, his duties were no longer totally focused on Rover products.

Back at Solihull, autumn 1970 brought the New Look or Series II P6 models, and it was only logical that the Federal 2000TC should be updated along with the others. The last of the Series I Federal 2000TC models was built in August 1970, and in November a Federal 2000TC Series II began to roll off the production lines. As was to be expected, it combined the main features of the New Look cars with the special lighting arrangements and other features already in use on the Federal 3500S.

However, the updated car came too late to make a big impact. It was on sale for just over a year, because production was stopped in August 1971 along with that of the Federal 3500S. Just 222 examples had been made – and the records show that sixteen cars in the numbering sequence were not built, presumably because of cancelled orders – which makes this one of the rarest of all P6 models.

NADA AND FEDERAL CHASSIS NUMBER SEQUENCES

1964–67 NADA cars

2000	403 series (1964–66)
2000 Automatic	408 series (1966–67)
2000TC	418 series (1966–67)

1967–71 Federal cars

2000SC Automatic	858 series (1967–69)
2000TC	859 series (1967–70)
3500S	433 series (1969–71)
2000TC Mk II	435 series (1970–71)

CHAPTER TEN

NEW LOOK OR 'SERIES II' MODELS, 1970–1973

The second half of the 1960s was an almost frantically busy time for Rover, with one new product after another lined up for introduction. First came the 2000TC and 2000 Automatic in 1966; next was the V8 engine (in the P5B 3.5-litre) in 1967; the Three Thousand Five came in 1968; and the Federal 3500S as soon as practicable after that, in 1969. There was then a pause before the planned launch of the Range Rover, which was expected to go on sale in early 1971 after a late-1970 press launch. This left mid-1970 as the only gap in the schedule (although Rover's careful planning was subverted when British Leyland brought the Range Rover launch forward by six months), and so that was the only realistic option for the introduction of the facelifted P6 range.

The new models were actually introduced at the Paris Salon, which opened on 1 October 1970, and for the domestic market they were announced at the Earls Court Motor Show on 14 October. The *Rover & Alvis News* of October 1970 described them as having 'a refreshing and eye-catching external appearance', and trumpeted the fact that the P6 assembly lines were 'at peak production to satisfy full order books'. The magazine also quoted sales figures for the earlier cars that represented a huge success for Rover, even if they seem quite small by modern standards. The company had sold nearly 156,000 4-cylinder P6s (of which almost 30 per cent had gone for export), and nearly 26,000 V8s (of which 33 per cent had been exported).

THE 1971 MODELS

The facelift – New Look in publicity material of the time, Mk II in some Rover company documents, and Series II to

Pictured in late August 1970, just before the launch of the Series II models, PXC 162J was a very early 2000TC numbered 446-00002A. The new grille, side trim strip and wheel trims are very clear in this picture, together with the shrouded door handles and the vinyl-covered rear pillar.

enthusiasts – was quite extensive and affected both the exterior and interior of the cars. However, it was essentially cosmetic and did not bring any major mechanical changes, except for power-assisted steering as an option for the 3500 models. Further changes, which included the long-overdue introduction of a manual-gearbox V8 model, were held over until the start of the 1972 model year.

Back in 1963, David Bache had imagined that a future facelift might be a straightforward re-skin of the original car, using the same base unit. However, by the time work began on the New Look cars, British Leyland were not prepared to grant Rover the budget for such a thing, and so exterior changes had to be limited to ones that were largely decorative. The earliest styling mock-ups appear to date from May 1969, but many of their proposals were not carried forward and it looks as if Bache and his team eventually had to use the Federal 3500S as their starting point (see Chapter 9) and build on that.

Two features obviously carried over from the Federal car were stainless steel trim strips on the flanks, noticeably wider than the ones used for some export markets from the mid-1960s, and Satin Black sill panels that slimmed the side elevation. The black was continued across the bottom of each front wing, just as it had been when Bache first used this visual trick on the V8-engined P5B in autumn 1967. Intriguingly, though, its appearance on the P6 range may well have been prompted by something else. Back in January 1968, Mr Robinson of the Rover Service Department had pointed out that the need to stock pre-painted P6 sills in a variety of different colours was causing his department problems; if the company could introduce one-colour sills, in aluminium or black, he said, the problem would disappear!

Completely new was a bonnet that featured a pair of 'power bulges' like those Bache had designed for the P6-based Alvis GTS (see Chapter 8) a few years earlier. Both 4-cylinder and 8-cylinder models had it, and the V8s lost their distinctive bright metal 'eyebrow'. The bonnet was slightly longer than before, carried a plastic Rover badge on its nose, and was accompanied by a new black plastic grille with an 'egg-box' design and bright silver highlights along its front edges. This idea could be traced back to the Zagato-designed TCZ show car in 1965, via the Federal 3500S. This new grille carried a small bright metal TC or V8 badge when appropriate, the single-carburettor 4-cylinder cars having no badge.

Other distinguishing features of the New Look models were wheel trims with a larger black central section around a plastic Rover emblem, and a black vinyl covering for the

This rear view of an early Series II 2000SC Automatic shows the new tail badges; the 2000 badge was carried over from the last of the Series I cars. HUMPHREY STEVENS

There were still minor variations for some export markets. This is a 2000TC for Austria, with the racing-type mirror that was standard equipment for that market.

rear quarter-panels, with a discreet bright metal Viking ship motif. Bache had been toying with quarter-panels in a contrasting colour ever since the days of the 2000S in 1962 (see Chapter 3), and of course white 2000TC models for North America had contrasting blue-painted quarter-panels. There were new door handles, too, with a stylish shroud around the release buttons. This met the latest safety regulations in Germany, and had not been on the Federal 3500S only a year earlier.

... and here is another dummy registration number, this time on one of the new Series II 3500 cars. The blacked-out sill panels and side trim strip made these models in particular look more slim and lithe than their predecessors.

This time, the registration plate is a real one but the car is actually a Three Thousand Five (425-06954D) that was used in April 1970 as a styling mock-up car for the Series II models.

This is another early styling car. Despite appearances, it was actually a Series I 2000SC Automatic numbered 405-11581J, and this picture was taken in December 1969. Interesting is that the printed chrome rings around the headlights were not carried forward to production.

The new instrument panel, first mooted some eight years earlier, was beautifully clear, and the sweeping dash top that accompanied it added fresh style to the passenger compartment.

At the rear of the car, the red reflectors were now fitted below the tail-light units instead of on the bootlid, and so the stick-on panels disappeared from the channels beside the boot. There were three new exterior paint colours as well. Badges were the same as on the 1970 models, though, with the 'lightweight' 2000 badges for 4-cylinder cars, supplemented by TC or Automatic badges as appropriate; one small change was that the TC badges were no longer fitted on the front wings. For the first New Look cars, the Rover name also remained as separate letters on the left-hand side of the bootlid.

On the inside, all the New Look cars had a new switch panel in the centre of the dash, with illuminated rotary switches and a new hazard warning lights switch; the old toggle switches had gone. This panel was another feature that had been pioneered on the Federal 3500S in autumn 1969, and there were several more. They included the passenger-side map light, the hazard warning light system, the intermittent wiper control with variable delay (a first on a British car, incidentally), the anti-theft lock incorporated in the ignition switch, and the gear-driven front quarter-lights operated by a turnwheel control. While the single-carburettor

Badges on the Series II cars were printed in black (earlier 3500 badges were cast with recessed numbers and frame), and it looks as if Rover experimented with this 'negative' version and made some trial copies before settling for the production style. CHRIS WILSON

cars retained the strip-type speedometer, the 2000TC and V8 models came with the superb new four-dial instrument panel that had entered production for the Federal 3500S and had been designed as long ago as 1962 for the 2000S that did not make production (see Chapter 3).

Completely new for the New Look models were the flatter, crushable grips on all interior door handles – except the front doors of the 3500 – and window winders. These met German safety standards introduced as long ago as 1968 and were presumably standardized on all models to save

A new option on the 1973-model cars was brushed nylon upholstery, initially always in Sandalwood.

Early Series II cars were provided with 'ET' headrests when these were ordered, but the teardrop style took over during the early 1970s.

Rover having to make special handles and winders just for Germany. The company no doubt reasoned that other countries would jump onto the safety bandwagon before long, anyway.

There was a new and darker rosewood-grain plastic laminate for the 'wood' trim on doors and dashboard. A non-slip parcels shelf mat was made standard, and all seat squabs now incorporated fittings for head restraints, although these were an extra-cost option on all models; seats came with a blanking plug as standard to cover the fitting slot. Front seats had also been modified to suit the option of inertia-reel safety belts, which would soon become available.

A new no-cost option across the range was stain-resistant brushed nylon upholstery material in place of the standard leather. This was available only in Sandalwood. As the promotional leaflet for this new upholstery claimed:

Leather... for so long the traditional facing material for high-quality car seats, is no longer the obvious choice, nor is it necessarily the most suitable one... what is the accepted type of material for the chairs we sit in at home has now become available for the cars we travel in day after day. Cars of high quality, with comfort to match.

Rover's plan was clearly to phase out the Ambla upholstery that could be had on entry-level versions of the 2000SC, and in practice that option did disappear at the end of the 1971 season.

All cars now had the battery relocated in the boot, and the 4-cylinder models took on the alternator that had been pioneered on the 3500. Bizarrely, the press release claimed that the battery box had been relocated on the 4-cylinder cars in order to allow larger batteries to be fitted – a piece of PR-speak that is hard to comprehend on any level, let alone to believe! For the 3500 only, the petrol reserve tap outlet was repositioned on the tank, so doubling the reserve capacity to 2.5 gallons (11.4ltr). Clearly customer feedback had suggested that the earlier small reserve, which had given a realistic range of only 20–25 miles (32–40km) in the worst conditions, was too small.

Several other features pioneered on the Federal 3500S in 1969 now found their way to the 3500 for other markets. Power-assisted steering became an extra-cost option and, as on the Federal car, was accompanied by a 16in (406mm) steering wheel with a black leather-covered rim. The brake pad wear warning system was now made standard (although the 4-cylinder cars did not get it), and the front doors now took on the combined armrest and door pull from the Federal cars, although in this case without the stowage bin below it. Presumably that deletion was made to contain costs, as the door bins were actually a very welcome feature in a car with a relatively small passenger cabin.

New Look Models: Press Reactions

'The changing standards of seven years have done nothing to mar our admiration for a fine product,' concluded *Motor* magazine in its 12 December 1970 road test of a 2000SC. Generally speaking, the British motoring press completely agreed with that assessment, and even three years later, *Autocar* still gave high marks to the Rover. In its 26 April 1973 test of a 2000SC, it said that 'there are so many features of the car which continue to set standards for others to attain… It is a tribute to the original design that with minor development and improvement, the car remains competitive in its class ten years after its introduction.'

The New Look visual changes met with approval, too. *Autocar* tried a 2000TC for its issue of 18 March 1971 and was particularly impressed by the new instruments, which had 'very clear lettering and are so well placed that we cannot think of a single car which is better arranged'. The same test concluded that, overall, 'Rover have made it a much more appealing car by the latest revisions'. Not everybody agreed, though, and the *Sunday Express* newspaper of 13 December 1970 described the changes as 'rather pitiful. The makers appear to have indulged in that old sinful habit of fiddling for fiddling's sake. By sticking strips of shining metal along the body, the original purity of line has been lost.'

Motor found the ride of the 2000SC 'still extremely good – almost on a par with the Jaguar XJ6' (which was generally considered to have the best ride of any car then in production). *Autocar* agreed in its test of a 2000TC: 'Ride, handling

and brakes are all more than good enough to take it on for a few more years.' Where the 4-cylinder P6s had fallen behind, however, was on performance. *Autocar* thought that the 2000TC's engine was 'really overdue for a substantial power boost. More capacity would mean more torque and this would give the greater flexibility one expects in a car of this class now.' The TC was 'not quick. The same kind of acceleration, through the gears in the lower speed ranges, is possible in a Ford Escort GT or a Hillman Avenger GT, both with much smaller engines than that of the Rover.'

Autocar was right, of course, although the two GT models appealed to a very different type of buyer from the 2000TC. They were both sporty versions of ordinary family saloons, while the TC was still a small luxury saloon, and was more expensive as a result. But what had been sporting characteristics in the mid-1960s no longer seemed so. The magazine complained of a need to row the car along with the gear lever, to keep the engine revs up to maintain speed, and of 'the rorty exhaust system, which seems totally out of character with the refined nature of the rest of the car'. Fortunately, Rover were already working on a more refined successor.

It should come as no surprise that the single-carburettor cars were also criticized for their lack of performance. In its 2000TC test, *Autocar* commented that the 2000SC was now 'something of a sluggard'. Testing a 2000SC in 1973, the same magazine complained that 'performance [was] not its best point' and that there was 'a disappointing lack of torque at the bottom of the rev range'. *Motor* was more charitable, simply commenting that the 2000SC was 'not quite a 100mph car, although quick enough away from rest to satisfy most owners not interested in the extra TC power'.

The specialist press did not retest the 2000SC Automatic and Rover seem to have been reluctant to submit cars for test, if the experience of the *Sunday Express* correspondent was typical. Yet he was full of praise for the example he was eventually lent to test. 'There are people,' he conceded, 'who can say this car is underpowered,' but overall it was 'quite exceptional… light to handle in traffic and a deceptively languid distance gobbler, it is ideal for so many people who have the proper respect for their blood pressure'.

The New Look 3500 received relatively little press attention, perhaps because Rover wanted the press generally to focus its attention on the manual-gearbox 3500S that would be introduced just a year after the facelift. Nevertheless, *Autocar* tried an example for its 15 October 1970 issue and liked it. 'Rover could easily have remained complacent with the continued demand for the 2000-3500 series,' the testers concluded, 'but instead they have made a big effort to improve the appeal of the cars. A really desirable car like the 3500 thus becomes even better.' Particularly good features were the new instruments, the optional power-assisted steering and brushed nylon seat facings, and the new Dunlop SP Sport tyres, 'adhesion in tricky conditions [being] made even more impressive by these excellent tyres'.

The maximum speed was 112mph (180km/h), slightly below the 114mph (183km/h) that *Autocar* had seen from its April 1968 road test of the Three Thousand Five, but all the acceleration figures were within half a second of the earlier times and the 1970 car actually took 1.3 seconds less to reach 100mph from rest. Perhaps the differences were due to minor variations between individual cars; the new one was very slightly heavier than the earlier example. It was quick enough, anyway, thought *Autocar*, finding it 'fast without having any pretensions to sporting performance'. It was also 'extremely quiet from the aspect of mechanical noise, though quite a lot of the characteristic exhaust beat is audible under acceleration'. That V8 exhaust note, of course, has always been much appreciated by driving enthusiasts!

NEW FOR '72: THE 3500S

As Chapter 6 explains, it had not been easy to find a manual gearbox that was both strong enough to take the torque

of the V8 engine and sufficiently refined to suit customer expectations of a Rover. The long drawn-out association with ZF ultimately failed to deliver what Rover wanted, and by the end of 1968 it must have been clear that something had to be done right away if a manual-gearbox P6B was ever going to go into production. The relationship with ZF was terminated, and Frank Shaw's Transmissions Department was asked to strengthen the existing four-speed gearbox from the 2000 to do the job.

The changes made were minimal, probably to minimize both costs and development time. The gearbox was re-engineered with double the oil capacity of the 2000 type, and a pump driven from the rear of the layshaft provided positive lubrication for gears and bearings. Although the gear ratios of the 2000 were not changed, there were shot-peened gears and taper-roller layshaft bearings in place of the needle-roller type of the 2000's gearbox. The outer casing, too, was strengthened and was given fins to aid cooling. The redesigned gearbox was just about capable of handling the torque of the V8 engine, although there seems to have been not much margin for error, and Rover played for safety by developing a heavy-duty police-specification version as well. This was both noisier and heavier to use than the standard type, and so was not adopted as standard.

No doubt prototypes of the redesigned gearbox had been tested in other development cars during 1969, but it was not until December that year that the first full prototype of the new Rover took to the road. Registered as KXC 676H, it had car number 70350001M, which clearly stood for 1970 model year, 3500, no. 1 manual. In specification, it was in effect a right-hand-drive Federal 3500S, complete with Federal-specification V8 engine, but of course with a manual gearbox. This car went on long-distance test in southern Spain over the summer of 1970, in the hands of brake specialist Jim Shaw. It looks as if the specifica-

The new 3500S took centre stage on Rover's motor show stand in autumn 1971.

And now there were two... This was the October 1971 sales catalogue for the 3500 and 3500S. SXC 216K was another dummy number – although there had been a genuine SXC 216J, which was a 3500.

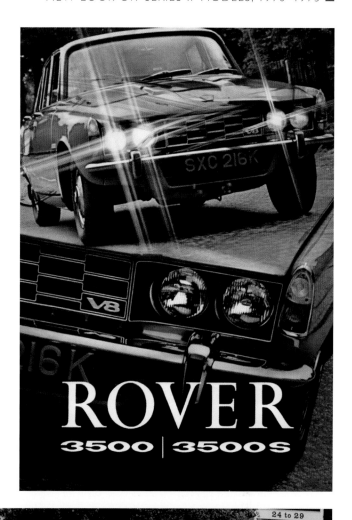

And now there were two... This was the October 1971 sales catalogue for the 3500 and 3500S. SXC 216K was another dummy number – although there had been a genuine SXC 216J, which was a 3500.

tion was already as good as it was going to get, because KXC 676H appears to have been not only the first but also the only full prototype of the new model before production began in mid-1971.

So, at long last, the manual-gearbox V8 engined car was announced as a 1972 model in early October 1971, wearing 3500S identification. Rover's decision to give it that name seems controversial in hindsight, but the car was introduced just as the Federal 3500S (*see* Chapter 9) was dropped from production – and besides, outside the USA very few people indeed knew that the Federal model had ever existed. With the four-speed gearbox, the new V8-engined P6 could reach 60mph from rest in 9.12 seconds and would continue accelerating strongly right up to its maximum speed of 125mph (201km/h). High gearing – gearbox ratios the same as in the 2000, plus the taller 3.08:1 final drive of the 3500 automatic – gave 24mph (39km/h) per 1,000rpm, and a touring consumption of 22.5mpg (12.6ltr/100km). Despite a somewhat heavy clutch, this was unquestionably the masterpiece of the P6 range, and it was also a car that outclassed every rival in its price range.

It almost goes without saying that **TXC 523K** was a dummy number as well... but the car shows all the correct features of a 3500S, with the full vinyl roof, bolt-through wheel trims, special badges and box-pleated seats.

Here are those box-pleat seats, which gave a distinctively sporting air to the 3500S – especially in black, like these.

The manual-gearbox car was distinguished from other New Look models by a vinyl-covered roof in brown or black, with sill panels painted to match, by the bolt-through wheeltrims of the Federal model, and by 3500S plate badges, which were printed rather than engraved like those of the Federal car. On the inside, it came with box-pleated Ambla upholstery (the first use of box-pleating outside the Federal cars) that gave a suitably sporting appearance and also certainly helped Rover to price the car attractively below the leather-upholstered 3500 with automatic gearbox. A leather option was cunningly held over until January 1972, and when it arrived it put the cost of the car above that of a standard 3500.

Right from the start of production, the new 3500S was a hot property. It seemed to be exactly what police forces in Britain wanted as a motorway patrol car, and there was an immediate and strong demand for that use.

3500S: Press Reactions

The comment that most accurately summed up the character of the new 3500S came from *Australian Motor Manual* in December 1972. 'The first thing that strikes you when you drive the 3500S,' they wrote, 'is the tremendous reserve of smooth power.' Without the losses through the torque

converter that affected the automatic models, the V8 engine could at last show its full potential.

The leading British magazines had already given their verdicts by this time, and were very enthusiastic about the car. 'With a top speed of 120mph [193km/h],' said the *Motor* test of 16 October 1971, 'it offers an unrivalled combination of high performance and reasonable economy, good handling and road-holding, an excellent ride, refinement with much luxury and, perhaps most important of all, quality.' For *Autocar* dated 21 October, the 3500S was 'more than a match for its competitors, both British and foreign', and 'we can best sum it up by saying that we cannot think of a single car we would prefer at the price'.

Autocar elaborated by saying that the effects of putting a manual gearbox into the V8-engined P6 were to 'surpass all expectations' and to give the car 'excellent mid-range performance'. *Motor* rather strangely argued that performance differences between the 3500S and the automatic car were 'rather academic and only apparent in the upper speed ranges'. The *Motor Sport* test did not appear until that magazine's May 1972 issue, and Bill Boddy, rather cross at having to wait several months for a road test car, expressed both praise and doubts. On the one hand, 'the V8 is a much faster car than the TC'; on the other, while 'there is no denying the impressiveness of the performance… On the road… I felt no very great improvement over the TC until the lower gears were stirred about to keep the engine turning at over 4,000 to 4,500rpm.'

The 3500S was certainly not perfect, of course. *Autocar* singled out the rather heavy clutch and gear whine in the indirect ratios; *Motor* agreed about the gear whine, also pointing out that the gearchange was 'a little heavy and ponderous in action with rather obstructive synchromesh which does not encourage snatched changes upwards or rapid changes downwards, especially from third to second'. *Autocar* also found that 'over-exuberance on tight corners soon has the inside rear wheel spinning furiously. With this amount of power on tap, a limited-slip differential would be a worthwhile proposition.'

Motor Sport complained of quite serious yaw at high speeds, and Bill Boddy had a long list of complaints about the car's appearance.

Air-conditioning became available on 1971 3500 models, but was always rare. It came with a single-scoop bonnet and an air cleaner like that on the NADA 3500S Automatic.

This was the layout of the air-conditioning system on the V8 models. The compressor was a proprietary type, manufactured by York.

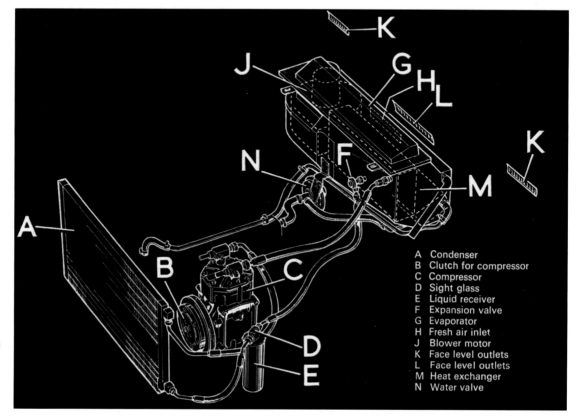

A Condenser
B Clutch for compressor
C Compressor
D Sight glass
E Liquid receiver
F Expansion valve
G Evaporator
H Fresh air inlet
J Blower motor
K Face level outlets
L Face level outlets
M Heat exchanger
N Water valve

With the air-conditioning came a different control arrangement on the centre console. Also visible in this picture is the later style of automatic selector grip that replaced the earlier ball type.

To me, Rover implies dignity and the garish trims on the V8's bolt-on wheels, intended to make them resemble 'boy-racer' magnesium alloy ones, the trim line along the body sides, the too-obvious type-badges and ROVER name on body and boot, the substitution of pleated Ambla upholstery for hide... and the grained plastic stuck on the steel roof did not seem in keeping with the best Solihull tradition.

EVOLUTION, 1970–73

Few changes were made to the P6 range during the 1971 model year, although at an unknown date in 1971 the 2000TC was given a rev limiter on the distributor, apparently to safeguard the engine against over-enthusiastic owners who had tried to out-accelerate V8 models. Meanwhile, the Ambla upholstery option for the 2000SC was not proving popular, and from around May 1971 it was replaced by an Ebony brushed nylon option. The material had nevertheless proved itself, and would become standard on the 3500S in the autumn, albeit with a box-pleated rather than flat-pleated design. At the same time, inertia-reel belts were made an option for the front seats, and their acceptance would persuade Rover to make them standard equipment a few months later.

It was also in May 1971 that air-conditioning became available as an option for the 3500 models, the installation being essentially the same as on the contemporary Federal 3500S. It was still listed as an option in 1975 but was always very rare. The timing of its introduction strongly suggests that Rover saw it as a way of using up stocks of the air-conditioning systems that had been ordered for the Federal cars, which were due to go out of production over the summer. The first dozen or so New Look 3500 models to have it had a single bonnet scoop that fed air directly into the top of the air filter box in exactly the same way as on the Federal cars. However, later examples seem to have managed without this. All the air-conditioned cars came with a viscous-coupled cooling fan, an electric fuel pump and power-assisted steering.

The 1972 cars introduced in autumn 1971 came with a mild facelift, in the form of new badges. Printed plate-type model badges became standard on all cars (in line with British Leyland corporate policy), with a plate badge for the Rover name instead of separate letters on the boot lid as well; there was now no identifying badge to distinguish a 2000SC Automatic from its manual equivalent. Development for the new 3500S had also led to the gear lever on all manual-gearbox cars being mounted on a gearbox extension instead of to the transmission tunnel, in order to reduce vibration.

Displaying its new plate badges is a 4-cylinder model. Other photographs in the sequence show that this one carried the registration plate TXC 524K – another dummy.

Also new for 1972 was a larger fuse box, now with twelve fuses to handle the car's electrical demands more effectively. Four-cylinder models gained a new pre-engaged starter motor in place of the old inertia type, and the TC's air cleaner now came with a new thermostatically controlled air intake – an award-winning piece of design from the Austin-Morris division of British Leyland that appeared on several of the group's engines at about this time. It shortened engine warm-up times and contributed to better fuel consumption, too. The V8 engines for 1972 came with a flat-bladed fan instead of the curved-blade type originally designed to reduce fan noise. Then there were more powerful (75-watt) inner headlamps for most markets, including of course the UK.

Interior changes for 1972 were limited at first to the ashtrays, which now had a modified design incorporating a spring-assisted lid with a release button, and a matt finish intended to reduce reflections that might distract the driver. Then from January 1972 came further changes, as inertia-reel front safety belts became standard on all models, and 'teardrop' headrests (first seen on the Federal 3500S) replaced the earlier 'ET' type on the options list. Rover still had some stocks of the older type, but these were gradually used up over the next few months.

Paint colours underwent only minor changes for 1972 and during the season, but for the 1973 models introduced in autumn 1972 the white option was changed and a new and distinctive colour called Lunar Grey (which was actually a light greyish-green) joined the range. Two interior colours were also replaced (see the panel below).

Long overdue was a quieter exhaust system for the 4-cylinder cars, which for 1973 took on a three-silencer system in place of the old one with only two silencers. However, other changes were not introduced until mid-season. In February 1973 came new round grips for the petrol reserve and choke control, which were now 'crushable' to meet safety requirements in some markets. Similar grips had been available earlier on cars sold in Germany, to meet local regulations. At the same time, the heated rear window was fused through the main fuse box and the fuse for the hazard warning lights was deleted. A more powerful battery-sensed 18ACR alternator also replaced the earlier machine-sensed type. There was then one more change in April 1973, when L92Y spark plugs were fitted to all V8 engines to counter the misfiring that occasionally occurred with the earlier L87Y type.

Probably dating from this period were some experiments done jointly with Triplex on demister elements for the front

The cost of living.

Compared with the average 2-litre saloon, the Rover 2000 may seem a little expensive.

Until you consider the extra safety you get for your money.

A steel safety cage to protect both you and your passengers.

A steel bulkhead to stop the engine penetrating the passenger compartment in a head-on collision.

Disc brakes on all four wheels.

And 30 other safety features that won us the first medal for safety ever awarded by the AA.

With all this safety built in, perhaps you can see why the Rover 2000 is Britain's most expensive 2-litre saloon.

And, with road conditions as they are today, why it's also Britain's most successful. ❀ ◉ ROVER ❀

The Rover Company Limited, Solihull, Warwickshire.

Safety was still an important element in the marketing of the Rover 2000. The registration number BXC 743J on the car pictured in this advertisement was one of the many dummy ones that Rover used in publicity material in the early 1970s.

door windows. The heating elements were orange Hotline types, printed on the glass, and while probably effective would also probably have hindered vision out of the car to an unacceptable extent. They were tried on at least one P6 but the idea was not pursued.

SELLING THE NEW LOOK MODELS

Rover advertisements in this period tended to focus on the P6's reputation for safety, perhaps partly to counter the success that the Volvo 144 was now having in Britain. One late 1970 advertisement for the 2000TC and 3500 models relegated the New Look features to second place, stressing that the tried and trusted ones had not been changed:

> In some ways, 1971's Rovers are exactly the same as 1970's Rovers. We haven't dropped any of the 23 safety features that gave us the first gold medal for safety awarded by the AA … Yet we've still managed to come up with some big improvements for 1971. There are 10 new or improved safety features…

> And as you can see, our body's taken on a rather advanced new look. So 1971's Rovers won't look any more old-fashioned in seven years' time than a seven-year-old Rover 2000 looks today.

The message remained substantially the same in May 1973. 'You are right to feel safe in a Rover,' ran the headline of one advertisement. Once again, there was a reference to the twenty-three safety features, and comfort was picked

PAINT AND TRIM OPTIONS

September 1970–September 1971

Three new paint colours were introduced – Almond, Cameron Green and Mexico Brown. They replaced Arden Green, Burnt Grey and Sage Green, leaving the total of colour options at eight again. Black vinyl rear quarter-panels were standard with all colours, and sills were painted Satin Black on all models.

Trim colours and materials remained the same as before, except that Ambla upholstery (in all four colours) became an option for the 2000SC only, and brushed nylon upholstery (in Sandalwood only) became an option for all models. The Ambla upholstery option for the 2000SC had gone by July 1971.
The combinations now available were:

Almond	with trim in	Buckskin, Ebony or Sandalwood
Brigade Red		Buckskin, Ebony, Sandalwood or Toledo Red
Cameron Green		Buckskin, Ebony or Sandalwood
Corsica Blue		Buckskin, Ebony or Sandalwood
Davos White		Ebony, Sandalwood or Toledo Red
Mexico Brown		Buckskin, Sandalwood or Toledo Red
Tobacco Leaf		Buckskin, Ebony or Sandalwood
Zircon Blue		Buckskin, Ebony or Sandalwood

October 1971–March 1972

Monza Red replaced Brigade Red, but the total number of colour options remained at eight. Trim colours remained as before, with brushed nylon upholstery only in Sandalwood at first; from approximately May 1971 there was an Ebony brushed nylon option as well. Ambla trim was standard on the new 3500S, which also had a choice of two colours for its vinyl roof covering and sills. The combinations were:

Almond	with trim in	Buckskin, Ebony, Sandalwood or Toledo Red
Cameron Green		Buckskin, Ebony or Sandalwood
Corsica Blue		Buckskin, Ebony or Sandalwood
Davos White		Ebony, Sandalwood or Toledo Red
Mexico Brown		Buckskin, Sandalwood or Toledo Red
Monza Red		Buckskin, Ebony, Sandalwood or Toledo Red
Tobacco Leaf		Buckskin, Ebony or Sandalwood
Zircon Blue		Buckskin, Ebony or Sandalwood

out as an important contributory factor in the car's safety record, '… but a Rover gives you far more than safety and comfort. It gives you confidence. The confidence that comes from control.' At the end, the Rover-British Leyland logo was accompanied by the discreet message, 'Rover: Travel First Class'.

The New Look models sold very well in Britain, helped no doubt by Rover's determination to keep prices at sensible levels despite the general inflationary trend. Over the three

seasons of its production, the New Look 2000SC increased in price by only 11 per cent. Nevertheless, strong sales at home were matched by a downturn abroad. Exports of the P6 range all but collapsed in this same three-year period. It was clearly time for something new to keep P6 sales alive; the V8 models were selling strongly wherever local taxation on large engines did not price them out of the market, but it was the 4-cylinder models that needed a boost.

Ebony vinyl rear quarter-panels remained standard on all models except the 3500S, which had a full vinyl roof covering with matching quarter-panels; sills on the 3500S were Satin Black with Ebony roof trim or Satin Brown with Huntsman roof trim. The roof trim colours on the 3500S were as follows:

| Ebony | with paint in | Cameron Green, Corsica Blue, Monza Red or Zircon Blue |
| Huntsman | | Almond, Davos White, Mexico Brown or Tobacco Leaf |

(From December 1971, Ebony roof trim on the 3500S was only available with Ebony interior trim.)

April–July 1972
Zircon Blue was discontinued, leaving seven paint options available. There were no other changes.

August 1972–August 1973
Arctic White replaced Davos White, and Lunar Grey made the total paint options up to eight again. Sills were painted Satin Black on all cars except those with Huntsman roof trim, when they were Satin Brown.

The Sandalwood and Toledo Red interior trim options were replaced by Bronze and Mango. Standard upholstery was still leather, but the brushed nylon option remained available (in Ebony or Sandalwood) and Ambla remained standard on the 3500S. Birch Grey carpets were fitted with all varieties of Ebony trim. The combinations were:

Almond	with trim in	Bronze, Buckskin or Ebony
Arctic White		Bronze, Ebony or Mango
Cameron Green		Bronze, Buckskin or Mango
Corsica Blue		Buckskin, Ebony or Mango
Lunar Grey		Bronze, Ebony or Mango
Mexico Brown		Bronze, Buckskin or Mango
Monza Red		Bronze, Buckskin or Ebony
Tobacco Leaf		Bronze, Buckskin or Ebony

Roof trim colours for the 3500S were as follows:

| Ebony | with paint in | Cameron Green, Corsica Blue, Lunar Grey or Monza Red (and other colours if Ebony interior trim was specified) |
| Huntsman | | Almond, Arctic White, Mexico Brown or Tobacco Leaf (except with Ebony interior trim) |

OPTIONAL EXTRAS, 1971–73 MODEL YEARS

For 1971 Model Year

Air-conditioning no longer available on 4-cylinder models

Air-conditioning for 3500, with electric fuel pump and PAS, from May 1971; first dozen or so cars with single bonnet scoop; available for 3500S as well from October 1971

Badge bar

Brushed nylon upholstery

Dipping interior mirror (standard for some export markets)

Driving lamp (Lucas Square 8)

Floor mats

Fog lamp (Lucas Square 8)

Head restraints, front

Head restraints, rear

Heated rear window (standard in UK and some other markets)

Laminated windscreen

Mud flaps, front and rear

Oil cooler for 2000TC (standard for all markets except the UK and Ireland)

PAS with 16in (406mm) leather-rim steering wheel, for 3500 only

Radio (type dependent on market)

Safety belts for front seats, inertia-reel type, from May 1971

Safety belts for rear seats, static type

Spare wheel mount on bootlid

Sundym tinted glass

Sunroof (Coenan metal type)

Sunroof (Hollandia metal type)

Sunroof (Tudor Webasto fabric type)

Wire wheels no longer available for 2000TC

Wooden gear-lever grip

Wood-rim steering wheel

For 1972 Model Year

As 1971, plus the following:

Ambla upholstery no longer available for 2000SC

Grab handle no longer available

Heavy-duty rear suspension for 4-cylinder models (primarily for police use)

Heavy-duty suspension, front and rear, for V8 models (primarily for police use)

Leather upholstery for 3500S, from January 1972

For 1973 Model Year

As 1972, plus the following:

Collapsible boot floor (for use when spare was stowed flat in boot well)

Towbar: shaped cross-piece, to give clearance for rear overriders

PRICES AND RIVALS, 1970–73

The totals shown here were basic showroom prices in the UK without extras. Also shown are the basic ex-factory cost and the purchase tax payable. The UK switched to a decimal system of currency in February 1971.

September 1970

	Total	Ex-factory	Purchase tax
2000SC (Ambla)	£1,660 6s 11d	£1,270	£390 6s 11d
2000SC (Leather)	£1,674 14s 2d	£1,281	£393 14s 2d
2000TC	£1,777 16s 11d	£1,360	£417 16s 11d
2000SC Auto	£1,802 13s 1d	£1,379	£423 13s 1d
3500	£2,049 8s	£1,568	£481 8s

January 1971

	Total	Ex-factory	Purchase tax
2000SC (Ambla)	£1,743 18s 1d	£1,334	£409 18s 1d
2000SC (Leather)	£1,758 5s 3d	£1,345	£413 5s 3d
2000TC	£1,866 12s 6d	£1,428	£438 12s 6d
2000SC Auto	£1,892 14s 9d	£1,448	£444 14s 9d
3500	£2,149 18s 7d	£1,645	£504 18s 7d

July 1971

	Total	Ex-factory	Purchase tax
2000SC	£1,683.12	£1,345	£338.12
2000TC	£1,786.88	£1,428	£358.88
2000SC Auto	£1,811.87	£1,448	£363.87
3500	£2,058.12	£1,645	£413.12

October 1971

	Total	Ex-factory	Purchase tax
2000SC	£1,683.12	£1,345	£338.12
2000TC	£1,786.88	£1,428	£358.88
2000SC Auto	£1,811.87	£1,448	£363.87
3500S	£1,976.88	£1,580	£396.88
3500	£2,058.12	£1,645	£413.12

January 1972

	Total	Ex-factory	Purchase tax
2000SC	£1,783.13	£1,425	£358.13
2000TC	£1,981.88	£1,512	£379.88
2000SC Auto	£1,908.12	£1,525	£383.12
3500S	£2,095.62	£1,675	£420.62
3500	£2,176.88	£1,740	£436.88

5 April 1972

	Total	Ex-factory	Purchase tax
2000SC	£1,723.44	£1,425	£298.44
2000TC	£1,828.56	£1,512	£316.56
2000SC Auto	£1,844.27	£1,525	£319.27
3500S	£2,025.52	£1,675	£350.52
3500	£2,104.06	£1,740	£364.06

24 April 1972

	Total	Ex-factory	Purchase tax
2000SC	£1,776.60	£1,469	£307.60
2000TC	£1,884.15	£1,558	£326.15
2000SC Auto	£1,897.44	£1,569	£328.44
3500S	£2,089.56	£1,728	£361.56
3500	£2,168.10	£1,793	£375.10

August 1972

	Total	Ex-factory	Purchase tax
2000SC	£1,868.44	£1,545	£323.44
2000TC	£1,983.23	£1,640	£343.23
2000SC Auto	£1,989.27	£1,645	£344.27
3500S	£2,206.77	£1,825	£381.77
3500	£2,285.31	£1,890	£395.31

Rivals

The main domestic competition still came from the Triumph 2000 and 2.5PI models, but there were also some serious new competitors from abroad. These included the Audi 100, BMW 2002, Citroën D Super and DS20, Peugeot 504 and Volvo 144 and 164. These cars offered varying combinations of more space, cheaper running costs, better performance and – an important one as British Leyland disease set in – better service support. They did severe damage to P6 sales outside the UK, especially in Europe.

ROVER 2000SC, 2000SC AUTOMATIC AND 2000TC, 1970–73

Rover 2000SC, SC Automatic and TC

Engine: (2000SC and 2000SC Automatic)
Type: Cast iron block and light alloy head
Cylinders: 4
Bore and stroke: 85.7mm × 85.7mm
Capacity: 1978cc
Five-bearing crankshaft
Single overhead camshaft
Carburettor: Single SU type HS6 carburettor
Compression ratio 9:1
Max. power: 99bhp SAE (90bhp installed) at 5,000rpm
Max. torque: 121lb ft SAE at 3,600rpm (113.5lb ft at 2,750rpm, installed)
Compression ratio 7.5:1 (export only)
Max. power: 87.5bhp SAE (80bhp installed) at 5,000rpm
Max. torque: 113lb ft SAE at 3,350rpm (106lb ft at 2,500rpm, installed)

Engine: (2000TC)
Type: Cast iron block and light alloy head
Cylinders: 4
Bore and stroke: 85.7mm × 85.7mm
Capacity: 1978cc
Five-bearing crankshaft
Single overhead camshaft
Carburettors: Two SU type HS8 carburettors
Compression ratio 10:1
Max. power: 124bhp SAE (109.5bhp DIN) at 5,500rpm
Max. torque: 132lb ft SAE at 4,000rpm (124lb ft DIN at 2,750rpm)
Compression ratio 9:1
Max. power: 107bhp at 5,500rpm

Transmission
2000SC and 2000TC:
Gearbox: Four-speed all-synchromesh manual
Ratios
  1st: 3.62:1
  2nd: 2.13:1

3rd: 1.39:1
4th: 1.00:1
Reverse: 3.43:1
2000SC Automatic
Gearbox: Three-speed Borg Warner Type 35 automatic
Ratios
  1st: 2.39:1
  Intermediate: 1.45:1
  Top: 1.00:1
  Reverse: 2.09:1
Axle ratio: 3.54:1

Suspension and Steering
Front: Independent suspension with transverse bottom links and leading upper links acting on coil springs mounted horizontally to the bulkhead; anti-roll bar; hydraulic telescopic dampers
Rear: Lower links and coil springs; De Dion tube incorporating sliding joint, with transverse location by fixed-length driveshafts and fore-and-aft location by Watts linkage; hydraulic telescopic dampers
Steering: Adamant Marles worm-and-roller type

Brakes
Type: Discs on all four wheels, mounted inboard at the rear; Girling discs and callipers; handbrake acting on rear discs; servo assistance standard
Size: 10.31in front, 10.69in rear
Tyres: 165 SR 14 radial
Wheels: Five-stud steel disc wheels 14in diameter
Rim width: 5in

Dimensions
Wheelbase: 103.375in (2,626mm)
Overall length: 178.5in (4,534mm)
Overall width: 66in (1,676mm)
Overall height: 54.75in (1,390mm)
Track: Front 53.375in (1,356mm)
Track: Rear 52.5in (1,333mm)
Running weight: 2,727lb (1,237kg), 2000SC
2,751lb (1,248kg), 2000SC Automatic
2,749lb (1,247kg), 2000TC

Performance

Max. speed: 100.2mph (161.3km/h), 2000SC
100mph (161km/h), 2000SC Automatic
112mph (180km/h), 2000TC

0–60mph: 13.9sec – 2000SC
17.75sec – 2000SC Automatic
11.45sec – 2000TC

Rover 3500

Engine

Type: V8 with light alloy block and cylinder heads

Cylinders: 8

Bore and stroke: 88.9mm × 71.1mm

Capacity: 3528cc

Five-bearing crankshaft

Single central camshaft, overhead valves

Carburettors: Two SU carburettors, type HS6 with 1.75in throats

Compression ratio: 10.5:1

Max. power: 184bhp SAE at 5,200rpm (144bhp DIN at 5,000rpm),

Max. torque: 226lb ft SAE at 3,000rpm (197lb ft DIN at 2,700rpm)

Compression ratio: 8.5:1

Max. power: 162bhp SAE at 5,000rpm

Max. torque: 210lb ft SAE at 3,000rpm

Transmission

Gearbox: Three-speed Borg Warner Type 35 automatic

Ratios
1st: 2.39:1
Intermediate: 1.45:1
Top: 1.00:1
Reverse: 2.09:1

Axle ratio 3.54:1

Suspension and Steering

Front: Independent suspension with transverse bottom links and leading upper links acting on coil springs mounted horizontally to the bulkhead; hydraulic telescopic dampers

Rear: Suspension by De Dion tube incorporating sliding joint, with transverse location by fixed-length driveshafts and stabilizer rod; fore-and-aft location by Watts linkage, with coil springs between front links and base unit

Steering: Burman recirculating-ball, worm-and-nut type with variable ratio. Power assistance optional

Tyres: 185 HR 14 radial

Wheels: Five-stud steel disc wheels with 14in diameter

Rims: 5.5in

Brakes

Type: Discs on all four wheels, mounted inboard at the rear; Girling discs and callipers; handbrake acting on rear discs; servo assistance standard

Size: 10.82in front, 10.69in rear

Dimensions

Wheelbase: 103.375in (2,626mm)

Overall length: 179.75in (4,565mm)

Overall width: 66in (1,676mm)

Overall height: 55.75in (1,416mm)

Track: Front 53.375in (1,356mm)

Track: Rear 51.75in (1,314mm)

Running weight: 2,861lb (1,298kg)

Performance

Max speed: 118mph (190km/h) with 10.5:1 compression engine
110mph (177km/h) with 8.5:1 compression engine

0–60mph: 10.5sec with 10.5:1 compression engine
11.0sec with 8.5:1 compression engine

3500S (1971–73)

As for contemporary 3500, except:

Gearbox: Four-speed all-synchromesh manual

Ratios
1st: 3.62:1,
2nd: 2.13:1
3rd: 1.39:1
4th: 1.00:1
Reverse: 3.43:1

Running weight: 2,868lb (1,301kg)

Performance

Max speed: 125mph (201km/h)

0–60mph: 9.58sec

CHAPTER ELEVEN

THE 2200s AND REVISED V8s, 1973–1977

The New Look models introduced in 1970 did give the P6 range a new lease of life, but by 1973 there was no denying that the cars were becoming dated. While the 3500 and 3500S still offered competitive performance and refinement, the 2000 models no longer did so: an engine that had seemed exciting back in 1963 was, frankly, dated ten years down the line. The P6's poor rear legroom was also increasingly counting against it as newer designs offered better accommodation. Sales were still strong in the home market, but export interest was declining quite dramatically – as indeed were the export sales of all British cars in this period.

Rover did have a replacement model in preparation. What had started out as the P10 in 1969 had evolved into the SD1 after Rover and Triumph had been brought together in British Leyland's Specialist Cars Division during 1971. But it was by no means imminent. The Rover-Triumph engineers believed they could have it ready for production by autumn 1975 at the earliest – and in practice it would be summer 1976 before the first examples went on sale.

By this stage, British Leyland were in no position to allocate Rover a large sum of money to fund any more major changes to the P6 range. The car would have to be kept saleable on a fairly minimal budget until the new SD1 was ready. Triumph faced much the same dilemma with their 2000 and 2.5PI saloons, still rivals for the P6 Rovers even though the two marques had now effectively amalgamated; the SD1 was to replace these models as well.

So Rover looked at ways of making maximum impact for minimum expenditure, and concluded that the most important thing to do was to improve the performance of the 4-cylinder cars. They also used this opportunity to increase commonality between the 4-cylinder and V8 models, so taking some costs out of the manufacturing process. By mid-1973 a package of changes was ready, and the final major

variants of the P6 range were launched on 1 October 1973 as 1974 models. The 3500 and 3500S remained available, but the 4-cylinder range was replaced by new models called the 2200SC, 2200SC Automatic and 2200TC, all of which had a new 2204cc version of the existing ohc 4-cylinder engine.

The new models were introduced at a pivotal time for Rover's parent company, British Leyland. Two events in late 1973 worsened the company's already precarious financial state, and by the end of 1974 the position had become critical. British Leyland were staring bankruptcy in the face and had to go cap-in-hand to Harold Wilson's new Labour government to seek financial support. This was granted – the alternative facing the government was to see thousands of motor industry employees suddenly out of work – but on a number of conditions. One was that the government itself would become a majority shareholder in the company and would have a say in its corporate future. A new holding company was created with the name of British Leyland Ltd (almost universally known as BL) so that this could happen. Both the company's budget and, bizarrely, its decisions about future products, became subject to government scrutiny and approval. In effect, BLMC had been nationalized.

The events of late 1973 also had their effect more directly on Rover. Sales of big-engined cars such as the 3500 and 3500S slumped in the wake of the oil crisis that erupted that autumn. In early October, Egypt and Syria had launched a co-ordinated attack against Israel in the hope of regaining territory lost during the 1967 Arab-Israeli War. Israel had successfully fought them off, seizing even more territory than before, and a cease-fire had been declared before the end of the month. However, the Arab association of oil producers (OPEC) now tried a form of blackmail to force territorial concessions by Israel that would allow the Palestinians their own state. They put pressure on Israel's western allies by cutting oil supplies to some and raising oil prices for others. In Britain, fuel prices escalated and car sales slowed dramatically – all at a time of serious inflation, which would reach 23 per cent by June 1975.

The second blow was from the five-month-long coal miners' strike that began in November 1973. The strike cost British Leyland an enormous amount of money – some three-quarters of a billion pounds sterling – as it generated emergency power to maintain production and air-freighted after-sales replacement parts to the UK from around the world in order to maintain limited production of new cars.

Sadly, the collapse of British Leyland seemed to be perfectly in tune with the socio-political atmosphere of the times. The early 1970s were a period when Britain had largely lost faith in itself, and so the 1974 collapse was just another highly public British disaster in a chain of many. In such an atmosphere it was hardly surprising that domestic car buyers came to the conclusion that BL's cars were somehow sub-standard. The public feeling was that if it had been made in Britain, it could not be any good, and of course foreign manufacturers were not slow to recognize their opportunity. The numbers of Volvos and Peugeots on suburban driveways in Britain began to increase – and Rover would never regain the market they had lost.

THE NEW 2200 ENGINE

The 2200 engine had come about almost by accident, and was actually based on an engine originally intended for the forthcoming P6 replacement model, then known as P10 but soon to become SD1. Work on this engine began in June 1970 and was led by Dave Wall from Jack Swaine's engines team at Solihull.

The plan was to develop the existing Rover ohc 4-cylinder with twin overhead camshafts and four valves per cylinder –

This cutaway view shows the new 2200TC engine with its cast top cover bearing the Rover name. The thermostatically controlled air intake is at the left of the picture.

a cost-effective way of getting more value from the existing engine and one that would certainly have received a nod of approval from the accountants at British Leyland. In principle, the original cylinder block was retained; it was also redesigned to save some weight, but not so extensively that it could not be machined on existing P6 transfer line tooling, which was to be modified to accommodate an increase in the bore size. The block was also designed to be mounted at an angle to fit under the sloping bonnet planned for the P10, and as a result was often called the 'slant-four' at Solihull.

Dave Wall told the author many years ago that the increase in bore size was made primarily to make room for the four valves above each cylinder. He settled for a 90.5mm diameter (the 2000 engine had an 85.7mm bore), which was the largest that could safely be achieved. This gave a swept volume of 2204cc. Five or six prototypes of the engine were built, and one, fitted with Bosch L-Jetronic fuel injection, was developing 170bhp on the test-bed when British Leyland brought the project to a halt.

What had happened was simply the resolution of a potential clash between the new Rover and a planned new

Triumph. British Leyland decided in favour of the new Rover but kept the Triumph engineers happy by allowing them to go ahead with a new 6-cylinder engine that Rover could use in the cheaper versions of their new saloon. In those

Rover were clearly rather proud of the new Paprika paint option, seen here on a 2000SC. The buyers were rather less impressed.

The steering wheel centre of course carried '2200' identification on the new 4-cylinder models. This is an early left-hand-drive 2200TC with km/h speedometer, showing the longer gearstick and the switchgear with crush-proof choke and fuel reserve knobs.

circumstances, there was no reason to proceed with further work on the 4-valve Rover engine, and the project was formally cancelled in May 1971. It was the last new engine ever designed by the old Rover Company; Rover and Triumph were formally amalgamated in early 1972.

Nevertheless, Dave Wall's work was not wasted. There was enough money available for a limited upgrade of the existing 4-cylinder P6, and so the 90.5mm bore was transferred to the existing single-ohc engine, where it allowed the cylinder head to be redesigned with larger exhaust valves. This improved breathing, and in tandem with the additional swept volume it improved the engine's power and torque outputs.

This was also a time when concern about exhaust emissions was spreading, and several countries were introducing legislation to limit those emissions. Carburettor maker SU had designed their new HIF series to meet the new legislation through more precise mixture control, and Rover chose 1.75in HIF6 types for both single- and twin-carburettor versions of its new engine. These also gave higher gas velocity at lower engine speeds than the 2in carburettors on the 2000 engines, so improving driveability quite noticeably.

It is difficult to compare the outputs of the 2.2-litre engines directly with those of their 2000 predecessors, because from autumn 1973, British Leyland generally started to quote engine figures to DIN standards instead of the earlier SAE figures. (DIN stood for Deutsche Industrie Normen or German Industry Standards, while SAE was for the Society of Automotive Engineers, an American body.) The DIN standards were more representative of the engine as installed in a car, complete with power-sapping ancillary equipment, while the SAE figures were closer to pure bench-test figures and were taken without ancillaries attached. So on paper, the 2.2-litre engines appear less powerful than the 2-litre ones they replaced. That was not quite the case, although the 1974-season 4-cylinder models had certainly gained a little more weight and could not reach the same maximum speeds as the 2-litre cars. By way of compensation, the new engines were much smoother and more refined than the old ones.

Other changes of detail played their part. A new ribbed and grey-painted rocker cover bearing the Rover name helped to distinguish the new engine at a glance, and a '2.2' identifier was cast into the cylinder block. The engines also had a new pre-engaged Lucas 2M100 starter motor, but the TC remained the only variant with a thermostatically controlled air intake.

THE 2200 MODELS

There was a greater degree of parts commonization between the 2200 models and the V8s than there had been between 2000s and V8s. This was at least partly in the interests of manufacturing economies, but it also provided stronger components to cope with the greater outputs of the new 4-cylinder engines.

All the 2200s were initially suffix A types. They took on the stronger final drive and rubber-mounted rear suspension that had been standard on the V8s since the beginning, plus the V8 models' larger 15-gallon (68ltr) fuel tank. This

There were no changes to the view from the rear, except of course that the 2200 models had new badges. This late 2200SC was once owned by the author and is carrying the optional extras of a passenger's side door mirror and rear fog guard lamps.

increased their theoretical range on a full tank by a useful 25 per cent. An uprated clutch with a tougher lining coped with the increased torque of the new engines, and the pinions of first, second and third gears were shot-peened as an additional precaution.

The new 4-cylinder cars were slightly quicker through the gears than the models they replaced, with a more reassuring depth of torque available. The difference was most noticeable on the 2200SC Automatic, which was a much more pleasant car to drive than the old 2000 model. Refinement was higher all round: a new design of intermediate silencer box reduced exhaust boom, and extra soundproofing at the front of the passenger cabin also made a contribution. All of this was most noticeable on the 2200TC, which had admittedly lost some of the sporty feeling of the old 2000TC but was a much better car for it, with refinement more typical of a Rover.

REVISED V8s

Europe followed the US lead on exhaust emissions regulation with the introduction of the first ECE Regulation 15

standards in 1970. These measured the amount of CO_2 in car exhausts over a stylized driving cycle that was said to represent typical driving conditions in busy European cities. The standards were tightened for 1974, with ECE Regulation 15-01, and to meet those Rover had to make some changes to its V8 engines. Other factors had an influence on those changes, too, notably the planned withdrawal of Five-Star (99–101 RON) petrol.

The major changes, then, were to the compression ratio and the carburation. All V8s now had a 9.25:1 compression ratio to cope with Four-Star (96–98 RON) petrol, and they had HIF6 carburettors – the same as those adopted for the 2200 engines – because these gave the more precise fuel metering that was needed to meet the new emissions regulations. Inevitably, there was a reduction in power output, which for the last engines with a 10.5:1 compression had been quoted to DIN standards as 152.5bhp at 5,000rpm with 203.5lb ft of torque at 2,750rpm; the 1974-season V8s had 143bhp at 5,000rpm and 202lb ft at 2,700rpm. Rover had clawed back a few bhp by fitting the large-bore exhaust system of the 3500S models to the 3500 as well, but in the real world, the difference between old and new high-compression engines was as negligible as it appears on paper.

This 1974-model 3500S looks every inch the sports saloon in Monza Red with Ebony vinyl roof trim. The bolt-through wheel trims of the early 3500S had now given way to the plainer push-fit type. Despite the convincing-looking Solihull registration plate, the number is a fake applied for the publicity picture: there were no genuine KXC-M registrations.

The new ECE 15-01 V8 engines also took on the rubber lip-type crankshaft seals that had already replaced the original rope-type seals on V8 engines destined for Range Rovers. The first ones were identified by a D suffix to the engine number.

The 3500S soldiered on with its just-about-adequate four-speed manual gearbox, but Rover chose to provide a new automatic gearbox for the 1974-season 3500 models, even though the old Borg Warner Type 35 was retained for the 2200SC Automatic. The new gearbox was a Borg Warner Type 65, lighter and smoother in operation and operated by a cable selector instead of the rod type associated with the Type 35. Its fluid dipstick was also mounted on the opposite side of the engine.

Cosmetically, the changes to the two V8 models for 1974 were the same as those for the 4-cylinder models, and those shared changes are described below. But there were also some specification changes that were unique to the 3500 and 3500S. Both models now came with Sundym tinted glass and front-seat head restraints as standard, and both models now had the full vinyl roof that had earlier been associated with the 3500S. The 3500S also lost its distinctive bolt-through wheel trims and took on the push-fit type of the 3500.

On the 1974 and later cars, a full vinyl roof covering was standard on the 3500 as well as the 3500S. This 3500 has the Huntsman Brown option. Once again, the registration plate is a dummy: there were no genuine UXC-N numbers!

The new box-pleat upholstery is clear in this picture of a left-hand-drive 3500 with km/h speedometer. This kind of steering wheel was used on cars with power-assisted steering.

THE DENOVO OPTION

The two V8 cars for 1974 could also be ordered with a brand-new option, actually announced in May 1973 but in practice not available until the start of 1974-model sales on 1 October. This was Dunlop's new Denovo run-flat tyre, and the Rovers became the first production cars in the world to have it. It was a feature very much in keeping with the P6's reputation for safety.

The Denovo was a low-profile tyre, like those that would become increasingly popular during the 1970s, and its key feature was the ability to sustain a complete loss of air pressure at high speed with almost no effect on the stability of the car. The tyre was then capable of running for limited distances at speeds of up to 50mph (80km/h) in deflated condition and, after repair at a Dunlop service centre, would be fully operational again.

Denovo tyres required special wheels, which had canisters of a special lubricant attached to the wheel rim inside the tyre. This lubricant was released automatically when the tyre deflated, reducing friction, keeping the tyre temperature down, sealing any small punctures and partially reinflating the tyre, all within the space of a few seconds. The special wheels were made in two parts that were bolted together, and had a larger diameter than the standard 14in disc wheels fitted to P6s in order to give the same rolling radius with the low profile of the Denovo tyres. Although the difference in size was not immediately noticeable, the wheels used on Denovo-equipped Rover P6B models had distinctive plastic trims with a radial-spoke design.

At parking speeds, a deflated Denovo tyre on a front wheel made the steering very heavy, and so Rover made power-assisted steering standard with the Denovo option. As there was theoretically no need for a spare wheel, Rovers with the Denovo option did not have one, but instead

The Denovo run-flat tyres came with distinctive vaned plastic wheel trims. This was the cover of the sales brochure for them.

The Denovo wheels had their own distinctive trims.

Denovo tyres were used on this armoured P6B. The car looks fairly standard but the side glass is fixed and there are no quarter-lights. It was pictured at FVRDE, the military testing ground at Chertsey. TANK MUSEUM, BOVINGTON

had a fully carpeted boot area. There was nothing to stop a customer ordering a fifth Denovo wheel and tyre as an extra, of course, but most minor problems could be solved with the aid of a temporary repair kit for small punctures that Rover provided with all Denovo-equipped cars.

In practice, the Denovo option did not prove very popular. Although the tyres remained available until the end of P6 production, they gained a reputation for rapid tread wear, and Dunlop were unable to find a quick solution. They also added £65 to the cost of a 3500 or 3500S (at September

1974 prices) and therefore looked like a poor investment to most customers. Denovos were offered for a time on the Rover SD1 and also on the Mini 1275GT, but by the end of the 1970s Dunlop had to admit defeat and owners of Denovo-equipped cars were offered a full set of standard steel wheels with ordinary tyres to replace the Denovo items on their cars. As a result, there are probably no P6s still running on their original Denovo wheels and tyres, although there may be some whose owners have kept a set for show use. Cars which once had the Denovo option can nevertheless still be identified by their fully carpeted boot areas.

1974: THE CROSS-RANGE REVISIONS

There was enough money in Rover's budget to allow a series of cross-range changes on all the 1974 models. None of these were major, but all of them contributed to the impression that these Rovers were better specified than the models they replaced – and that mattered in the showrooms when prices for the new cars were around 10 per cent higher than they had been a year earlier.

Recently introduced European regulations ensured that the 1974-season cars all had a driver's-side door mirror of the type that had earlier been optional. All cars also had a heated rear window (except for markets where it was unnecessary for climatic reasons), although this had been routinely fitted as a matter of course to UK-market cars despite being

The 2200TC sold well in Europe and Scandinavia. This left-hand-drive example was for Switzerland. Note how the windscreen wipers park on the opposite side from those on right-hand-drive cars.

an extra-cost option. A few revisions to the paint options brightened things a little, as Scarab Blue replaced Corsica Blue and a ninth option of Paprika – a rather bright orange that never proved popular – was added. Out of sight, a new breather system cured the long-standing irritation of a fuel filler that blew back when petrol was pumped in at full flow.

There were several changes inside the passenger cabin, too. The most obvious was new box-pleated upholstery, in twin high-cord brushed nylon as standard or leather at extra cost. Ambla upholstery was no longer available for the 3500S. Sandalwood, unavailable since spring 1972, was reintroduced as an interior colour option, and extra padding at the front of the seat cushions improved knee and thigh support while reshaped front seat backrests gave a little extra rear legroom. A new tufted type of carpet material was introduced, and extra sound-deadening material below the facia and on the transmission tunnel improved refinement.

All the manual-gearbox models now had a new gear lever, 2in (50mm) longer than before and designed to improve the 'feel' of the gearchange. The single-carburettor 4-cylinder models retained their strip speedometer but now gained a switch panel with some illuminated rotary controls, different in detail from the one fitted to the 2000TC and V8 models. On these more expensive cars, the wiper control had an additional 'delay' setting, and the length of that delay could be varied by a rather fiddly control on the steering column shroud. To make room for this function, the parking lights position was deleted from the light switch.

Interior mirrors had a new safety 'break-out' stem, and theoretically had convex glass on cars for the home market but a flat dipping mirror on export models (in practice, supply difficulties led to most home-market cars having the flat mirror). Reshaped sun visors fitted around the new mirrors, and the passenger's side visor now had a vanity mirror that was made of flexible acrylic to minimize injuries in a collision. However, optional extras remained as they had been in summer 1973 before the 1974-model cars were introduced.

EXPORT MODELS

With the new 2200 models, Rover drew their horns in. Production of the single-carburettor 2200SC and 2200SC Automatic was confined to right-hand-drive markets. Just one left-hand-drive automatic car was built as a pilot-production example in June 1973, so the decision not to go

The old strip speedometer was still used in the single-carburettor cars, and this is a 2200SC with manual gearbox and the new 'long' gear lever. The switchgear continued to feature non-illuminated controls for windscreen wipers and interior lights.

ahead with volume production must have been taken over that summer. There would only ever be small numbers of right-hand-drive cars for export, too, most of them destined for Ireland or as individual exports through the Personal Export Division.

Nevertheless, the 2200TC did look as if it would appeal to buyers outside Britain, and in the event export sales of both right-hand-drive and left-hand-drive variants proved satisfyingly healthy over the next few years. As with the 2000TC, an oil cooler was standard equipment for all markets except Britain (and, in this case, Ireland as well).

For two of Rover's export markets, the introduction of the 2.2-litre engine caused complications, because engines larger than 2 litres incurred extra taxation. So Rover offered them special variants of the P6 range. One of those markets was Nigeria, but far more important to Rover was Italy. In that country, the tax on petrol engines up to 2000cc was 16 per cent, but on larger engines it was 38 per cent. Adding that extra 22 per cent to the showroom price of a 4-cylinder P6 would have made the cars unsaleable.

The Rover solution was straightforward. The company simply built cars for both countries with the old 2-litre engine. Pilot-build models were assembled in January 1973 and volume production got under way later in the year, run-

The special 2000TC for Italy came in the same colours as the contemporary 2200 models. The small round indicator repeater on the wing was an Italian requirement. FERRUCCIO, VIA NICK DUNNING

ning in parallel with that of the new 2200 types. The cars were badged as 2000SC and 2000TC types respectively, and in every other respect were identical to the mainstream manual-gearbox 2200SC and 2200TC models. They did, however, have their own commission number sequences: the twin-carburettor cars were identified by an 868 prefix, and the single-carburettor cars by an 869 prefix.

Very little is known about the single-carburettor models, of which exactly 100 were built. They were intended only for

Both cars and engines had a special numbering sequence for Italy. FERRUCCIO, VIA NICK DUNNING

Nigeria, and 98 were shipped to BEWAC, the Rover importers in that country, the remaining two being sold through the personal export division. Deliveries probably began in or around August 1973, and the last example was completed on 2 December 1974 – although the last six 869-series cars were not actually shipped until April 1975.

There were very many more of the 868-series twin-carburettor models, and a total of 845 examples were built. Of these, 104 went to Nigeria via BEWAC, and two were sold through the Personal Export Division. Deliveries of the Nigerian examples ended during 1974. The remaining 739 cars were all intended for Italy, and all seem to have been sold there even though one car (868-13827) was diverted to the Henlys dealership in London. There was a nine-month pause in production of the 2000TC models during 1975: 560 cars were built up to December 1974 (454 of them for Italy), and then production began again in September 1975, 285 more examples being built before the last one left the assembly lines on 9 March 1977.

Essentially, the twin-carburettor engines used in these special export 2000TC cars had the same specification as the 'detoxed' European export TCs built since 1970, with charcoal run-on filters, a wax rheostat air box, and an oil cooler. They were nevertheless distinguished by the grey-painted rocker covers associated with the contemporary 2200 types.

THE PRINCESS GRACE ROVER

Famously, Princess Grace of Monaco, formerly the actress Grace Kelly, died at the wheel of her 3500S. On 13 September 1982, she was driving with her daughter Stephanie back to Monaco from the family's holiday home at Roc Agel. As she approached a hairpin bend on the Route de la Tourbie, the car was seen to swerve and then to accelerate before crashing through a stone barrier and then going over the edge of the slope.

After the car had come to rest, Stephanie was able to get out but Princess Grace was unconscious. She was rushed to the Monaco Hospital where she underwent emergency surgery, but the following morning she was taken off life support equipment and died.

On hearing of the accident, Rover immediately despatched two engineers with the aim of finding out whether there had been a mechanical problem with the vehicle. However, it turned out that in fact the Princess had suffered a stroke at the wheel, causing her to lose control of the car.

As for the V8 models, both the automatic 3500 and manual-gearbox 3500S continued to find customers outside the UK. Examples of these cars and of the 2200TC exported to West Germany still had some special features to meet local regulations: there were protective rubber fairings on the rear bumper ends, special rear number-plate lights, and glovebox lids with curved and padded inner ends to protect occupants' knees from the hard plastic of the console in an accident. Cars for Austria, Norway, Sweden and Switzerland all had twin brake servos and dual brake lines, and there was a headlamp wash-wipe system for Sweden as well.

PRESS REACTIONS

Unsurprisingly, the motoring press took very little interest in the V8 models, which had only been very mildly revised for 1974. Besides, there was occasional coverage for the 3500S in *Autocar*, whose managing director, Tim Gold-Blyth, provided long-term ownership reports on his 1972 car, WCL 130L. There was also the problem that the cars were no longer as far ahead of the opposition as they once had been; by January 1975 they had been relegated to the 'Boring' category in *Car* magazine's pithy review feature, 'The Good, the Bad and the Ugly', which commented: 'Replacement is long overdue.'

The new 2200s did attract their fair share of press attention, although the major specialist magazines in the UK ignored the entry-level 2200SC in favour of its automatic-gearbox and twin-carburettor stable-mates. *Autocar* tested a 2200SC Automatic for its issue of 4 October 1973, and

Motor tested the same car for its 6 July 1974 issue. This was KXC 840L, car number 476-00001A, which had been registered in June 1973: only a few factory-registered 2200s attracted L-suffix registrations because sales to the public did not begin until October, by which time M-suffix registrations were being issued in the UK. Both of these magazines and *Autosport* also tested the same 2200TC, the *Motor* test appearing on 6 October 1973, the *Autocar* test on 6 July 1974 and the *Autosport* one on 19 December 1974. It is perhaps revealing of the times that Rover were still offering an L-registered car (KXC 838L, 491-00004A) for test so late during the currency of the M-suffix registrations.

Rover were probably well pleased with the *Autocar* test of the new 2200SC Automatic. The magazine reported that overtaking performance was now enough to quell its earlier criticisms of the 2000SC in this area, and that 'the improvement in performance that the larger engine gives to the Rover 2200 has turned what was an extremely sedate car into a more sporting saloon which is the equal of its immediate four-door competitors'. It went on to say that the improvement 'cannot be fully appreciated from mere figures, as the 2200 feels a different car altogether from its predecessor, especially in automatic form'. *Autocar* also had praise for the car in more general terms: 'As ever, the engineering of the car is to a very high standard, and the finish both inside and out is good. Despite the length of time that this design has been in service, there is little to show its age.'

By the time *Motor* tested the same car, several months later, some minor build-quality faults were detectable. There was also bad engine shake at idle with Drive engaged – surely the result of inadequate preparation by the Rover press garage. The overall impression that the car made was nonetheless favourable: 'Attention to detail design put it at the top of its class when it was introduced, and after all these years it's still not far off.' Performance was not so good, though, and *Motor* felt that it could 'at best be described as sluggish if not downright poor'. They also pointed out that its 0–60mph acceleration times were bettered by a Hillman Avenger 1600 automatic, a Morris Marina 1.8 automatic and by a whole gaggle of lesser manual-gearbox cars. 'The real weakness,' they complained, 'lies in an almost disastrous lack of acceleration which is quite out of keeping with a car of this price and class.' In fact, the differences between the figures they obtained and those that *Autocar* had achieved earlier were relatively small – but the negative comments cannot have helped sales during 1974.

As for the 2200TC, *Autocar* felt that it 'remained entirely competitive in 1974'. *Motor* thought that it was not much quicker than its predecessor although it was more flexible; and *Autocar* reported that it was quicker through the gears and felt 'decidedly brisk', although maximum speed had not increased over that of the 2000TC it replaced. Fuel consumption was also worse. Nevertheless, all three magazines agreed that the real improvement in the TC was its new-found engine refinement. *Autosport* wrote of 'the astonishing metamorphosis of the somewhat unrefined engine into a notably smooth and quiet unit', and John Bolster's summary spoke for all the magazines:

> For fast, long journeys, the performance of the 4-cylinder Rover has been transformed. Whereas the 2000 seemed to need urging along, the 2200 is more than willing to get on with the job. People who would normally have bought the 3500 may be in doubt as petrol costs rise. The old 2000 would have seemed rather sluggish to the V8 owner but this new model, with its greatly increased torque and smoother performance, is not so far behind the more powerful Rover.

THE FINAL YEARS, 1975–77

Just before Christmas 1974, Rover introduced a new identification numbering system for its cars. It is still not clear why this was done, although it may have been intended as a trial run of a system that used a common serial number sequence with variable prefixes, as the new VIN system would do when it became standard on the SD1 models in 1976. The new system, however, was not as complex as the VIN system would be.

Under the old Rover system, each sub-variant of a model had its own serial numbering sequence. So, for example, the 2200TC had home market variants starting at 491-00001, RHD export variants starting at 492-00001, and LHD variants starting at 494-00001. The new system retained the same three-digit prefix codes, but now had a common sequence for each major type. So, for the 2200TC, the serial numbers began at 8000 but all sub-variants were numbered within the same sequence. It thus became possible for three cars with successive serial numbers to have three different prefixes; an example occurred early on with 491-08132, 492-08133 and 494-08134.

At the start of 1975, Rover were still building six major variants of the P6 range. The 4-cylinder types were the 2200SC manual, 2200SC Automatic and 2200TC, plus the special 868-series 2000TC for Italy. The V8 types were the 3500 and the 3500S. The 2200SC and 2200SC Automatic came only with right-hand drive, and the overwhelming majority were destined for UK dealers; most of the RHD export types went to Ireland or were sold through the personal export division. By far the strongest seller was the 2200TC. Most were for the home market, and there were some RHD export types for Ireland and for personal export, but there was also quite a strong demand for left-hand-drive models, particularly in Europe.

The 3500, meanwhile, sold over twice as well as the manual-gearbox 3500S in the last two and a half years of P6B production. Demand for both models was strongest in Britain, while far smaller numbers of RHD export cars went to Australia, New Zealand, or through the Personal Export Division. As for the LHD cars, which were built in much smaller quantities, most went to Europe, like the LHD 4-cylinder models. The last export 3500S built for Belgium in July 1976 was also the last export-specification 3500S of all. Sales of the 3500 gradually dwindled outside the UK, and a number of LHD cars were actually re-imported in early 1977 and converted to RHD for sale in Britain. (They nevertheless retained their original LHD chassis prefix identifiers.)

EVOLUTION, 1973–77

There were no important specification changes during the first year's production of the 2200s and revised V8s, although supply shortages in December 1973 meant that 162 4-cylinder cars were built with V8-type front swivel assemblies and front brake callipers. All had right-hand drive, and there were eighty-seven 2200SC models, fifty-six 2200TCs and nineteen 2200SC Automatics.

Meanwhile, sales of all big-engined cars were slow after the October 1973 oil crisis as petrol costs increased and the British government threatened to introduce fuel rationing. Many 1974-model Rovers remained unsold by the autumn of that year, and Solihull's main concern was to dispose of these. So in spite of a massive price increase in October 1974, which added more than 30 per cent to the base price of some models, buyers of 1975-season 2200 and V8 models were offered nothing new – except that P6s produced from autumn 1974 came with a rocker switch for the heated rear window in place of the earlier push-pull type. Nor were any significant changes considered for the remainder of the P6's time in production. The only revision during the 1975 season came in the spring, when the 'wood' trim changed from Rosewood to a lighter type known as Planked Teak.

There were nevertheless a few running modifications. On the 2200 Automatic, the loop-type handle of the gearbox oil filler changed (at 476-00935A) to a round type. There were also changes to the final drives of the 2200 models, marked by a change to Suffix B in the cars' identification numbers. On late cars, dual sourcing of components meant that Adwest and Burman steering boxes were fitted interchangeably on the assembly lines.

For the 1976 season cars that became available in October 1975, it became possible to order the 2200 models with the full vinyl roof trim that was standard on the two V8s, and the whole range was freshened up with a set of new paint colours. These previewed some that would become available for the forthcoming SD1 replacement model. However, they were also associated with a major change in the production process, as explained in Chapter 13. In theory, the change to a new and more modern paint plant should have worked well, but unfortunately, it was less than wholly successful. Some areas of the bodies were not sprayed as effectively as before, and teething troubles with the new process allowed moisture to become trapped under the paint, causing it to lift prematurely and the metal below to start rusting.

THE VIP MODELS

Meanwhile, Solihull had been making plans for a special run-out edition of the P6B 3500. Two pilot-production

The 3500 VIP was the only P6 derivative ever to have metallic paint when new. This example has a pair of optional auxiliary lamps mounted below the bumper.

Among the stickers on the inner wing of the VIP cars was one revealing the paint colour – in this case, Platinum Silver.

examples were built in summer 1975, and both were painted in one of the new metallic colours that were planned for the SD1 range. This was a silver called Platinum, and it became the only metallic paint ever to be used on a production P6 of any kind. Right from the start, this special edition was given its own number prefix of 861, although the serial numbers were within the standard sequence for 3500 models.

This special edition was also planned to try out some of the other features planned for the SD1 range. It was to have a light brown brushed nylon headlining on a fibreglass supporting pad, and the seats were also to be upholstered in box-pleat Nutmeg brown velour. Air-conditioning would be widely available on the SD1 as an option, and so the special-edition P6 model was also provided with air-conditioning as standard. The special-edition cars would also have a bootlid-mounted spare wheel, rear seatbelts and a laminated windscreen as standard – all items taken from the P6 options list. A further special feature was that they all had compression struts in the doors, as seen on the NADA 3500S; the likelihood is that these were simply left-over stocks that Rover wanted to use up. Lastly, as these were 3500 models, they would all have Sundym tinted glass and a full vinyl roof trim.

A first batch of forty-six cars was built between February and May 1976, and a further twenty-nine between August 1976 and January 1977. All the first group except for one were painted in Platinum; the odd one out was painted in Brasilia, a standard P6 colour of the time, and all the second batch were also painted in Brasilia. This made up totals of forty-five Platinum cars (plus two pilot-production models in this colour) and thirty Brasilia examples. All cars of both colours had Huntsman Brown sills, roof trims and spare wheel covers.

This special edition was known as the VIP, and the first examples were registered for the road in April 1976. However, it very much looks as if some of the impetus behind the idea disappeared when it became clear that the SD1 would not replace the P6 cleanly in summer 1976 because the 6-cylinder models were delayed. As production and sales of the 4-cylinder models were now going to continue for several months, the VIP was clearly not going to be an end-of-line celebration edition. This may be a reason why no sales literature was ever produced for it.

All the VIP models were intended for the home market, although one car (861-30981E) was diverted to a dealer

in Ireland in October 1976. No dealer took delivery of more than one example, and this has led to speculation that the cars were intended as 'dealer specials' for the use of those who owned Rover dealerships. From quite an early stage, the Platinum examples were recognized as rarities, although the less immediately obvious Brasilia cars were largely ignored. One Platinum car, 861-30975E, ended up with two sets of initials and an inscription scratched behind the rear number-plate: 'Last of 50 made, 12/5/76. B.K.H, E.J.' It was in fact neither the last of fifty made nor completed on the date that this inscription suggests, but somebody clearly thought the inscription might enhance its value!

A small point of interest is that probably all the VIPs had a radio-cassette ICE unit as standard, but that there seem to have been differences between the two groups. The early 1976 cars came with a second speaker mounted in the rear parcel shelf, which was perforated for the purpose. The cars built from August onwards had speakers in the front door trims and no perforations for a rear parcel shelf speaker. They were the only P6s ever to be so equipped on the assembly lines.

THE 1977 MODELS

The delays in getting the 6-cylinder SD1 models into production probably ensured that more P6s than originally intended were built during what can be called the 1977 model year – although as far as Rover and the newly renamed Leyland Cars were concerned, they were not 1977 models. Although they may have been built after September 1976, they were old models and the company was no longer promoting them; there were no P6s on the Leyland Cars stand at the London Motor Show in October 1976. Nor were there any specification changes from the 1976 models.

In fact, only one P6 model went out of production over the summer of 1976 as the first volume-production SD1s were being built. This was the 3500S, of which the final example was probably built in July. The 2200SC, 2200SC Automatic, 2200TC, 2000TC for Italy and 3500 all remained in production until early 1977, and a total of 1,577 P6s were built in that calendar year. Production of base units had meanwhile ended at Pressed Steel in December 1976, and the last ones were built up into cars in late January and early February 1977.

The first of the remaining models to go out of

This picture was taken to commemorate completion of the last P6 base unit at the Pressed Steel works in Cowley. Unfortunately, the calculated total of base units built was wrong.

... and here is that same base unit at Solihull, now built up to create a left-hand-drive 2200TC, although the outer panels have yet to be fitted. The commemorative sign seems to have travelled to Solihull with the base unit!

production was the manual-gearbox 2200SC, of which the last one numerically (471-10908) entered the Despatch Department on 25 January 1977. Some cars with earlier serial numbers nevertheless entered Despatch later than this. Next to go was the 3500, and the last of these numeri-

cally was 451-31837, which was a Pendelican car that entered Despatch on 27 January. Production of the 2200SC Automatic ended numerically with 476-07130 on 1 February, and the last 2200TC was 492-15871, which was completed on the same day.

This Avocado 3500S, VVC 700S, was declared to be the last P6, but it had actually been built several months before the real last-of-line car, which has never been satisfactorily identified.

ROVERP6MAN/WIKIMEDIA COMMONS

OPTIONAL EXTRAS, 1974–77 MODEL YEARS

For 1974 Model Year
As for 1973 list, plus:
Denovo wheels and tyres, with PAS, for V8 models only; cars with the Denovo option had a fully carpeted boot area
Door mirror on passenger's side
Floor mats: black rubber front and rear sets, with Rover name on front pair, in place of earlier link type and charcoal grey rubber type
Fog lamp, Lucas Square 8 type
Heavy-duty suspension, front and rear, for 4-cylinder models (police spec)
Leather box-pleat upholstery
Roof rack: third type replaced earlier design

Sliding sunroofs: Coenan and Hollandia types probably no longer available
Spot lamp, Lucas Square 8 type
'Wooden' gear lever knob no longer available

For 1975 Model Year
No changes.

For 1976 Model Year
As for 1974, plus:
Full vinyl roof for 4-cylinder models

For 1977 Model Year
No changes.

AN INGLORIOUS AWARD

As British Leyland sank lower and lower in the public estimation during the early 1970s, the Automobile Association decided to ginger things up a little by creating a Square Wheel Award, to be given to the company that produced the most troublesome new car in the year under review.

To Rover's shame, they won the first award, which was presented during 1975. The car that earned it for them was a Mexico Brown 3500 model, registered VYU 472M and supplied by Rover dealers Harvey Hudson of Woodford in east London to a Mr Robert Rouse. When first supplied in June 1974 (as a substitute for a Paprika example that Mr Rouse had ordered but was delayed), the car had a faulty engine. Harvey Hudson remedied this fault, but it would not be the last.

Before the car had clocked up 6,000 miles (10,000km), the dealer claimed to have fitted three new replacement engines, two new replacement gearboxes, two new bell housings and a new wiring loom. More faults were discovered: faulty paintwork on the wings, a gearbox oil leak, a collapsed off-side rear seat, an exhaust pipe fouling the rear suspension, and a second gearbox oil leak.

Mr Rouse asked Rover to replace the car, but was told this was the dealer's responsibility. The dealer asked Rover to replace the car, but without success. When Mr Rouse called in the AA for legal and technical advice, a vehicle inspector who examined the Rover judged that several significant mechanical defects needed immediate attention.

That car survived for nearly ten years before being taken off the road. The DVLA records that it was last taxed in January 1984.

However, identifying the last-of-line P6 is a far from simple matter. Typically, car manufacturers hold a small ceremony – often inviting the press along – to mark the end of production of a long-running model, but there was no such ceremony for the P6. Leyland Cars were too busy looking into the future to care very much about the past – and besides, a last-of-line P6 ceremony was not going to generate any more of the income that the company needed so badly at this stage.

So the whole question was overlooked until March, when a 3500S that had actually been built the previous summer was located somewhere on the Solihull site and was notionally 'completed' on the production line on 19 March 1977. This Avocado car, number 481-14890D, was designated as the last P6, was registered as VVC 700S, and was presented to the Heritage Collection. And there it remained until, in 2003, the Heritage Collection had a clear-out of some of its less interesting cars. Probably well aware that this 'official' last P6 was nothing of the sort, they sold it off and it entered private ownership.

So what was the identity of the real last-of-line P6? Logically, it must have been one of the last two 2200 models that were completed on 1 February 1977: the line produced no more cars after that. Nevertheless, a small number of cars did not go straight into the Despatch Department but were retained in the assembly hall for rectification work. Two cars

were not signed-off until 8 April, and these were a 2200SC (471-10648) and a 2200TC (491-15829), so it would be possible to argue that these were completed after the two that left the lines on 1 February. There was one final straggler, too: 3500 number 454-31550 had been completed on 27 October 1976, but languished unwanted in the Despatch Department until 27 June 1977, when it went to Henlys in London.

And finally, to round off the story.... a few years after P6 production had ended, a former assembly line employee purchased one of the spare base units and built it up from parts as a 2200 in Avocado with a Triplex glass roof. This car also has a claim to being the last-ever P6!

Selling the Final P6s

Britain was in the grip of rampant inflation in the mid-1970s, and Rover increased the showroom prices of their P6s dramatically between 1973 and 1977. The 2200SC, for example, nearly doubled in price between October 1973 and July 1976. The strongest seller globally was the 2200TC, but sales of all models were on the decline. The V8s suffered heavily because they were large-engined and thirsty cars at a time when petrol prices were volatile and fuel consumption was becoming an important issue. Public perceptions shifted so much during this period, however, that even the 2200 models came to be seen as large-engined cars. As the basic design was now well over ten years old and had lost its freshness, simple old age also proved a hindrance to sales.

This change in public perception was reflected in Rover's advertising for the P6 range. In October 1973, advertise-ments for the 2200 range still stressed the car's reputa-tion for safety: 'The new Rover 2200,' read one, '... more power, but still playing it safe.' After listing some of the new model's features, it went on to say that 'the overriding reason for choosing a Rover is unaltered: safety'. Contrast that with the position in August 1974, when all references

---

PRICES AND RIVALS, 1973–77

The totals shown here were basic showroom prices in the UK without extras. Also shown are the basic ex-factory cost and the car tax and VAT payable.

October 1973

	Total	Ex-factory	Car tax	VAT
2200SC	£2,018.69	£1,694	£141.17	£183.52
2200TC	£2,139.04	£1,795	£149.58	£194.46
2200SC Auto	£2,147.39	£1,802	£150.17	£195.22
3500S	£2,444.11	£2,051	£170.92	£222.19
3500	£2,531.10	£2,124	£177.00	£230.10

September 1974

	Total	Ex-factory	Car tax	VAT
2200SC	£2,531.88	£2,164	£180.33	£187.55
2200TC	£2,681.64	£2,292	£191.00	£198.64
2200SC Auto	£2,689.83	£2,299	£191.58	£199.25
3500S	£3,010.41	£2,573	£214.42	£222.99
3500	£3,168.36	£2,708	£225.67	£234.69

December 1974

	Total	Ex-factory	Car tax	VAT
2200SC	£2,716.74	£2,322	£193.50	£201.24
2200TC	£2,877.03	£2,459	£204.92	£213.11
2200SC Auto	£2,886.39	£2,467	£205.58	£213.81
3500S	£3,230.37	£2,761	£230.08	£239.29
3500	£3,398.85	£2,905	£242.08	£251.77

March 1975

	Total	Ex-factory	Car tax	VAT
2200SC	£2,933.19	£2,507	£208.92	£217.27
2200TC	£3,106.35	£2,655	£221.25	£230.10
2200SC Auto	£3,116.88	£2,664	£222.00	£230.88
3500S	£3,487.77	£2,981	£248.42	£258.35
3500	£3,671.46	£3,138	£261.50	£271.96

July 1976

	Total	Ex-factory	Car Tax	VAT
2200SC	£3,768.57	£3,221	£268.42	£279.15
2200TC	£3,986.19	£3,407	£283.92	£295.27
2200SC Auto	£4,003.74	£3,422	£285.17	£296.57

Although P6 models remained on sale into 1977, no further price lists were issued in Britain.

Rivals

In this final period of Rover P6 production, competition for the 4-cylinder models once again came from the Triumph 2000, but the Peugeot 504 and Volvo 144 were gaining ground. The Volvo was replaced by a 244 model during 1974, presenting the Rover with an even stronger challenge. Further up the scale, the V8 models were hard-pressed by cars like the BMW 2002Tii, Opel Commodore and, most notably, by the top-of-the-range Ford Granadas.

In its January 1974 issue, *What Car?* magazine ran an interesting comparison test that pitted a Rover 3500 against its more serious competitors from Ford (a Granada GXL) and Opel (a Commodore GS) and against a pair of also-rans from Vauxhall (the much cheaper Viscount) and Toyota (the Crown 2600). The 3500 fitted into the middle of the price bracket that these cars encompassed, but came out top in the personal preferences, along with the Opel. The writing was on the wall, however: if head ruled heart, the testers concluded, they would choose the Ford.

PAINT AND TRIM OPTIONS

September 1973–September 1975

Scarab Blue replaced Corsica Blue, and Paprika was added, making the total options up to nine. Sandalwood, absent since August 1972, was reintroduced as a trim colour and took the options up to five. All trim colours were now available with either leather or brushed nylon upholstery. The combinations were:

Almond	with trim in	Bronze, Ebony or Sandalwood
Arctic White		Bronze, Ebony or Mango
Cameron Green		Buckskin, Mango or Sandalwood
Lunar Grey		Bronze, Ebony or Sandalwood
Mexico Brown		Buckskin, Mango or Sandalwood
Monza Red		Buckskin, Ebony or Sandalwood
Paprika		Bronze, Buckskin or Ebony
Scarab Blue		Buckskin, Ebony or Mango
Tobacco Leaf		Bronze, Buckskin or Ebony

As before, all cars had Ebony vinyl rear quarter-panel trim and Satin Black sills unless Huntsman roof trim was specified, in which case the sills were in Satin Brown. The full vinyl roof trim was now standard on both 3500 and 3500S models. Combinations were:

Ebony	with paint in	Cameron Green, Lunar Grey, Monza Red, Paprika or Scarab Blue (and other colours when Ebony interior trim was specified)
Huntsman		Almond, Arctic White, Mexico Brown or Tobacco Leaf (except with Ebony interior trim)

September 1975– February 1977

A new range of six paint colours completely replaced the earlier options. A full vinyl roof covering was now optional on 2200 models. Interior trims remained as before. The combinations were:

Atlantis	with trim in	Buckskin, Ebony or Mango
Avocado		Bronze, Ebony or Sandalwood
Brasilia		Buckskin, Mango or Sandalwood
Pendelican		Bronze, Ebony or Mango
Richelieu		Buckskin, Ebony or Sandalwood
Turmeric		Bronze, Ebony or Sandalwood

(Note: Turmeric was misspelled as Tumeric on some colour cards.)

Roof trim colours were Ebony and Huntsman, as before, with sills painted in Satin Black and Satin Brown respectively. The colour combinations were:

Ebony	with paint in	Atlantis, Avocado, Pendelican, Richelieu (and others specified with Ebony trim)
Huntsman		Brasilia, Pendelican, or Turmeric (unless specified with Ebony trim)

In addition, the special-edition 3500 VIP models were available with either Brasilia or Platinum (metallic) paint, in either case with Huntsman roof trim and Satin Brown sills. These cars had Nutmeg velour interior trim and a brushed nylon headlining. (Note that two pilot-production examples were built in summer 1975, before the period under review here.)

to fuel consumption and performance had been deleted, and even the safety angle was no longer to the fore. The focus was now on the marque's twin reputations for value for money and low depreciation that resulted from durability. So one advertisement showed a 2200TC in the City of London attracting admiring glances from a couple of bowler-hatted City gentlemen. The only text read: 'If you understand investments, you own one.'

There is little doubt that the generally negative image of all British Leyland products in these years also depressed Rover sales – and with reason. Build quality undoubtedly suffered, even though the excellence of the Rover design was never questioned. Morale was low within the workforce, particularly after the three-day working week imposed by Edward Heath's Conservative government early in 1974 as a response to the oil crisis-induced slump, and some very poor-quality cars came out of Solihull. Among them was the 3500 that won the AA's Square Wheel Award in summer

---

THE 2200s AND REVISED V8s, 1973–77

2200SC and 2200SC Automatic, 1973–77
Engine
Type: Cast iron block and light alloy head
Cylinders: 4
Bore and stroke: 90.5mm × 85.7mm
Capacity: 2204cc
Five-bearing crankshaft
Single overhead camshaft
Compression ratio: 9:1
Carburettor: Single SU type HIF6 carburettor
Max. power: 98bhp DIN at 5,000rpm
Max. torque: 126lb ft DIN at 2,500rpm

Brakes
Type: Discs on all four wheels, mounted inboard at the rear; Girling discs and callipers; handbrake acting on rear discs; servo assistance standard
Size: 10.36in front, 10.69in rear

Running weight
2,822lb (1,280kg) with manual gearbox
2,855lb (1,295kg) with automatic gearbox

Performance
Max. speed: 101mph (162km/h)
0–60mph: 13.4sec with manual gearbox
14.5sec with automatic gearbox

Transmission, suspension, steering, wheels, tyres and dimensions all as for earlier 2000SC models

2200TC, 1974–77
Engine
Type: Cast iron block and light alloy head
Cylinders: 4
Bore and stroke: 90.5mm × 85.7mm
Capacity: 2204cc
Main bearings: Five-bearing crankshaft
Valves: Single overhead camshaft
Compression ratio: 9:1
Carburettors: Two SU HIF6 carburettors
Max. power: 115bhp DIN at 5,000rpm
Max. torque: 135lb ft DIN at 3,000rpm

Brakes
Type: Discs on all four wheels, mounted inboard at the rear; Girling discs and callipers; handbrake acting on rear discs; servo assistance standard; some export models with twin servos and dual-circuit brakes
Size: 10.36in front, 10.69in rear

Running weight
2,829lb (1,283kg)

Performance
Max. speed: 108.3mph (174.3km/h)
0–60mph: 11.75sec

Transmission, suspension, steering, wheels, tyres and dimensions all as for earlier 2000SC models

3500, 1973–77
Engine
Type: V8 with light alloy block and cylinder heads
Cylinders: 8

1975 when a panel of experts judged it to be the 'worst, most troublesome, new car of the year' (see panel on p.199).

As the SD1 came on-stream during 1976, export sales of the P6 range more or less collapsed. To clear stocks quickly, Rover held back a number of the last left-hand-drive 2200TCs and diverted them to the home market, converting them to right-hand drive but not changing the commission number prefixes that revealed what they once were. (The switches in the centre of the dash were not changed to their RHD locations, which makes these cars interesting oddities.) These helped to hold the fort for the Rover marque until the 6-cylinder versions of the SD1 became available. In Britain, these late sales can be recognized by their registration suffixes: a P suffix denotes the last full year (1975–76) for P6 production, but later sales attracted R (1976–77) and S (1977–78) suffixes. A small number of cars even lingered in the showrooms long enough to attract T-suffix plates.

Bore and stroke: 88.9mm × 71.1mm
Capacity: 3528cc
Five-bearing crankshaft
Single centred camshaft, overhead valves
Compression ratio: 9.25:1
Carburettors: Two SU HIF6 carburettors
Max. power: 143bhp DIN at 5,000rpm
Max. torque: 202lb ft DIN at 2,700rpm

Transmission
Gearbox: Three-speed Borg Warner Type 65 automatic
Ratios
   1st: 2.39:1
   Intermediate: 1.45:1
   Top: 1.00:1
   Reverse: 2.09:1
Axle ratio: 3.54:1

Suspension and Steering
Suspension: As contemporary four-cylinder models
Steering: Burman recirculating-ball, worm-and-nut type with variable ratio; power assistance available
Tyres: 185 HR 14 radial
Wheels: Five-stud steel disc wheels with 14in diameter; Denovo wheels and tyres optional
Rim width: 5.5in

Brakes
Type: Discs on all four wheels, mounted inboard at the rear; Girling discs and callipers; handbrake acting on rear discs; servo assistance standard; some export models with twin servos and dual-circuit brakes
Size: 10.82in front, 10.69in rear

Dimensions
Track: Front 53.375in (1,356mm)
Track: Rear 51.75in (1,314mm)
Wheelbase: 103.375in (2,626mm)
Overall length: 179.75in (4,565mm)
Overall width: 66in (1,676mm)
Overall height: 55.75in (1,416mm)
Running weight: 2,872lb (1,303kg)

Performance
Max. speed: 115.5mph (185.8km/h)
0–60mph: 10.95sec

3500S, 1973–77
As for contemporary 3500, except:

Transmission
Gearbox: Four-speed all-synchromesh manual
Ratios
   1st: 3.62:1
   2nd: 2.13:1
   3rd: 1.39:1
   4th: 1.00:1
   Reverse: 3.43:1

Running weight: 2,878lb (1,306kg)

Performance
Max speed: 122mph (196km/h)
0–60mph: 10.18sec

CHAPTER TWELVE

P6s IN POLICE SERVICE

Rover made no effort to market a police-specification 2000 in the early days because demand from the civilian market kept the factory at full capacity. However, W. R. Taylor of *Police Review* magazine had tried an early car and had been immediately impressed with its potential as a police patrol car. For the magazine's issue of 25 February 1966, he reported on more recent experience and was full of praise for the car. The brakes were extremely impressive and 'the suspension, coupled with Pirelli Cinturato tyres, gives this car the most amazing road-holding powers'. He went on to say that 'this car will do things safely that are beyond the imagination of most sane-thinking drivers on the road… other than for a straight run down the motorway, there is no other car in this country that can catch, or get away from, the Rover 2000 when it is being driven properly'.

Not long after that review appeared, the 2000TC model became available, and at that stage police forces began to sit up and take notice of the Rover. Among the earliest users were London's Metropolitan Police, who took both 2000TC and Three Thousand Five models from 1968. Hertfordshire

was another early user of the Three Thousand Five, and both the City of London Police and the Kent Police had 2000TC models from around 1969.

Rover seem to have used the introduction of the 3500S in autumn 1971 as the occasion for a big effort to gain police sales in Britain. They were already pushing police sales of their still-new Range Rover, with considerable success, and before long the two models (accompanied by some automatic-gearbox 3500 types) became a familiar sight in police livery all over the country. The high performance of the saloon models was particularly welcomed for motorway patrol work, and the stereotypical police motorway patrol car of the 1970s had the 'jam sandwich' livery – white with a red and blue or red and yellow stripe, and often with the force crest on the front doors. In practice, of course, the police livery and markings varied from one force to the next, as did the equipment. So did the colours: the Metropolitan Police, for example, took its Area cars in blue and its Traffic cars in white.

The precise specification of a police P6B inevitably depended on its intended use, but Rover did offer a special equipment package to meet police requirements, though different police forces took different items from the police specification list. Heavy-duty suspension (introduced in autumn 1971 alongside the 3500S) and battery

The Metropolitan Police was an early user of the 2000TC, and its publicity department produced this dramatic picture of two cars driving through London at night. METROPOLITAN POLICE

Here is one of the Met's 2000TC models at rest, complete with smiling crew. There are no wheel trims: the police took them off for safety. POLICE VEHICLE ENTHUSIASTS' CLUB

The Met was also an early user of the Three Thousand Five. Two of its first examples were pictured here on delivery, the darker (blue) car being for area duties and the white one for the traffic division.

This rear view of an early Met traffic car shows the discreet police sign carried on the bootlid.

A calibrated speedometer was fitted to traffic cars. This is an early one in a Met Three Thousand Five; later ones were neater.

Another Met Three Thousand Five; the car belonged to the traffic division but did not have the side stripe associated with motorway patrol cars.

Motorway patrol cars soon began to sport the 'jam sandwich' livery. This 1970 model belonged to the Hertfordshire Constabulary, and had a loud-hailer mounted on the rear bumper. STEVE WOODWARD

This 2000TC belonged to the Inverness force, and is quite sparingly marked – although there would be no mistaking that side stripe. STEVE WOODWARD

Liveries and fittings differed quite markedly from one force to the next. This West Yorkshire traffic car – an early Series II model – has its side stripe higher up the body than most, and carries a simply enormous illuminated police sign on the roof. POLICE VEHICLE ENTHUSIASTS' CLUB

EUE 71K was a 2000TC that belonged to the West Midlands Police, and has quite plain markings, with no force crest on the door.

were recommended fitments, and there would typically be a special wiring harness to power lights and sirens mounted on the roof. This came with a special headlining with zips at front and rear to permit access to that wiring.

Rover also supplied an extra fuse box, and an additional switch panel that fitted into the space above the standard radio position. A calibrated speedometer could be fitted in the centre of the dashboard and an observer's rear-view mirror was listed. Lights and police signs were typically fitted in the purchasing force's own workshops, and inevitably there was a wide variety of different configurations. Some forces favoured a relatively discreet complement of additional lights and police signs, but the motorway patrol cars usually had an illuminated police sign on the roof for maximum visibility. Some had one on the bootlid as well, and the cars generally had a variety of radio aerials, sirens and lights. Not all police cars were identified as such, of course, and unmarked ones used by the Metropolitan Police often had a 'Police Stop' sign

This South Wales Police Series II 3500 typifies the motorway patrol Rover of the early 1970s.

The 3500S proved popular as a traffic car, and this one served with the Kent Police. In this case, the standard vinyl roof covering was deleted. KENT POLICE MUSEUM

When the Hampshire Police complained of handling quirks at speed, Rover modified a 3500S with a crude metal front spoiler and lent it to them for trials.

This later 3500S belonged to Strathclyde Police and retained its standard wheel trims. It also shows the 'production' version of the police-specification front spoiler. STEVE WOODWARD

The Greater Manchester Police coped with the problem by ensuring that there was always a spare gearbox in the workshops waiting to be fitted in case of need, and by rebuilding the damaged gearbox immediately after the replacement operation. The same force soon began to provide a replacement gearbox service to neighbouring police forces that did not have the capability of rebuilding the gearboxes themselves. In the south of England, several forces came to rely on the services of a specialist firm in Maidstone to do their rebuilds.

However, the widespread stories of modified engines were simply urban myths. Reliability was the most important factor in police service, and force workshops were unwilling to sacrifice this for a little extra performance. London's Metropolitan Police, an early user of the 3500, had a particular concern about accidental selection of first gear in the automatic gearbox leading to over-revving of the engine, and so their cars had a metal plate (supplied by Rover) that prevented the lever being pulled back into the first-gear lock-up position.

A particular worry to police forces was that the push-fit wheel trims could rotate under hard acceleration and cut into the tyre valve. As a result, police P6s were often seen without their wheel trims. However, there was no such problem with the bolt-through wheel trims of the 3500S, and so the users of this model tended to retain the trims, and some even fitted them to automatic-gearbox 3500 models.

Rover had not anticipated one problem that became apparent in police use, but soon heard about it from the Hampshire Police. Motorway patrol officers complained that their 3500S cars could change lanes on the M3 motorway all by themselves at sustained speeds of 90mph (145km/h) or more. Rover were contacted at once about the problem, which was most noticeable at an area called Black Dam, around Junction 6 near Basingstoke.

Fleet sales manager Stan Faulkner insisted that he had never had such a complaint before; perhaps the drivers might be at fault. Hampshire's Sergeant Nick Carter took exception to this, and invited the Rover man down to see for himself. Several tests later, it became apparent that the front axle weight was half a hundredweight (56lb/25kg) lighter when the car was loaded than when it was unloaded. It then became clear that the weight of all the emergency equipment carried in the boot raised the front of the car by 3in (76mm), with the result that front-end lift at speed would leave the car with no steering!

mounted on the rear parcel shelf that could be flipped up to become visible through the rear window.

On 3500S models, the vinyl roof trim was sometimes deleted and, well aware that the car's manual gearbox was near the limit of its capacity, Rover also introduced a heavy-duty gearbox option. This was always a 'police specification' item that was not offered to the public, and although it was a little stronger than the standard type, it was certainly not a complete cure for the gearbox's weaknesses. A particular problem was that the oil feed was inadequate in reverse, and if reverse was selected in a hurry (as often occurs on police duty), the gearbox would seize solid.

So Rover hastily developed a crude spoiler to reduce front-end lift, fitting it to a 3500S registered YXC 763K (481-00813A) and delivering the car to the Basingstoke Traffic Section in around March 1972. The police experimented for a few weeks and trimmed the spoiler to achieve a compromise that gave the right aerodynamic effect while looking more attractive. Rover then produced the spoiler from GRP in two handed sections that bolted to the front apron, and made them available as part of the police specification package and as a retro-fit for forces that needed them. However, the spoilers were never made available for cars sold to the public.

The Greater Manchester Police took a batch of sixty 3500S models with the Denovo run-flat tyre option, which was provided free of charge by Dunlop, who probably hoped that a successful outcome would prove beneficial to sales. However, one of the tyre's strengths also proved to be its downfall. It was designed to re-inflate after a puncture, with an almost undetectable effect on the stability of the car, and could then be driven for a limited distance at speeds up to 50mph (80km/h) before being changed. Unfortunately, the 'undetectable effect' was literally that, with the result that police officers would carry on driving at high speed until the tyre began to disintegrate and pieces flew past the window. The effect of that disintegration was potentially disastrous, and on one occasion it actually tore the front wing off a patrol car.

An even bigger problem was that replacement tyres could only be fitted by a Dunlop specialist. As a result, cars would have to be taken off the road for long periods, especially if they suffered a puncture out of normal working hours. The whole problem was compounded by the Denovo tyres' tendency to wear much faster than standard tyres. After trying the tyres for a period of eighteen months, GMP went back to standard tyres and ordered no more Denovos.

The quantities of P6s in use with each force varied widely. Some bought just a few at a time but some of the larger forces bought large batches year after year. The Metropolitan Police, for example, bought thirty V8 models during the currency of the L-suffix registration, and in 1975–76 took delivery of one batch of forty-six cars (451-28805 to 451-28850) and a later one of fifty cars (451-31330 to 451-31379). Many were not in the Pendelican (white) that would have been used for motorway patrol cars: 451-28850, for example, was in Almond, and all of the later batch of fifty cars were in Atlantis (blue). At least one late car was delivered in Avocado.

Greater Manchester also trialled Denovo run-flat tyres, and their distinctive wheel trims can just be seen in this picture of 3500S GNC 253N. STEVE WOODWARD

On duty: the view through the windscreen of a Hertfordshire patrol car. This one was a Series II 3500, registered GJH 447K. The calibrated speedometer installation on these later cars was far neater than the early type. POLICE VEHICLE ENTHUSIASTS' CLUB

Despite the well-known drawbacks of the P6B, those police forces that used the cars tended to remain loyal to the type – and after 1976 several of them bought its replacement, the SD1 3500. The Rover did not have things all its own way as a high-performance Traffic Division car, of course, and after March 1972 faced keen competition from the new Ford Granada 3-litre. Police forces tended to be Ford users or Rover users; very few had examples of both cars. No reliable list of the forces that used Rovers exists, and compiling one is severely complicated by the fact that the cars were in service at the time (1974) when there were multiple amalgamations of forces and the introduction of new force names and identities.

Patrol work apart, some UK police forces used 3500 and 3500S models for special duties in the 1970s. The Ministry of Defence Police had some, and these may well have been used alongside their long-wheelbase armoured Range Rov-

ers to escort convoys of nuclear material. The Metropolitan Police's Royalty Protection Group also had two armour-plated examples. One was later deliberately destroyed (the army drove a tank over it on Salisbury Plain) but the other has survived and belongs to the Metropolitan Police Heritage Museum – although some of its armour plating and other special features have now been removed.

Registered MMC 501L, this is a Corsica Blue car that was delivered in June 1972 but was not issued for duty until June

XVU 610M belonged to the Greater Manchester Police. Note the gap in the high-mounted side stripe – probably to allow spilled petrol to drain off the wing without causing damage to the stripe. STEVE WOODWARD

This Hertfordshire traffic car is a late 3500S, with the police-spec spoilers just visible at the front. STEVE WOODWARD

The spoilers are in evidence again on this Lanarkshire car, an unmarked vehicle that was the first in Scotland to be fitted with the Vascar speed monitoring system. Vascar stands for Visual Average Speed Computer And Recorder. POLICE VEHICLE ENTHUSIASTS' CLUB

Old police cars never die – they just get relegated to training duties. Kent's TKP 958N was pictured on skid-pan duties, with suitably misshapen front air intake. KENT POLICE MUSEUM

There is a strong interest in preserved police vehicles, and this former Met area car was pictured at an enthusiasts' gathering. Note the bolt-through 3500S-type wheel trims, even though this is a late 3500. POLICE VEHICLE ENTHUSIASTS' CLUB

Most police equipment was hidden out of sight in unmarked cars. This is the police radio in a former Regional Crime Squad car that belonged to the Metropolitan Police. LEE KINGHAM

The Met took large quantities of cars very late in the P6B's life. This one entered service late enough to attract one of the S-suffix registration numbers current in 1977/78. METROPOLITAN POLICE

1973. Car number 451-14428B had fixed side windows of armoured glass with a sliding steel sunroof that was intended as a means of escape in an emergency. There was also an armoured windscreen, said to have been so thick that a specially dished steering wheel was needed to leave room for the driver's hands to turn it. The car had an air filter system for the passenger compartment. As the Royalty Protection Group operates all over the UK and not just within the Metropolitan Police's area, the car also had several different radios permanently fitted in the boot to suit the frequencies used by different forces around the country.

(*Special thanks to Paddy Carpenter, Lee Kingham and Steve Woodward for information used in this chapter.*)

Now preserved in the Metropolitan Police's museum, MMC 501L was an armoured model used by the Royalty Protection Group of the Metropolitan Police. Note the sliding sunroof, which was fitted as an 'emergency exit'. POLICE VEHICLE ENTHUSIASTS' CLUB

CHAPTER THIRTEEN

HOME AND ABROAD: BUILDING THE P6

By far the majority of Rover P6 models were assembled at the company's factory in Lode Lane, Solihull, to the south-east of Birmingham. A few thousand cars were also assembled outside the UK, using major assemblies shipped out from Solihull and sometimes adding locally supplied items to suit local requirements. These cars were known as CKD (completely knocked down) types.

Rover's Solihull factory had been built by the British government on farmland in the late 1930s as a 'shadow' factory intended to duplicate the manufacturing capabilities of Britain's aircraft makers in case of war. The Rover Company had the job of managing it during the hostilities that lasted from 1939 to 1945. Part of the arrangement was that Rover should be given first refusal when the factory was sold on after the war, and the company seized that opportunity when it arose. The old Rover premises in Coventry had been destroyed during the Blitz in 1940, and so from late 1945 Solihull became the new home of Rover.

This Rover factory at Solihull was wholly dedicated to Land Rover manufacture from early 1982, and remains the primary Land Rover plant under what is now Jaguar Land Rover.

ASSEMBLY AT SOLIHULL

The assembly area for all Rover P6 models built at Rover's Solihull factory was constructed specially for the purpose on the northern side of the site. In consequence, it was generally known as the North Works. After P6 assembly ended in 1977, the North Works was mothballed, and part of it became a temporary storage area. However, in 1979 it was extensively rebuilt and enlarged to become the new assembly plant for Range Rovers.

Several major components for the P6 were manufactured off-site, and were delivered to the assembly plant by road; the Solihull plant has never had a dedicated rail link. Base units and panels were manufactured by Pressed Steel at their Cowley plant near Oxford. Engines were built at Rover's own Acocks Green plant, which was located about 4 miles (6km) north-west of Solihull in the Yardley district of Birmingham (and had also started life as a Rover-managed shadow factory). Transmissions came from the Rover plant at Pengam in South Wales, which had been specially built in the early 1960s (see Chapter 1). Meanwhile, smaller components, from exhausts and windscreens to speedometers and brake pads, were delivered direct to the Solihull plant by their various manufacturers.

New base units were delivered with a protective oil coating that was simply washed off before corrosion protection was applied, and were typically stored in the open. The protective coating was designed to be effective for two or three weeks, which was more than adequate in the early days, but as production volumes increased and base units sometimes stood in the open for longer, the protective coating could fail before a base unit reached the assembly lines.

When base units were taken forward to the assembly hall, their first port of call was a special 'acceptance' jig. The assembly method of the Rover P6 depended heavily on dimensional accuracy, and this jig checked that each base unit complied and also drilled four datum holes in it for subsequent machining and inspection locations. The base unit then went on to a fully automated jig, which drilled and spot-faced sixty-two holes, tapping forty-six of them to UNF thread sizes in preparation for mechanical and panel-fitting work later in the assembly process. A final acceptance fixture then checked the accuracy of the drilling, spot-facing and tapping operations.

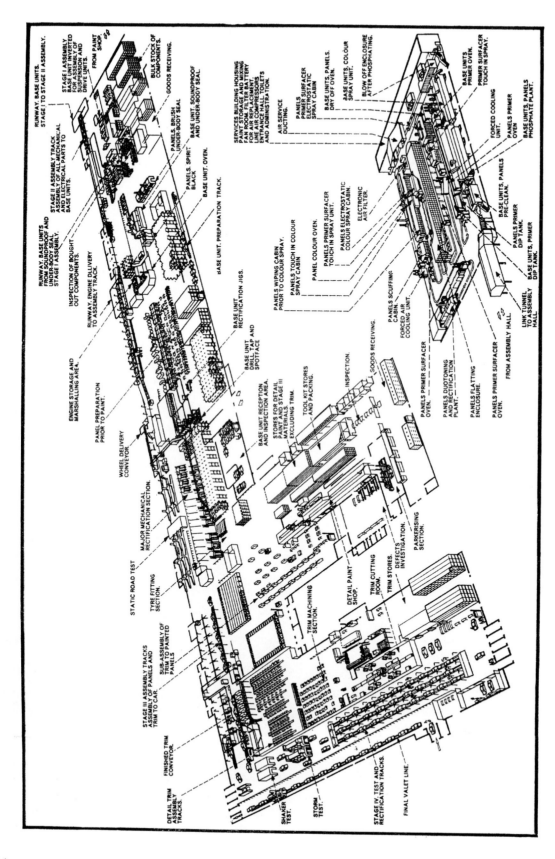

RUNWAY. BASE UNITS. STAGE I TO STAGE II ASSEMBLY.

STAGE I ASSEMBLY BASE UNIT INVERTED FOR ASSEMBLY OF SUSPENSION AND DRIVE UNITS.

FROM PAINT SHOP.

RUNWAY. BASE UNITS FROM UNDERHOOD AND UNDER-BODY SEAL. STAGE I ASSEMBLY.

STAGE II ASSEMBLY TRACK ASSEMBLY OF ALL MECHANICAL AND ELECTRICAL PARTS TO BASE UNITS.

BULK STOCK OF COMPONENTS.

GOODS RECEIVING.

PANELS. BRUSH UNDER-BODY SEAL

INSPECTION OF BOUGHT OUT COMPONENTS.

PANELS. SPIRIT BLACK

RUNWAY, ENGINE DELIVERY TO ASSEMBLY TRACK.

BASE UNIT, SOUNDPROOF AND UNDER-BODY SEAL.

ENGINE STORAGE AND MARSHALLING AREA.

BASE UNIT, OVEN.

SERVICES BUILDING HOUSING PAINT STORAGE AND MIXING FAN ROOM, FILTER BATTERY FOR AIR REPLACEMENT. LINE COMPRESSORS, ENTRANCE HALL, TOILETS AND ADMINISTRATION.

PANELS PRIMER SURFACER ELECTROSTATIC SPRAY CABIN.

BASE UNITS, PANELS. PRIMER SURFACER TOUCH IN SPRAY.

PANELS PRIMER SURFACER ELECTROSTATIC SPRAY CABIN.

BASE UNITS, PANELS. DRY OFF OVEN.

BASE UNITS, COLOUR SPRAY UNIT.

BLOW OFF ENCLOSURE AFTER PHOSPHATING.

AIR SERVICE DUCTING.

BASE UNITS. PRIMER OVEN.

PANEL PREPARATION PRIOR TO PAINT.

BASE UNIT. PREPARATION TRACK.

PANELS ELECTROSTATIC COLOUR SPRAY CABIN.

PANELS PRIMER SURFACER TOUCH IN SPRAY UNIT.

ELECTRONIC AIR FILTER.

FORCED COOLING UNIT.

PANELS PRIMER OVEN.

BASE UNIT RECTIFICATION JIGS.

PANEL COLOUR OVEN.

BASE UNITS, PANELS PHOSPHATE PLANT.

WHEEL DELIVERY CONVEYOR.

BASE UNIT DRILL TAP AND SPOTFACE.

PANELS WIPING CABIN PRIOR TO COLOUR SPRAY.

PANELS TOUCH IN COLOUR SPRAY CABIN.

BASE UNITS, PANELS. PRE-CLEAN.

STATIC ROAD TEST.

MAJOR MECHANICAL RECTIFICATION SECTION.

BASE UNIT RECEPTION AND INSPECTION AREA.

STORES FOR DETAIL PAINT AND STAGE III MATERIALS. EXCLUDING TRIM.

GOODS RECEIVING.

PANELS SCUFFING CABIN.

FORCED AIR COOLING UNIT.

PANELS PRIMER DIP TANK.

BASE UNITS, PRIMER DIP TANK.

LINK TUNNEL TO ASSEMBLY HALL.

TYRE FITTING SECTION.

TOOL KIT STORES AND PACKING.

INSPECTION.

PANELS PRIMER SURFACER OVEN.

FROM ASSEMBLY HALL.

SUB-ASSEMBLY OF TRIM TO PAINTED PANELS

PANELS DUOTONING AND RECTIFICATION PLANT.

STAGE III ASSEMBLY TRACKS ASSEMBLY OF PANELS AND TRIM TO CAR.

PANELS FLATTING ENCLOSURE.

DETAIL PAINT SHOP.

PANELS PRIMER SURFACER OVEN.

FINISHED TRIM CONVEYOR.

TRIM CUTTING ROOM.

TRIM STORES.

TRIM MACHINING SECTION.

DETAIL TRIM ASSEMBLY TRACKS.

DEFECTS INVESTIGATION.

PARKERISING SECTION.

SHAKER TEST.

STORM TEST.

STAGE IV. TEST AND RECTIFICATION TRACKS.

FINAL VALET LINE.

The P6 assembly plant at Solihull was specially built for the new model, and Rover were very proud of it. This schematic picture was issued when the car was launched in 1963. Base units entered the plant at the top right in this picture, and the line ended at top left. Completed cars then turned 90 degrees left to pass through the test sequence. Inset is the paint shop, again specially built to handle the P6; its overhead conveyor to the assembly hall is pictured in the foreground.

Meanwhile, body panels newly arrived from Pressed Steel passed through their own acceptance fixtures for dimensional checking, after which they were also jig-drilled at their fixing points. Contours were checked by eye and clearances by gauge, and the panels were hand-filled and surface-finished before being stored in special racks until required for painting.

Each base unit now met up with a complete set of panels and was taken with them by overhead conveyor into the paint shop. Here, a seven-stage pre-clean and phosphate process prepared the metal for painting, and base unit and panels were then dipped in a phenolic primer, which was baked on at high temperature. Base units, still suspended from the overhead conveyor, were then hand-sprayed with two colour coats of synthetic enamel, which in turn was also baked on.

Meanwhile, panels were transferred from the overhead conveyor onto special trucks on a floor conveyor, which took them into an electrostatic spray booth for primer-filler coats. A waist-level conveyor then took them past trackside operatives for hand-flatting and rubbing of the filler coats, after which two finish coats were electrostatically applied and baked on. Inspection followed, and the panels were then loaded once again onto the overhead conveyor, which took them, together with their base unit, back into the main assembly hall.

Base unit and panels then parted company again as the former first had its weld lines and joints crack-sealed and was then undersealed. The wings were given their sound-deadening and then went with the rest of the panel set to the panel sub-assembly shop, where all panels were covered with loose protective covers before being fitted with their 'furniture': windows, window frames and so on for the doors, and light units for the wings.

Next came the first stage of vehicle assembly. Here, the base units were turned upside down on the track to simplify the fitting of steering, suspension, differential, wiring harness and brake and clutch pedals. Some items were fitted with the base units stationary and others were added as they progressed along the line.

The next major station on the line was Assembly Stage II, where the base units were turned the right way up. Here, the windscreen, rear window, engine, gearbox and transmission, exhaust, wheels and tyres were added to make each base unit into a driveable assembly. They next passed over a suspension-settling grid and the steering was set.

At this point, the new cars were actually driven for the

A painted P6 base unit emerges from the paint plant on its way to the main assembly hall.

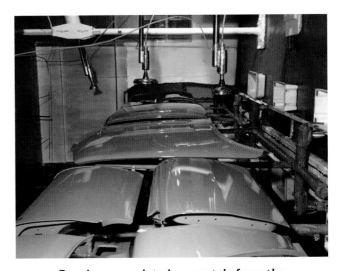

Panels were painted separately from the base unit, and this is a complete car set in Tobacco Leaf, from the early 1970s.

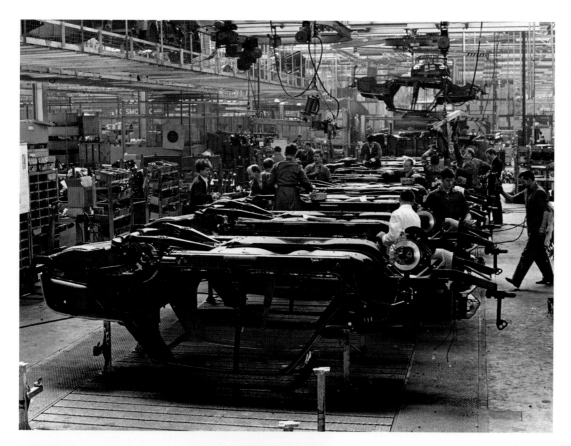

At the first stage of assembly, base units were turned upside down to allow easier fitting of suspension, hubs and brakes to the underside.

first time, travelling under their own power into an almost soundproof booth where they were driven on rollers at speeds up to 75mph (120km/h) while engine and transmission checks were carried out. Brakes were also tested on the rollers for efficiency and balance; test reports were made out and vehicles in need of rectification were dealt with in an adjacent ramp area and then retested.

At Assembly Stage III, panel sets from the panel subassembly shop met up with their base units again and were bolted to them. This stage also saw the cars receiving exterior finish details, plus upholstery and trim, which had been fed through to an overhead staging post by conveyor from the trim shop that was located next to the Stage III assembly line.

Placed on the track the right way up, base units were gradually built up with items such as engine bay ancillaries, lights and even the windscreen before the engine was lowered in from above.

Now fully assembled, each P6 went through a series of three tests. From the assembly line, it was driven into the shaker test house where its suspension was subjected to simulated rough-road conditions for approximately five minutes. Loose or chattering body panels or other fittings shown up by this test were then rectified before each car passed on to a second booth for a storm test, in which a fine spray of water blown all over and under the car simulated 70mph (113km/h) gale conditions. In one of the two storm test booths, the wheels could turn on rollers and throw water under the wheel arches to simulate road conditions and test for waterproofing.

After these tests, the cars passed to Assembly Stage IV, where any necessary rectification was carried out. They were then handed over to the Quality Control Department, who proof-tested each one on the test track within the factory grounds. Once signed off by an inspector, each car then entered the Despatch Department's parking area, where it was suitably protected from the elements. When required for delivery, it would then be driven through a wash-deck and back into the assembly hall to a final valet line for polishing and preparation.

When a car entered the Despatch Department, the date would be recorded by hand in a ledger, and the date of its departure (together with the destination) would be recorded in that same ledger. These ledgers now belong to the British Motor Museum at Gaydon, and provide the information about manufacture that is used for the Heritage Certificates that are issued to owners today. It is worth noting that by the 1970s the Despatch Department was so busy that the ledgers were sometimes not filled in until time was available, with the result that dates may in some cases not be entirely accurate!

Some cars were delivered to their destination by road on transporter lorries. A small number would have been collected directly from the factory. Others were delivered by rail, and as the Solihull factory did not have its own rail link, Rover made use of the railway sidings at Tyseley. Brand-new vehicles, Land Rovers and Rover cars alike, would be driven from the factory on trade plates to the dispersal yard there, where they would be loaded onto railway wagons for onward delivery.

There were some changes to the production process at Solihull in summer 1975. Rover had built a new, state-of-the-art paint plant for the forthcoming SD1 models, and tested it out on the final P6s. However, the new plant was designed to handle completed bodies, because the SD1 had a mono-

Engine securely in, work is continuing here to connect it up as necessary and to add the radiator. The car is an early 4-cylinder model.

Further down the line, the door seals are in, but there are still no outer panels on the body.

This is the end of the Stage IV test and rectification tracks, some time around 1968. There has clearly been a problem on the line because two cars are missing rear wing panels. They have been allowed to proceed to avoid holding up the line, and will be taken off to the major fault rectification area seen on the right of the picture.

These P6 saloons and Land Rovers have passed through Despatch and are seen at Tyseley railway sidings, awaiting onward delivery. The date is approximately 1974. Note that the wheel trims have been removed to avoid damage in transit. JONATHAN STOCKWELL

coque structure, so the P6 production process had to be adapted to suit.

The bodies, with the doors and skin panels already attached, would be primed electrophoretically, and then sprayed with a tough new thermoplastic top coat. When the P6s were put through the plant, they bypassed the first stage of this process because their base units and panels had already been primed by Pressed Steel. However, a major difference from the earlier production sequence was necessary in order for complete bodies to pass through the plant. So, on arrival at Solihull, the primed panels were now mounted to the base units and the P6 bodies received their top coats as complete assemblies. One result was that their door hinges were now painted in the body colour.

ASSEMBLY FROM CKD

CKD operations were established in overseas territories where P6s imported in fully built condition would have been prohibitively expensive because of local taxation. There was no universal standard CKD specification. One reason is that assembly facilities and the skills of the assembly staff differed from one country to another. A second reason is that some assembly plants added locally sourced items (typically paint, glass, battery and tyres) to the kits of parts shipped from the UK in order to increase the percentage of 'local content', which was usually a factor in avoiding punitive taxation.

Shipping of CKD kits was subcontracted to Export Packing Ltd of Banbury, who would have kept their own records, but these appear not to survive. In the records of the Despatch Department at Solihull, cars are often recorded only as 'CKD' and no destination is shown. For these reasons, very little information is available about individual cars built from CKD, and there is only partial information about the CKD operation as a whole.

In order to minimize shipping costs, CKD cars were normally packaged in groups of six at a time. To save space and costs, the P6 base units had their roof sections cut off at waist level for shipping, and these were then stowed upside down within the passenger compartment and welded back in place as part of the assembly process.

Six overseas assembly plants for CKD P6s have been iden-

tified, although the list may not be exhaustive. These six were in Belgium, Costa Rica, Malta, New Zealand, South Africa and Trinidad.

Belgium

The assembly plant at Malines (Mechelen) had started life under Standard-Triumph and had passed to Leyland when the car company was taken over in 1961. Assembly of Rover 2000SC models began at Malines at the end of April 1967, just a few months after Rover had joined the Leyland fold. The cars were 404-series models with left-hand drive, destined for sale in Europe.

By the end of 1967, Rover was having doubts about its involvement with the Malines operation because the devaluation of the British currency in November had removed its cost benefits. Nevertheless, the Belgian operation seems to have continued, and records show that it assembled forty-two 2000TCs in 1970, plus thirty 3500s. No other figures are currently available.

Costa Rica

The Costa Rican operation seems to have been tiny. The cars were presumably built at the San José plant that had been assembling Land Rovers since 1963. Records so far discovered show only six 3500s assembled there in 1970; they presumably had the left-hand drive that was normal in Costa Rica.

Malta

Car Assembly Ltd of Marsa in Malta was established in 1963 and over the years built a variety of British cars from CKD kits, including the Austin Mini, the Triumph Herald 13/60 and the Morris Marina. The company was scheduled to begin assembly of right-hand-drive P6 models in May 1968, for sale through Muscat's Garage Ltd, of Msida, who had been appointed Rover distributors in November 1967.

Surviving records show that the plant assembled twenty-four 2000SCs and eighteen 2000TCs in 1969, six 2000TCs in 1970 and eighteen 2000TCs in 1971. The later TCs were 448-series cars. There may have been some later assembly as well.

The P6s assembled in Malta had a small badge with a Maltese Cross on each rear quarter-pillar. The Maltese-built cars were sold locally and were also exported to Greece, Israel and Tunisia.

New Zealand

Local assembly of the Rover P6 from CKD in New Zealand began in April 1968, and more than 5,600 examples had been

This small emblem, seen on a 2000TC, was added to P6s assembled in Malta by Car Assemblers Ltd. PHIL HOWARD

built there by the time the operation closed down in 1976. This made it by far the largest of the P6 CKD operations.

All the first cars were 4-cylinder types, and there were 402-series 2000SC, 407-series 2000SC Automatic and 417-series 2000TC models in 1968 and 1969, although the 2000SC manual models were dropped for 1970. Assembly was at Nelson, in the plant owned by Motor Bodies that also assembled other British Leyland models. In 1970, Motor Bodies became part of the New Zealand Motor Corporation (NZMC) that united all four assembly plants in New Zealand.

The Rovers seem to have been a step up for the Nelson plant. Mark Webster's book, *Assembly*, quotes a former member of the company as saying that, 'This was our first foray into real quality build, complete with genuine leather seating and door panels. We had no end of problems obtaining the requisite standard of hides at that time so that the whole car interior could be trim matched.'

Assembly of the 4-cylinder models continued until December 1971, later including 448-series Series II 2000TC cars. Meanwhile, assembly of 453-series 3500 models had begun in May 1971. The V8 models were assembled for the domestic market until April 1975. Between June 1972 and October 1976 they were also assembled in quantity for export to Australia under the NAFTA free trade agreement between the two countries. Although the exact figures are in dispute (see below), it is clear that more 3500s were assembled for Australia than for the New Zealand domestic market.

There was a quite substantial local content added to the UK-sourced kits at Nelson, and with the New Zealand labour input of welding, assembly, underseal and painting, this reached the required figure of 45 per cent of each car's value. From 1971 and possibly earlier, locally made components were seats, carpet, interior trim, headlining, door cards, radiators, batteries, exhausts, road springs, tyres, brake hoses and some wiring. All the window glass was locally sourced (although the first cars in 1971 incorporated glass from the UK), and original windscreens were clearly marked 'Pilkington New Zealand'. Most of the locally sourced components gave no trouble, but it has been said that there were recurrent quality control problems with some local parts such as the Repco brake hoses.

The assembly process at the Nelson plant was quite different from that in Solihull. As explained above, the roof and its supporting pillars were cut off each base unit before it left Solihull, and an early part of the assembly process was to reunite the two parts. Also notable was that the bodies

The glass in New Zealand-assembled P6s was supplied locally and had its own distinctive markings.

This is another example of local manufacture: on the early New Zealand CKD cars, all front door armrests were black. This one dates from 1971. KEN WATTS

always remained the right way up during assembly, so that suspension and other components were fitted from underneath; at Solihull, the base units were turned over for this part of the assembly process.

The paint colours used on the New Zealand-built 3500 models were shared with other cars being assembled there, notably some Triumph saloon models. There were at least ten of them for the Rovers, all different from colours used at Solihull. Those ten colours were:

Bitter Apricot
Country Cream
French Blue
Honeysuckle
Ice Blue
Maple
Pimento Red
Saffron
Spanish Olive
Turquoise
(In addition, the Nelson plant used three standard Rover colours, which were Arden Green, Cameron Green, and Turmeric.)

This late 3500 was built up from CKD in New Zealand and was shipped to Australia under the NAFTA agreement. It has commission number 453-30187E and is painted in Bitter Apricot, which was unique to the New Zealand plant. By the time this one was built, UK-assembled cars had a full vinyl roof, but these cars did not. Note also the bolt-through wheel trims, once associated with the 3500S but no longer used on the Solihull lines. ROBERT PENN BRADLY

The dashboard of the same car combines a km/h speedometer with right-hand drive. ROBERT PENN BRADLY

The ADR compliance plate was not always fitted in the same place. Here it is on a February 1976 3500, number 453-29897E.

The New Zealand-built cars that were shipped to Australia were fitted at the port of entry with an ADR (Australian Design Rules) compliance plate. In this picture of an October 1974 car, it is the large silver plate. Note that the car is described as a product of the Leyland Motor Corporation of Australia, despite its origins. The two black tags welded to the inner wing show the commission number (453-03834E) and what is assumed to be a build code from the assembly plant.

Other distinctive features were that none of the cars assembled at Nelson had the vinyl roof that became standard on later Solihull-built 3500 models, and that by 1976 3500S-type wheel trims appear to have become standard. By 1976, the chrome door mirror that was standard had been replaced by a rather less attractive black 'racing' mirror.

The figures so far discovered for Rover P6 assembly at the Nelson plant are as follows:

2000
Total: 2,473 of all models, 1968–71, *including*:
1969: 36 SCs, 120 TCs and 48 Automatics
1970: 216 TCs and 78 Automatics

3500
Total: 3,151, 1971–76, *including*:
1971–75: 1,345 for the domestic market
1972–76: 1,806 for Australia
1971: 894

Note that the figure of 1,806 3500 models for Australia is taken from a 1987 circular to NZMC staff, which added that some production schedules were missing. This figure should therefore perhaps be considered a minimum. The 1976 NZMC annual report to shareholders states that 541 Rovers, with a value of NZ$2.9 million, had been exported to Australia in the year to 31 March 1976. If a comparable number of Rovers had been exported every year, there would have been a total of well over 2,000 cars in the four years when Australia was receiving New Zealand-assembled cars.

The first exports to Australia under the NAFTA agreement were made during the New Zealand winter (which lasts from June to August) in 1971, and the very first batch of cars left the port at Wellington en route to Sydney aboard the ro-ro ship MV *Maheno*. Exports continued through Wellington until October 1976, and it was probably that month that the last batch of seventy Rovers reached Sydney aboard the *Union Sydney*, again a ro-ro vessel. Some cars remained unsold in showrooms into 1977, and the very last were not sold until 1978.

The cars were shipped with the wiper arms and blades, head restraints, door mirrors, hubcaps and tool kits stored separately in a locked security box, for fitting on arrival in Australia. There were few optional extras, but the bootlid-mounted spare wheel was available, there were several different radios, and a Smiths air-conditioning unit could be ordered as an aftermarket fit. Some late cars had a locally made ClimbAir Imperial air-conditioning system, with the same York compressor that was used with the Smiths system.

Most interesting is that the New Zealand-assembled Rovers did not get a warm welcome in Australia. Roger Harding of NZMC told author Mark Webster that he had to visit Australia to '… answer for our sins. Generally, New Zealand goods don't get a big hand in Australia… You try and sell them an expensive motor car and see how you go – we had problems. Not that the cars were bad, but Australian dealers just didn't want them.' Harding found Australian workers using sandpaper to remove every sign that the cars had been made in New Zealand; he claimed that they were even grinding the logos off the tyres!

South Africa

Early CKD cars were built at the Rover plant in Port Elizabeth, which also assembled Land Rovers. These were 402-series 2000SC models with right-hand drive; 2000TC and 2000 Automatic models were brought in as fully built vehicles.

Under British Leyland, the South African operations were named Leykor from December 1968 and production of all car makes was centralized at Blackheath (Cape Town), a former BMC plant. Assembly of CKD 2000 models ceased with the move to Blackheath, where assembly of 427-series CKD 3500 models commenced in 1969.

Local content was probably limited to paint and interior trim. South African 3500 models initially had an 8.5:1 compression ratio (to suit the local 90-octane petrol) and an annular ring around the radiator fan to aid cooling, but the

cars regularly overheated in the local temperatures of 105°F (40°C). The 8.5:1 engine was probably generally similar to the early Range Rover engine (which had the water pump mounted higher), and South African *Car* magazine tested a locally built Three Thousand Five to a maximum speed of 110.5mph (177.8km/h) and recorded a 0–60mph time of 11 seconds.

This late Australian car has a locally made ClimbAir Imperial air-conditioning system. It was not original to the car but is of the type that could be ordered as an aftermarket fit. MARK ROBERTSON

Local accessories: this sun visor was pictured on a P6 in Australia, but was never available (or needed) on cars for the home market. The sheepskin seat covers are another reminder of the local climate: leather suffers in prolonged direct sunlight, and so do the backs of the occupants' legs!

All the V8 cars built by Leykor had base units suitable for air-conditioning, but several were built without it. These had a special rubber seal to prevent air entering the passenger cabin around the standard heater box, which was smaller than the type on air-conditioned cars. They also had a yellow-tinted rear window of local manufacture, which was intended to prevent the sun ruining the interior trim, and also to protect the rear-seat passengers.

Build quality of the cars from Blackheath was generally considered poor, and in particular the roof rusted out. By the time the Series II cars arrived in 1971, higher-octane petrol had become more generally available in South Africa and so these had 10.5:1 compression engines and were advertised as '3500 Sport Automatic' models, although there was no change to the badges.

Surviving figures show that 372 kits were shipped from the UK in 1969, 1,098 in 1970 and 402 in 1971. The evidence suggests that no CKD kits were brought in after 1973, although the 3500 remained on sale in South Africa until 1976.

Trinidad

The Rover assembly operation in Trinidad opened in May 1968, and was located at Tumpuna Road in Arima. It was owned by Amalgamated Industries Ltd, which had been established when the local BMC, Ford and Rover importers agreed to pool resources. Rover assembled Land Rovers there from the beginning, adding P6 assembly in April 1969. The cars had right-hand drive.

In 1969, Amalgamated Industries assembled thirty 2000TCs and twenty-four 2000 Automatics; in 1970 it built six 2000TCs and twenty-four 2000 Automatics; and in 1971 it built six 2000TCs and six 3500s. There may also have been some later cars, but information is not currently available.

CHAPTER FOURTEEN

BUYING AND OWNING
A ROVER P6

Even though the Rover P6 was a technically advanced car for its time, its maintenance is well within the scope of the average home mechanic. All models can be rewarding to own, but the most sought-after models are the 'shark's-tooth' 2000, the 1968–71 Three Thousand Five, and the manual-gearbox 3500S. There are also strong cult followings for the NADA 3500S and for the rare 3500 VIP. All these models are likely to be more expensive to buy than others in comparable condition, simply because of demand.

It is not difficult to find the consumable parts to keep a P6 on the road. There are several specialists in Britain, and some of them can also provide good second-hand panels and general expertise as well. With good online support through Facebook and owners' forums, plus two dedicated owners' clubs and an overall Rover club (the Rover Sports Register), help and advice are never far away.

STRUCTURE

When buying, it is important not to rely on first impressions. All the body panels are unstressed items that can be unbolted and replaced, and glossy panels can easily conceal corrosion in the base unit underneath. Even the factory-applied underseal can hide corrosion in the base unit.

That is not to say that corrosion in the skin panels can be ignored. It will usually be only too obvious. Front wings rust around the wheel arch and on their vertical trailing edges. The front valance is often corroded (thanks largely to its vulnerability to stone chips), and it is worth knowing that the larger valance on the V8 models is hard to find in good condition.

Check the underside of each door, and the rear door inners where they close over the wheel arch. Rear wings corrode at their leading edges and around the wheel arch lips. The rear valance will rust, too.

The bonnet and bootlid are made of aluminium alloy, so do not corrode. But paint does flake off around the washer jets on the bonnet, and sometimes around the badge on Series II models. The paint on late cars painted in the SD1 plant gave endless trouble, and many cars of that era will have been repainted. Beware of large areas of DIY touching-in, though. Bumpers and overriders rust because they are chromed steel, but they unbolt easily enough and can be re-chromed if necessary. However, the housing for the rear number-plate lamps can rot through and is now unobtainable.

A good place to begin examination of the less visible areas of a P6 is at the rear wheel arches, where their forward ends are normally concealed by the rear door. Rust will be very obvious here, as will poor-quality repairs. With the doors open, check the bottom of the B-posts. Doors should always shut cleanly, and they will drop if there is rust in the bulkhead (where the front door hinges) or in the B-post (where the rear door hinges). A sound bulkhead is vital because the front suspension forces act on it and will soon cause damage to one that has been weakened by rust. Repairs are not impossible but proper repairs may be impossibly expensive.

The structural sill panels are not visible; they are concealed behind the cosmetic outer panels. Always check these carefully, first by feeling for weak or crumbling areas; then take a look from the inside by peeling back the carpets. The sills and floor area can rust badly at the rear, in the area of the rear seat pan, so always lift the rear seat cushions and associated soundproofing felt to get a good look at the metal in the outer corners. If there are problems here, the car may also have rust holes in the rear inner wings.

Check the boot floor very carefully, and the vertical sides of the boot alongside the central well. Peel back the trim to check the soundness of the metal around the rear suspension arm mountings in these side panels; once the area is weakened by rust, the arms will soon pull through.

ENGINES

All 4-cylinder engines should be good for 100,000 miles (160,000km) before needing a major overhaul. However, they suffer from several maladies.

Look for coolant leaks from the side cover pates, which can rust through, and check the mounting flanges for the exhaust manifold on single-carburettor cars because these can crack. Timing-chain rattle is common on a cold start, but should soon disappear – although there is often a hollow ringing noise at around 1,200rpm with a warm engine. Otherwise, a persistent ringing noise suggests a worn lower timing chain, while a clattering noise means that the upper timing chain needs replacement. Overheating may result from corrosion of the waterways in the cylinder head – common if the use of antifreeze or corrosion inhibitor has been neglected.

The 2000TC may idle roughly, run on and even pink a little; its high (10:1) compression ratio was designed for 100-octane fuel, which is no longer available, and it takes patience to get the engine to run satisfactorily on lower grades of fuel. On both the 2000TC and 2200TC, the throttle spindles and linkage can wear, but flat performance usually indicates that the carburettors need balancing. An odd rattle at high engine speeds might be a cracked carburettor heat shield, and a rattle inside the inlet manifold might be a dislodged spacer – which can eventually disappear into the engine and cause further damage.

The V8 engines need regular oil changes, and many owners halve the recommended intervals to change oil and filter every 3,000 miles (5,000km). A top-end rattle that does not disappear quickly after start-up usually indicates wear in the tappets, the camshaft or the rocker shafts. Oil pressure is low on these engines, so 15–20psi in a warm engine is not a cause for alarm. However, a leak from the rear crankshaft seal on the pre-1973 (10.5:1 compression) engines is common. The rope-type seal fails and, although it can be replaced with the later neoprene type, the work involved is quite major and includes machining the block. Changing an original rope seal for a new one is also a fiddly

operation and requires a special tool known as a Chinese finger.

The coolant also needs regular attention on a V8 engine. If antifreeze or corrosion inhibitor are not used correctly, the internal waterways will corrode and the corroded particles will eventually block waterways or the radiator. The best cure is to flush the system out – but prevention is even better.

TRANSMISSION

The four-speed manual gearbox is fairly robust but the Series I cars have a linkage that can wear and cause rattles. In the manual 3500S, gearboxes were near their limits and will eventually suffer from difficult gear selection or jumping out of gear. Repair parts are becoming scarce. Owners sometimes fitted the five-speed LT77 gearbox from the Rover SD1 when these were readily available. This is a worthwhile modification but donor gearboxes are becoming rarer now.

Check automatic gearboxes for the condition of the fluid, which should be pink (not black) and clean. The early Type 35 is slow to change up and to kick down by modern standards, but is quite long-lived. The later Type 65 is smoother but slightly less durable.

Clonks in the driveline are usually caused by nothing worse than UJs in need of replacement. Differentials can leak, especially on pre-1967 cars where an unsatisfactory breather system allowed pressure to build up and blow the seals out. However, most will have been modified by now.

STEERING AND SUSPENSION

Most cars have manual steering, which is quite precise but not as sharp as modern rack-and-pinion systems. Beware of tight spots, which usually mean that an owner has over-tightened a box to remove play in the steering. Some people find the manual steering heavy at low speeds, especially on the 2200 models. Power-assisted steering was available only with the V8 engine and is valuable at parking speeds although it reduces high-speed stability to some extent.

The front suspension is odd but rarely gives trouble. If there is a clonk over rough surfaces, the cause is probably a worn ball joint at the bottom of the suspension leg. The rear suspension can be more troublesome, as the sliding joint in the De Dion tube may seize up if the rubber gaiter splits, letting grease out and dirt in. By modern standards, body roll in a P6 may be alarming, but that roll was standard when the cars were new.

WHEELS AND BRAKES

Most P6s have steel disc wheels. The optional wire-spoked type were available only on the Series I 2000TC and are therefore rare. They are not interchangeable with the disc type and need special splined hubs. Worn splines can be a problem (the wheel will be loose) and of course the spokes can rust and work loose.

The servo-assisted all-disc braking system gives superb stopping ability. However, the early Dunlop callipers tended to stick and seize and could crack discs; parts for these are now hard to find, and many owners have converted to the later Girling type, at least on the rear axle. Accessibility to the inboard rear discs is tricky, and many owners have neglected maintenance, with the inevitable results.

INTERIOR

Worn leather seats can always be re-trimmed, although the nylon fabric trim on later cars is no longer available, and owners sometimes switch to leather for this reason. Find-ing good second-hand seats in the early (pre-1966) colours is difficult, and a re-trim is often the only solution. On the 1971–73 cars, the leather can shrink, leaving wavy piping until the stitching eventually gives way under the pressure and the seat splits open.

On very early cars, the wood trim was real wood veneer on an aluminium backing, and this is now impossible to replace. On most cars the 'wood' was actually Formica, of which there were three different finishes. On all types the door sections slide into place, and can also slide out of place if the spring clips that hold them fail or are missing, resulting in trims cracking when the doors are closed.

ELECTRICS

The electrical systems on all these cars are simple by modern standards and are fairly robust. The exception is the twelve-position fuse box used on the Series II cars, which can melt.

All the 4-cylinder cars before the 1970 facelift had a dynamo, and all those before March 1966 had a positive-earth electrical system. Later cars changed to a negative earth, and after 1970 an alternator was fitted. The original Lucas 11AC type came with a separate regular that can fail, and some owners have changed to an 11ACR alternator with an integral regulator.

IDENTIFICATION NUMBERS AND STATISTICS

COMMISSION NUMBERS AND BUILD TOTALS

Rover P6 models were identified by what the company knew as a commission number. This was equivalent to the traditional chassis number and is today used as the VIN (vehicle identification number) on documentation.

Commission numbers followed the established pattern of Rover chassis numbering. Each major sub-type had its own three-figure identifying prefix, which was followed by a five-figure serial number. This serial number was then followed by a letter suffix, which indicated modifications of importance when servicing the vehicle. Note that the numbers are shown here (and throughout the book) with a hyphen for clarity between prefix and serial number. This hyphen does not appear in the number on a car's identity plate.

From December 1974 the numbering system was simplified. The original sub-type prefixes remained in use, but all variants of a major type shared a common serial number sequence.

The commission number of a Rover P6 was located in different places over the years. On the first cars, it was stamped into a plate screwed to the left-hand front door pillar. From September 1966, it was stamped into a small black tag that was brazed to the left-hand front inner wing. After December 1974, all cars had the commission number stamped directly into the left-hand inner front wing, with the BL flying wheel symbol at each end. On these late cars, it is also found stamped into the rear decker panel beside the bootlid hinges, and occasionally on the right-hand front inner wing as well.

The records that form the basis of the lists below are those of the Rover Despatch Department, which survive at the British Motor Museum in Gaydon, Warwickshire. The Despatch Department received completed cars from the assembly lines and was responsible for sending them on to the dealer or customer who had ordered them.

However, sets of CKD parts intended for overseas assembly did not pass through the Despatch Department and were not included in that department's records. As Chapter 12 explains, no complete set of records for CKD cars has been found. The figures shown below for CKD cars have therefore been calculated on the basis of surviving examples and are the best available at the time of writing; they are identified by an asterisk (*) and should not be considered as definitive.

The commission numbers shown in the lists below do not include suffix letters.

2000 and 2000SC

400-00001 to 400-62986	Home Market	Jan 1963 to Sep 1970	62,986
401-00001 to 401-05006	RHD Export	Mar 1964 to Aug 1970	5006
402-00001 to 402-01797 (*)	RHD CKD	(Dates not known)	1797
403-00001 to 403-11027	LHD Export	Feb 1964 to Aug 1970	11,027
404-00001 to 404-00011 (*)	LHD CKD	(Dates not known)	11
Total			80,827

Note: The highest number so far traced for the RHD CKD cars is 402-001797E, which was a assembled in New Zealand, and the highest number so far traced for LHD CKD cars is 404-00011E

2000 Automatic, 2000SC Automatic and Federal 2000SC Automatic

405-00001 to 405-13476	Home market	Jun 1966–Sep 1970	13,476
406-00001 to 406-01554	RHD export	Dec 1966–Aug 1970	1,554
407-00001 to 407-00228 (*)	RHD CKD	(Dates not known)	228
408-00001 to 408-01486	LHD export	Jul 1966–Aug 1970	1,486
858-00001 to 858-00940	LHD Federal	Jul 1967–Nov 1969	940
Total			17,684

Notes: The highest number so far traced for RHD CKD cars is 407-00228J, which was assembled in New Zealand in 1970 or 1971. There is no evidence that any LHD CKD cars were ever built.

2000S (Pilot Build Only)

410-00001 to 410-00012	Home market	Oct 1965–Nov 1965	12
413-00001 to 413-00003	LHD export	Nov 1965	3
Total			15

2000TC and Federal 2000TC

415-00001 to 415-35686	Home market	Jan 1966–Sep 1970	35,686
416-00001 to 416-03231	RHD export	Apr 1966–Sep 1970	3,231
417-00001 to 417-00576 (*)	RHD CKD	(Dates not known)	576
418-00001 to 418-01486	LHD export	Jan 1966–Aug 1970	11,851
419-00001 to 419-xxxxx (*)	LHD CKD	(Dates not known)	42
859-00001 to 859-04987	LHD Federal	Jul 1967–Aug 1970	4,987
Total			56,373

Notes: The highest number so far traced for RHD CKD cars is 417-00576G, which was assembled in New Zealand. At least forty-two LHD CKD cars were built (in Belgium), but no more detailed figures are known.

Three Thousand Five and Federal 3500S

425-00001 to 425-16986	Home market	Jul 1967–Aug 1970	16,986
426-00001 to 426-01866	RHD export	Mar 1968–Aug 1970	1,866
427-00001 to 427-01335 (*)	RHD CKD	(Dates not known)	1,335
428-00001 to 428-03438	LHD Export	Sep 1967–Aug 1970	3,438
429-00001 to 429-xxxxx (*)	LHD CKD	(Dates not known)	30
433-00001 to 433-02043	LHD Federal	Jun 1969–Aug 1971	2,043
Total			25,698

Notes: The highest number so far traced for RHD CKD cars is 427-01335, which was assembled in South Africa. There is evidence that as many as 1,470 cars may actually have been assembled there before the end of 1970, but that figure may include some Series II 3500 models. At least thirty LHD CKD cars were built (in Belgium), but no more detailed figures are known.

2000SC Mk II

436-00001 to 436-17875	Home market	Sep 1970–Sep 1973	17,867
			(8 cars not built)
437-00001 to 437-00697	RHD export	Sep 1970–Sep 1973	697
439-00001 to 439-00515	LHD export	Sep 1970–Sep 1973	515
869-00001 to 869-00100	LHD export	Oct 1973–Dec 1974	100
Total			19,179

Notes: The 869-series cars were a special series for Nigeria only. There were no known CKD models.

2000SC Mk II Automatic

441-00001 to 441-09798	Home market	Aug 1970–Sep 1973	9,798
442-00001 to 442-00456	RHD export	Oct 1970–Sep 1973	456
444-00001 to 444-00164	LHD export	Sep 1970–Sep 1973	164
Total			10,418

Note: There were no known CKD models.

2000TC Mk II and Federal 2000TC Mk II

435-00001 to 435-00238	LHD Federal	Nov 1970–Aug 1971	222
			(16 cars not built)
446-00001 to 446-26282	Home market	Aug 1970–Sep 1973	26,282
447-00001 to 447-01730	RHD Export	Sep 1970–Aug 1973	1,730
448-00001 to 448-00040	RHD CKD	(Dates not known)	40
449-00001 to 449-03814	LHD export	Sep 1970–Sep 1973	3,814
868-00001 to 868-00560	LHD export	Feb 1974–Dec 1974	560
868-xxxxx	LHD Export	Sep 1975–Mar 1977	285
Total			32,933

Notes: At least forty RHD CKD cars were built (in Malta and New Zealand), but no more detailed figures are known. The 868-series cars were a special series for Italy and Nigeria only. Between 1975 and 1977, they were numbered within the contemporary sequence for 2200TC models with 491, 492 and 494 prefixes; see below.

3500 Mk II

451-00001 to 451-26536	Home market	Aug 1970–Dec 1974	26,536
451-xxxxx	Home market	Jan 1975–Jan 1977	3,212
452-00001 to 447-01885	RHD export	Sep 1970–Dec 1974	1,853
			(32 cars not built)
452-xxxxx	RHD export	Jan 1975–Dec 1976	63
453-00001 to 453-xxxxx (*)	RHD CKD	(Dates not known)	2,419
453-xxxxx	RHD CKD	Jan 1975–Dec 1976	732
454-00001 to 454-04532	LHD export	Aug 1970–Dec 1974	3,814
454-xxxxx	LHD export	Jan 1975–Dec 1976	705
861-xxxx	VIP	Jun 1975–May 1976	77
Total			39,411

Notes: The CKD figures are, as usual, problematical. There appear to have been no LHD CKD cars. The figure of 2,419 for the early 453-series cars has been calculated from other figures and relates to New Zealand only; there was probably also CKD assembly of 453-series cars in South Africa, so this figure must be seen as a minimum. The records show that there were 732 CKD cars between January 1975 and December 1976; probably all of them were 453-series cars for New Zealand – but this is an assumption. The January 1975 to December 1976 combined sequence covers 451-, 452-, 453- and 454-series cars, plus the 861-series VIPs. Serial numbers ran from 27000 to 31837, and forty-nine numbered cars were not completed. These are recorded as cancelled (presumably before build began) or as written off (typically because of severe damage during assembly); they have been deducted from the figures shown above.

2200SC

471-00001 to 471-04360	Home market	Jun 1973–Dec 1974	4,360
471-xxxxx	Home market	Dec 1974–Jan 1977	4,738
472-00001 to 472-00053	RHD export	Oct 1973–Aug 1974	53
472-xxxxx	RHD export	Jan 1975–1976	165
Total			9,316

Notes: The January 1975–January 1977 combined sequence covers both 471- and 472-series cars. Serial numbers ran from 06000 to 10908 and six numbered cars were not completed. These are recorded as cancelled (presumably before build began) or as written off (typically because of severe damage during assembly); they have been deducted from the figures shown above. There were never any LHD or CKD cars.

2200SC Automatic

476-00001 to 476-02979	Home market	Jun 1973–Dec 1974	2,979
476-xxxxx	Home market	Jan 1975–Feb 1977	3,097
477-00001 to 477-00025	RHD export	Jan 1974–Dec 1974	25
477-xxxxx	RHD export	Jan 1975 –1976	24
479-00001	LHD export	Jun 1973	1
Total			6,126

Notes: The January 1975–February 1977 combined sequence covers both 476- and 477-series cars. Serial numbers ran from 04000 to 07130 and ten numbered cars were not completed. These are recorded as cancelled (presumably before build began) or as written off (typically because of severe damage during assembly); they have been deducted from the figures shown above. There were no 479-series cars in the later combined sequence, and there were never any CKD cars.

3500S

481-00001 to 481-11747	Home market	Jun 1971–Dec1974	11,747
481-xxxxx	Home market	Jan 1975–Dec 1976	1,675
482-00001 to 482-01097	RHD export	Nov 1971–Dec 1974	1,096
			(1 car not built)
482-xxxxx	RHD export	Jan 1975–Dec 1976	33
484-00001 to 484-02275	LHD export	Aug 1971–Dec 1974	2,275
484-xxxxx	LHD export	Jan 1975–Dec 1976	189
Total			17,015

Notes: The January 1975–December 1976 combined sequence covers 481-, 482- and 484-series cars. Serial numbers ran from 13000 to 15002 and 106 numbered cars were not completed. These are recorded as cancelled (presumably before build began) or as written off (typically because of severe damage during assembly); they have been deducted from the figures shown above. There were never any CKD cars.

2200TC

491-00001 to 491-06664	Home market	Jun 1973–Dec 1974	6,664
491-xxxxx	Home market	Jan 1975–Feb 1977	6,050
492-00001 to 492-00516	RHD export	Sep 1973–Dec 1974	516
492-xxxxx	RHD export	Jan 1975–Feb 1977	152
494-00001 to 494-01339	LHD export	Jun 1973–Dec 1974	1,339
494-xxxxx	LHD export	Jan 1975–Feb 1977	1,362
Total			16,083

Notes: The January 1975–March 1977 combined sequence covers 491-, 492- and 494-series cars, plus the special 868-series 2000TC models (see above). Serial numbers ran from 08000 to 15871 and twenty-three numbered cars were not completed. These are recorded as cancelled (presumably before build began) or as written off (typically because of severe damage during assembly); they have been deducted from the figures shown above. There were never any CKD cars.

OVERALL BUILD TOTALS

There are some problems in establishing exactly how many P6s were built in all.

The total of the cars listed above comes to 331,078 but this must be considered a minimum quantity because the CKD totals shown in the lists are minimum figures.

Other totals have been quoted. The 'official' figure of 325,317 is demonstrably wrong and it is not clear how it was calculated. The figure of 327,208 base units that was used during the closing-down ceremony at the Pressed Steel plant in Cowley in 1976 (and again on the Rover assembly lines) is also clearly inaccurate.

ENGINE NUMBERS

On early 4-cylinder cars, the engine number will be found low down on the right-hand side next to the lifting lug at the back of the cylinder block. On later 4-cylinder models, it is on a ledge at the front of the engine, between two access plugs for the timing chain tensioners. On the V8 engines, the identifying number is stamped into a ledge next to the dipstick.

In all cases, there is a three-digit type identifier. This is then followed by a five-digit serial number and a letter suffix. The breakdown of type identifier prefixes is shown below; the letter suffixes indicate specification changes of importance when servicing the engine.

An example of an engine number is 481-00937A (as always in this book, the hyphen is included for clarity but is not present on the actual engine). The description 'detoxed' indicates an engine with emissions control equipment.

Prefix code	Type	Gearbox	Compression
400 (with suffixes A–K)	2000	Manual	9:1
400 (with suffix L)	2000 (Ser II)	Manual	9:1
401 (with suffixes A–K)	2000	Manual	7.5:1
401 (with suffix L)	2000 (Ser II)	Manual	7.5:1
405 (with suffixes E–K)	2000	Automatic	9:1
405 (with suffix L)	2000	Automatic	9:1
410	2000S	Manual	Not known
415 (with suffixes A–E)	2000TC	Manual	10:1
415 (with suffix F)	2000TC (Ser II)	Manual	10:1
416 (with suffixes A–E)	2000TC	Manual	9:1
416 (with suffix F)	2000TC (Ser II)	Manual	9:1
425 (with suffixes A–B)	3500	Automatic	10.5:1
425 (with suffix C)	3500 (Ser II)	Automatic	10.5:1
425 (with suffix D)	3500 (Ser II)	Automatic	9.25:1
427 (with suffixes A–B)	3500	Automatic	8.5:1
427 (with suffix C)	3500 (Ser II)	Automatic	8.5:1
427 (with suffix D)	3500 (Ser II)	Automatic	9.25:1
430	3500S (Federal)	Automatic	10.5:1
432	3500S (Federal)	Automatic	8.5:1
436	2000SC (Ser II)	Manual	9:1
438 (with suffixes A–B)	2000SC (Ser II)	Manual	9:1
	Service exchange for 436 and 440 engines		

438 (with suffix C)	2000SC (Ser II) Service exchange for 869 engines	Manual	Not known
440	2000 (Ser II)	Manual	Not known Detoxed
441	2000SC (Ser II)	Automatic	9:1
443	2000SC (Ser II) Service Exchange for 441 and 445 engines	Automatic	9:1
445	2000SC (Ser II)	Automatic	9:1 Detoxed
446	2000TC (Ser II)	Manual	10:1
447	2000TC (Ser II) Service exchange for 446 engines	Manual	10:1
448 (with suffixes A–B)	2000TC (Ser II) Service exchange for 449 and 450 engines	Manual	9:1
448 (with suffix C)	2000TC (Ser II) Service exchange for 868 engines	Manual	Not known
449	2000TC (Ser II)	Manual	9:1
450	2000TC (Ser II)	Manual	9:1 Detoxed
451 (with suffixes A–C)	3500 (Ser II)	Automatic	10.5:1
451 (with suffixes D–E)	3500 (Ser II)	Automatic	9.25:1
452 (with suffixes B–C)	3500 (Ser II) Service exchange for 451, 453 and 455 engines	Automatic	10.5:1 and 9.25:1
452 (with suffix D)	3500 (Ser II) Service exchange for 451 engines	Automatic	Not known
453	3500	Automatic	8.5:1
455 (with suffixes A–C)	3500	Automatic	10.5:1 Detoxed
455 (with suffix D)	3500	Automatic	9.25:1 Detoxed
461	3500 EFI (no production)	Manual	Not known
466	3500S (Federal)	Automatic	10.5:1 Detoxed
471	2200SC	Manual	9:1
473	2200SC Service exchange for 471 engines	Manual	9:1
476	2200SC	Automatic	9:1
478	2200SC Service exchange for 476 engines	Automatic	9:1
481 (with suffixes A–C)	3500S	Manual	10.5:1
481 (with suffixes D–E)	3500S	Manual	9.25:1

483 (with suffixes B–C)	3500S		
	Service exchange for 481 and 485 engines	Manual	9.25:I
483 (with suffix D)	3500S		
	Service exchange for 481 suffix D engines	Manual	9.25:I
485 (with suffixes A–C)	3500S	Manual	10.5:I Detoxed
485 (with suffix D)	3500S	Manual	9.25:I Detoxed
491	2200TC	Manual	9:I
493	2200TC Service exchange for 491 engines		9:I
858 (from suffix H)	2000SC (Federal)	Automatic	Not known
859 (from suffix F)	2000TC (Federal)	Manual	Not known Detoxed
868 (from suffix C)	2000TC (Italy & Nigeria)	Manual	Not known Detoxed
869 (from suffix C)	2000SC (Nigeria)	Manual	Not known

GEARBOX NUMBERS

Identifying numbers are stamped into the underside of the casing on manual gearboxes. On automatic gearboxes, they are stamped into a plate attached to the side of the gearbox casing. Manual gearbox numbers follow the same principles as chassis and engine numbers; automatic gearboxes have a different numbering system.

Prefix code	Model	Remarks
400	2000 and 2000SC	From Suffix A
401	2000TC	From Suffix D
436	2200SC and TC	From Suffix A
481	3500S	From Suffix A
483	3500S Police-spec	From Suffix B
EU	2000 and 2000SC Auto	From serial 1001
461	2200SC Automatic	From serial 1001
3FU	3500	From serial 1001
7FU	3500	From serial 1001
9FU	3500	From serial 1001
267	3500	From serial 1001
303	3500	From serial 1001
013	3500	From serial 1001

FINAL DRIVE NUMBERS

Identifying numbers are stamped into the underside of the final drive casing. They follow the same principles as chassis and engine numbers.

Prefix code	Model	Remarks
400	2000 and 2000SC	From Suffix A
	2000TC	From Suffix B
	2000 and 2000SC Auto	From 400-48929D
425	3500	From Suffix A
471	2200	From Suffix A

BASE UNIT NUMBERS

Base units were also numbered, in this case at the point of production by Pressed Steel. The aluminium plate carrying the base unit identity number is mounted to the lip at the lower edge of the boot aperture, and directly behind the spare wheel; it is usually concealed by rubber matting.

The numbers consist of a type prefix followed by a six-digit number. In each sequence, the six-digit number began at 000001. The prefix codes are as follows:

A	4-cylinder with automatic gearbox
M	4-cylinder with manual gearbox
BA	V8 with automatic gearbox
BM	V8 with manual gearbox

As a guide, the M-coded base units (the most numerous) are numbered up to around 215629. The identification numbers show no distinctions between Series I and Series II base units.

FACTORY REGISTRATION NUMBERS

Some enthusiasts take a special interest in cars registered by 'the factory'. The British system normally ensures that a car retains its original registration plate for life, and so a factory car can be easily identified many years down the line. Numbers are usually only lost if they are replaced by a personalized one or if a car is exported.

It is quite true that some factory-registered cars served as test and development vehicles, and also that some became part of the press fleet, from which they were lent out to members of the press and often featured in magazine articles of the time. However, it is important to put all this into perspective.

By far the majority of cars registered by the factory had no such interesting history. Many were allocated to staff as company cars, and many were given a British registration as a temporary measure before collection by an overseas buyer (typically under the Overseas Delivery Scheme). After the car had left UK shores, it was re-registered in its destination country.

Early prototypes of the Rover P6, and the pilot-production batch, were deliberately registered with local authorities some distance from the factory, so that keen observers were less likely to be able to guess their origin. The very first prototype, P6/1, had a London registration (WUL 432), and so did many of the pilot-production (FGO, FJJ and FLK) cars.

However, once the P6 had become public knowledge, the factory began to register cars with its own local authority. There were three 'eras' of factory registrations, as follows.

1963–64

A few early cars were registered with AC and WD numbers, which were issued by the Warwickshire registration authority. Examples are 65 JAC (October 1963) and 666 JWD (February 1964).

1964–75

From 1964, the borough of Solihull was granted its own local registration letters of XC, which had previously been a London mark. These letters were for use only with the new year-suffix registrations and, as they began in 1964, the first ones had a B suffix. The earliest one known to have been allocated to a factory Rover P6 was AXC 81B in April 1964. (AXC 1B was allocated to the Rover Chairman's P5 3-litre saloon.)

Numbers were generally allocated to Rover in batches; the company put them on cars as they were needed, and would periodically send somebody down to the local registration office with a list of what they had done. The appropriate details would then be transferred to the handwritten official ledgers, which survive today at the Coventry Transport Museum.

Note that several non-existent numbers were shown in press photographs. So, for example, there never was a KXC 203M; that number was nevertheless displayed on a 2200TC used for publicity pictures, which were air-brushed to provide the equally non-existent KXC 203N a year later.

1975–76

British Leyland centralized its registration procedures during 1975, and as a result some late Rover factory registrations were in sequences such as GAC-P (Warwickshire) and CUD-P (Oxfordshire). It is quite likely that some of these were also non-existent numbers invented purely for publicity pictures. The official last-of-line car, a P6B, carried the genuine number plate VVC 700S, which was a Coventry issue.

INDEX